The Great Within

The
Great Within

*The Transformative
Power and Psychology of
the Spiritual Path*

Han F. de Wit, PhD

SHAMBHALA
BOULDER
2019

Shambhala Publications, Inc.
4720 Walnut Street
Boulder, Colorado 80301
www.shambhala.com

This work is a revised edition of *The Spiritual Path: An Introduction to the Psychology of the Spiritual Traditions* (Duquesne University Press, 1999), published originally in Dutch under the title *De Verborgen Bloei* by Kok Agora.

9 8 7 6 5 4 3 2 1

First Edition
Printed in the United States of America

⊛ This edition is printed on acid-free paper that meets the American National Standards Institute Z39.48 Standard.
♻ This book is printed on 30% postconsumer recycled paper. For more information please visit www.shambhala.com.

Shambhala Publications is distributed worldwide by Penguin Random House, Inc., and its subsidiaries.

Designed by Howie Severson

Library of Congress Cataloging-in-Publication Data
Names: Wit, H. F. de, author.
Title: The great within: the transformative power and psychology of the spiritual path / Han F. de Wit.
Other titles: Verborgen bloei. English
Description: First edition. | Boulder: Shambhala, 2019. | "[I]ts first version was published in 1999 by the Duquesne University of Pittsburgh and translated from Dutch by Henry Jansen"—Author's acknowledgments. | Includes bibliographical references and index.
Identifiers: LCCN 2018034137 | ISBN 9781611806816 (pbk.: alk. paper)
Subjects: LCSH: Psychology, Religious. | Wit, H. F. de. Contemplatieve psychologie. | Contemplation.
Classification: LCC BL53 .W57713 2019 | DDC 200.1/9—dc23
LC record available at https://lccn.loc.gov/2018034137

Contents

Preface

Many years ago, my spiritual mentor told me, "Practice more, study more, and then go back to psychology." He said this after I had expressed my doubts about Western psychology as a means to explore, understand, and cultivate the human mind. Even though I had just received my PhD in psychology at the University of Amsterdam, I doubted the discipline's value.

When I first decided to study psychology, I set myself two goals: to learn what had been discovered about the human mind so far and to become a good scientific researcher of that mind. It did not take long, however, to discover something slightly disturbing about academic psychology; it appeared that studies at the time were not so much about the "psyche," as the name suggested, but about physical and verbal behavior. It was the time of behavioral psychology, which neither offered nor intended to offer a theory of mind in which the interplay between thoughts, emotions, perceptions, motivations, consciousness, and mental phenomena could be understood. Of course, outside of psychology as a science, the most interesting theories of mind were based on philosophical or conventional assumptions and even religious dogmas. However, these were not based on research or empirical testing. Why was that? Because systematic, direct observation of the mental domain was held to be impossible; one cannot research or investigate one's own mind because the research subject and the researcher have to be independent of each other. In empirical research, this is supposed to guarantee that the results are not spurious. So, it seemed that it was better to leave the black box of the mind alone.

Now, decades later, many sophisticated forms of research into the workings of human beings have been developed, with methods and technologies that look at the highly interesting relationship between the *brain* and experience. These include neuropsychological research that make the effects of meditation and mindfulness on the human brain visible. Of course, I use the word *brain* here purposefully, as neuropsychology tends toward the materialistic view that all human experience depends on neural brain activity; no nonmaterial mind or consciousness is believed to be operating. Like all other psychological study, this research is still done by psychologists on the minds of others (third-person research). This involves knowing something indirectly rather than directly, which would entail researchers looking at their own minds. It seems the assumption that reliable observation of one's own mind is impossible still endures. This might explain why the black box called mind remains ignored by researchers, even to the extent of denying the existence of mind by simply equating it with the brain.

Even though that is the way empirical research has always been conducted, as a young psychologist, I wondered if it had to be the case. How would Wilhelm Wundt—the famous nineteenth-century German physiologist and psychologist who is generally acknowledged as the founder of experimental psychology—feel about this? According to Wundt, all our ongoing everyday experience is only available as sensory mediated perceptions and perceived mental contents, like thoughts and emotions. These are directly available to their perceivers only through introspection.[1] His view greatly encouraged me. Wundt, however, was unable to develop a systematic and reliable method of introspection. Could something in that direction be found outside of academic psychology? How about in the spiritual traditions? Didn't most religions and spiritual traditions talk about getting to know one's mind? Didn't they discuss confusion and wisdom, thought and emotion, perception and self-deception, mental suffering and well-being, care and compassion, self-centeredness and altruism, and much more? In short, topics that we would nowadays call psychological?

But could a serious research psychologist really look into this direction without losing scientific credibility and status, or being seen as soft in the head or going off the deep end? Fortunately, Frits Staal, a highly respected researcher at the University of California, wrote a little pamphlet about just this dilemma.[2] He said that mysticism can be studied rationally, and that without such study, no theory of mind is complete. I found that very encouraging as a young researcher, for that was exactly the type of study I wanted to undertake. I contacted him, and at Frits's invitation, I moved to the United States as a visiting scholar at his university in 1975. Frits graciously received me at the San Francisco airport and drove me around in his scarlet convertible. Still jet-lagged but highly inspired, I asked him how he conducted a rational study of mind. He glanced at me and smiled. Then, looking out over the beautiful San Francisco Bay, he said, "I'd rather go surfing."

My Encounter with Buddhism

I had discovered Buddhism before coming to the United States. Two things struck me about that tradition. First, it claimed to contain an empirical method for exploring the human mind called *shamatha-vipashyana*. This struck me as the kind of controlled introspection that Wilhelm Wundt had advocated. Second, as Buddhism is not a theistic religion, it did not involve speculations about God, but it did have concrete theories about the human mind based on a systematic form of introspective research. This is why I decided to make Buddhism the object of my field study of a spiritual tradition.

In 1973, I had already made written contact with the Tibetan Buddhist meditation master Chögyam Trungpa, and

I decided to study under his guidance. In 1975, I moved from San Francisco to Karmê Chöling, his Buddhist practice center in the Vermont countryside. He encouraged me to explore my own mind and experience thoroughly by means of the Buddhist practice of meditation. Then, based on my acquired insights, he advised me to revisit and restart a dialogue with Western psychology. He was the one who told me to meditate and study more before going back to psychology.

My time as a student of Buddhism had a profound influence on my way of thinking about not only psychology but also other spiritual traditions. It became clear to me that many traditions, like Buddhism, included a way of exploring the landscape of the mind and that they all somehow involved changing our mistaken perceptions of reality, including our perception of reality *as we think it to be*. Even though spiritual traditions are all very different on a theological level, they are not so dissimilar in terms of the means they offer to explore and change the mind. I must admit that, from a conventional scientific point of view, their methods of exploring the mind and experience have suspicious names, like *meditation, prayer*, and *contemplation*. Nevertheless, these methods clearly lead to a certain kind of knowledge about the human mind.

In a way, the seeds of contemplative psychology began to sprout at this time. That brought me back to the United States in 1983, now as a visiting scholar to Naropa University (then Naropa Institute) in Boulder, Colorado. It had been founded by my teacher, the venerable Chögyam Trungpa Rinpoche, holder of the Kagyu, Nyingma, and Shambhala lineages of Tibetan Buddhism. At the time, the staff were having a lively discussion about what contributions and change of outlook Buddhist practices could bring to the Western practice of psychotherapy and psychiatry. I enjoyed these conversations with Edward Podvoll and Marvin Casper in particular, as they were exploring the possibility of what they would later call contemplative psychotherapy.

Contemplative Psychology

Still, I was after something else—to explore the psychological insights that I suspected were, and in fact found to be, present in the contemplative traditions of most religions. These traditions appeared to contain a psychology of their own. Actually, they provide the oldest form of psychology we have, certainly older than Western practice. I coined this *contemplative psychology*. In Boulder, I started to write what became my first publication in this field, "On Contemplative Psychology."[3]

Nowadays, we often associate methods or disciplines of contemplation with Buddhism. However, such methods are much more widespread; we find them in almost all religious traditions and even beyond. Whether we use *meditation* or *mindfulness* or *contemplation*, these terms all describe universal practices. The classical Greek word was *theoria*, meaning "mentally looking or gazing." This practice was aimed at developing wisdom or gnosis, which is insight into the nature and dynamics of the human mind and experience. The Latin translation of this same concept is *contemplatio*, which again refers to a mental way of looking at what takes place in our heads; thus, we have the common Christian term *contemplative prayer*. Whatever the name, it is a method of acquiring knowledge about the mind. I prefer the use of the old Latin term to indicate that the insights and discoveries of this type of psychology are the fruits of contemplation. As we will see, such methods are forms of first-person research, an empirical method of systematically studying one's own mind.

Exploring Other Contemplative Traditions

Having discovered the Buddhist methods of contemplative investigation and their resulting theories, I took the lead from that tradition and began to explore others—foremost, the contemplative practices of Christianity and other traditions that make use of methods to acquire insight into the human mind and experience. This brought me into contact with interreligious dialogue, in particular the dialogue among the contemplative orders of the Catholic tradition in the Netherlands and Belgium. These orders would invite me to speak about contemplative psychology, although they knew I was a Buddhist practitioner. Being contemplative orders themselves, they thought contemplative psychology might well have something to offer them. I readily accepted the invitation, because these lectures offered me the opportunity not only to exchange insights about contemplative psychology but also to check the hypothesis about the existence of some common form of such psychology. The dialogue conducted by people who lead the contemplative life is, in fact, the cradle of contemplative psychology. I gave ten lectures that later became the basis for the ten chapters of this book.

In the evening, the male and female novice masters and I would sit together, enjoying each other's company, with cigars and some strong Trappist beer. These occasions would turn into more informal interreligious dialogue about spiritual notions and our experiences. They were curious about a Buddhist practitioner writing about the contemplative life. For me, it was an opportunity to ask Benedictines about the experiential qualities of their key notions such as the Holy Spirit. I wanted to ask this because in the Buddhist tradition we have the notion of Buddha-nature. It is said that the Buddhist path is open to everyone because all human beings have this Buddha-nature. Moreover, there are moments in which we experience our Buddha-nature, even if it is only a glimpse that soon passes. Such moments can offer a different way of experiencing life. With the notion of Buddha-nature in my mind, I asked, "Is the experience of the Holy Spirit working through your heart more or less like this?" And they replied, "Yes, that is part of it." Later on, when they found out what I did, they would do the same thing to me; while having the notion of the

Holy Spirit in their mind they would use the word Buddha-nature when asking me about its experiential qualities.

Our exchange became joyous and interesting, as we started to have this kind of exchange about other terms as well, such as *compassion* and *mercy, wisdom,* and *blindness.* Even the notion of the devil was discussed from a contemplative psychological point of view. The Greek word *diabolos* is related to the verb *diaballein,* which means "splitting into" or "creating discord." This is very close to the Buddhist notion of the dualistic split that makes us see the world in terms of "I" and "other" and makes us suffer. No wonder, we concluded, that we will never see the devil, as he is active as a way of seeing!

This kind of exchange inspired me to dialogue with other traditions as well, in particular the theistic traditions like Judaism and Islam, to search for their understanding of the human mind. Again, I found that beneath or beyond the theological level, the traditions shared a lot on an experiential—or we could say "psychological"—level. In particular, the notion of ego-centeredness, or selfishness, appears to be recognized as *the* source of mental suffering by almost all spiritual and religious traditions. This theme can be found in the contemplative psychology of all traditions, which see ego-centeredness leading to mental blindness and confusion.

For Whom Did I Write This Book?

What I aspire to present in this book is a psychology that contains insights acquired through the systematic practice of contemplation, meditation, or introspection. Such insights are both personal and universal: personal in the sense that we alone can see and investigate the movement of our own minds; and universal in that the discoveries we make are valid and applicable for human beings in general, so these discoveries form a psychology of their own.

Why would we study this psychology? There are many reasons, but one is that it offers us a way to work with our own minds and experiences as well as those of others. How is this different from psychotherapy and the kind of theories on which it is based? Psychotherapy is meant to alleviate individual psychological suffering and promote psychological health, whereas contemplative psychology offers insights and methods to overcome spiritual stagnation and support spiritual growth. That is, a contemplative path goes beyond what psychotherapy calls mental health or sanity. It is directed, for lack of a better description, to the cultivation of our fundamental humanity in thought, word, and deed.

Is contemplative psychology then a form of what is today called "positive psychology"? It would be if we could equate happiness with humaneness. However, it is clear that in certain (life-threatening) situations, upholding one's fundamental humanity can be a very painful thing to do. It can lead to imprisonment, torture, and even death. How then can we qualify contemplative psychology as different from positive psychology? It is about elevating our personal and social life in the direction of—dare I say—sainthood. Even though the various contemplative traditions have different names for this quality or state, they largely agree on the description of it. This description closely relates to the unimpeded flourishing of our fundamental humanity on which all the positive virtues of love, compassion, and mercy rely.

So, who might benefit from reading this book and getting acquainted with contemplative psychology? Obviously, people who are practicing some kind of contemplative discipline or who are thinking about doing so because it may deepen their psychological understanding of their path and its practices. Helping to clarify the nature of mind and experience elevates their lives and that of others in the direction of genuine humanity.

Furthermore, people who are practicing psychotherapy, counseling, or positive psychology in some form will also benefit from becoming somewhat familiar with contemplative psychology, if only because some of the issues with which their clients may present are of a spiritual nature and may best be addressed from this point of view. Becoming familiar with this psychology will also clarify the distinction between introducing and using popular contemplative notions in Western psychotherapy and the opposite to that approach—using psychological terms to clarify the profound nature of spiritual growth as defined by the contemplative traditions themselves.

Also, getting acquainted with contemplative psychology may broaden our concept of what empirical science is, making us aware that there is an empirical science of mind that is based on first-person rather than third-person research. Without being acknowledged or even perceived as such, this contemplative science has been alive for millennia. I hope this book will contribute to making this kind of psychology, its methods, and its benefits more well known.

Acknowledgments

Of course, there are more stories connected with the personal story I have presented. There are also more people than those mentioned here who helped and supported me in my attempts to unearth the psychological notions and methods that have remained almost invisible for those—scientists, psychologists, and others—who have no personal experience with a contemplative tradition. As my personal story has made clear, I am most grateful to my own mentor, the venerable Chögyam Trungpa, also known as the Druk Sakyong of Shambhala; it was his broad, nonsectarian vision of the nature of spirituality that inspired me to this excavation of contemplative psychology.

The publication of my books—in the Netherlands and later in the United States, Germany, France, and Spain—was made possible by the interest of publishers and translators. As for this book, its first version was published in 1999 by the Duquesne University of Pittsburgh and translated from the Dutch by Henry Jansen. When Shambhala Publications offered to reissue this book for a broader readership, I was pleasantly surprised. And even more so, when they assigned Kathleen Gregory, PhD, as the editor for this republication. Not only did she turn out to be highly professional, but she also came up with interesting suggestions and improvements for this text. I would like to thank Karen Steib for the careful final editing and Shambhala Publications for making this book available for a new and wider audience than it had previously. May it be of benefit.

The Great Within

Introduction

The Flourishing Within

Why is it that one human being becomes wiser and gentler during her lifetime while another becomes more hard-hearted and shortsighted to the needs of others? What is it that causes some people to experience and radiate progressively more joy in their lives while others become increasingly anxious and fearful? And why do some people develop the ability to cope with suffering while others fall apart under the same sorrow? How is it that two such divergent psychologies can develop under similar circumstances, whether favorable or unfavorable? And, finally, can we influence this development, or does it lie beyond our control?

These questions are central to contemplative psychology. They are questions that concern an inner flourishing— sometimes willed, sometimes not—that can occur inside us. It takes place so deeply within our being that its presence or absence can determine our attitude toward life in its totality.

Even though this flourishing occurs in a certain sense in the hidden depths of the heart, it is not something abstract and detached from our lives: it becomes manifest in how we live every day. Its fruit is visible in the specific ways in which we relate to our environment, our fellow beings, and ourselves— ways that deepen and elevate our lives and those of others.

We all know or have heard of people who (at moments or perhaps continually) radiate something—a certain warmth, an unconditional interest in their surroundings, and a clarity of mind that is catching and inspiring. This is not necessarily because their situation in life provides them with a special opportunity or because they are especially fond of others; rather, it is because these qualities of warmth, interest, and clarity appear to belong to their very nature. Sometimes we wonder where this mental power comes from, where people find the courage and inspiration to keep going in very difficult circumstances, and even more difficult to answer, where they acquire the power to encourage and inspire others as well.

In this category, we may think of people such as Nelson Mandela; Dag Hammarskjöld; Martin Luther King Jr.; Mother Teresa; the Dalai Lama; or Thich Nhat Hanh. Or we may think of the United Nations general Philippe Morillon who, out of solidarity with the Bosnians, refused to withdraw from Srebrenica so that he could witness with them the inhumanities that occurred there. Or we may have read Etty Hillesum's biography about living in Nazi concentration camps and wondered how she managed to deal with the situations she encountered and give so much encouragement and warmth to those around her.

We sometimes say that such people have "risen above themselves." By this we mean that people who were (or seemed to be) primarily concerned with their own private projects and personal ambitions suddenly abandoned those ambitions when faced with an actual crisis and began to act from a much broader perspective. Improving the situation for everyone involved took precedence over what they initially saw as their self-interest.

Even though we may be pessimistic about people and their abilities, it cannot be denied that such moments occur—moments when something breaks through, like a flood that washes away our pettiness; moments when the protection or cultivation of the situation in which we find ourselves becomes more important to us than our own interests. These are moments when the usual distinction between our personal well-being and the well-being of everything around us is no longer relevant. When this happens, it is more than a blessing in disguise; it is a moment of liberation that reveals new possibilities. This also explains why people, even in the most difficult of circumstances, can experience freedom and strength in a very fundamental sense and are able to experience genuine happiness and encourage and inspire those around them.

We sometimes tend to view people who act from this broader perspective as special and regard them as far above us spiritually, as people who simply possess a spiritual power or capacity that is beyond our reach. However, even if we view these people this way, it is because we *recognize* something in them. The spiritual power and joy in life that we recognize is not essentially alien to us. We ourselves have moments when our attitude toward life is like this—moments when our own fundamental humanity is awakened and manifests itself.

Fundamental Humanity

The inner flourishing we have been examining concerns the uncovering of our fundamental humanity. Because this term is a central theme of this book, it is important to know what we mean by it. The term *fundamental humanity*, or *humaneness* for short, may sound pompous or theoretical. We may even be inclined to view it as somewhat moralistic. In this book, however, we will use these terms interchangeably to refer to a concrete experience that is actually quite familiar to us. Let us take a closer look at humaneness—not how we think it can be perceived in others, but how we experience it in our own lives.

Because fundamental humanity manifests itself under circumstances of both prosperity and adversity, it is difficult to express the way in which it does so in one word. In times of personal adversity, it takes the form of courage in life. Confronted with the misfortunes of others, it manifests itself as compassion, or unselfish caring. It enables us to work with adversity in a way that elevates us and others. In times of personal prosperity or in the viewing of others' prosperity, it manifests itself as joy in life.

In addition to these three forms, there is yet a fourth aspect: clarity of mind. This clarity allows us to see sharply what needs to be done and, just as important, to be realistic about ourselves and the world. It can occur in both good and bad times; in this sense, it is independent of the situation. Moreover, this clarity is not intellectual, as we will see in chapter 4, but rather appears in many respects to resemble the open inquisitiveness and interest that we see in healthy young children. Yet age has little to do with it. It is more the attitude we take toward the richness of color and shape, sound, odor, and physical touch offered by the world of phenomena. It is the universal human capacity and desire to be able to learn, to see, to be aware. It belongs to all people in all times and cultures. As we grow older, this open, eternally youthful inquisitiveness—if it is not choked—can lead to an increasing understanding of our own existence and to a capacity for understanding other people and evoking understanding in them.

By means of these four aspects of our humaneness, we are capable of working in a wholesome way with the reality of our existence—with prosperity and adversity, happiness and suffering, love and hate, certainty and uncertainty.

Let us attempt to word this even more concretely. We experience our fundamental humanity at the moment when we feel we are "at our best"—not in the sense that we could make a top-notch job of something or feel blissfully happy but in the sense that we experience that we are human beings who have been born fully equipped for all of life's ups and downs. At such moments, we realize that we are born first and foremost as human beings and not as the particular person our names and identities denote. There is a fundamental difference here, which we will examine thoroughly in chapter 3. In identifying as a particular person—say, someone called Han—we can often feel that we must justify, explain, defend, or earn our existence. And as Han, with our past history and our expectations, our oversensitivities and insensitivities, we do not always feel capable of coping with life. But at the moment we experience our humaneness, we feel strong and gentle at the same time, filled with youthful vitality and evident self-confidence. We feel strong, not in the sense of "I'm on top of the world!" and could conquer or resist anything, but in the sense that we can allow the world to be as it presents itself to us, to make room for it and work with it. On one hand, this power lifts us above ourselves as individuals, and on the other hand, it brings us closer to ourselves as human beings. It is experienced as a joy and courage that makes us open to our surroundings and reinforces our sense of being able to live with them. At such moments, even if we are in poor health or have other limitations, we still have something to offer—not because we *need* to give something, but because these moments are of themselves wide of view and great of heart.

These moments of being at our best do not occur because we have succeeded in satisfying certain desires or needs or in fending off dangers—although this could happen. Rather, such moments go beyond or, better yet, lie hidden under the satisfaction or frustration of our desires; they occur when every attempt at satisfaction is absent, either because our desire has been met or because we have had to let it go. It is as if rich soil for genuine humaneness exists within us independent of our desires. We are aware of this soil sometimes in happy circumstances and sometimes in suffering. More often, however, it does not manifest itself at all in either prosperity or adversity. Why not? Let us examine this more closely.

Joy in Life and Satisfaction

When we are born, we know nothing. We are naive; in a sense, our existence is veiled in darkness, unarticulated. There are no instructions for life lying beside the cradle. But small and helpless as we are, we are not out of the game; from the first moment of our birth, there is an open, unconditional interest in and devotion to the world of phenomena. We are apparently born this way. It is our fundamental humanity and is just as much a part of being human as are crying and the absence of toilet training. It remains a part of us for the rest of our lives, even when we have long outgrown the need for diapers.

With some people, it seems that this unconditional zest for life increasingly determines their paths, whereas with others, it seems to disappear as they grow older. In our own lives as well, there seem to be periods in which it manifests itself to a greater or lesser degree. Why this happens is, as stated earlier, one of the central questions to which contemplative psychology seeks and also gives an answer (as we will see in detail in chapters 2 and 3).

Here, let us give a broad indication of the answer to this question on the basis of one of the four aspects of humaneness—joy in life—and thereby make a distinction between satisfaction and joy in life. When using the word *life* in phrases such as "joy in life," "attitude toward life," and "courage in life," we indicate that we are talking about a state of mind or attitude that is directed toward life *in its totality* and not specific circumstances. This state of mind or attitude is therefore independent of any situation. Rather, the connection is the reverse: the way in which we respond to our circumstances depends on this state of mind. It determines how we deal with prosperity and adversity.

Thus, when we talk about joy in life, we mean a joyful state of mind that permeates the way we relate to any circumstances and is, in that sense, independent of them. Of course, circumstances can lead us to lose contact with this unconditional joy so that it is seldom evident. While at those moments when it does manifest itself, it transcends our circumstances. Such a moment can occur in distressing situations as well as happy ones—working in a hayfield on a sunny day or on walking through the city on a rainy morning. All of us experience these moments, although they are often concealed from us because, driven by our expectations, we pass them by. Leo Tolstoy wrote about these moments of joy in life:

> They mowed long rows and short rows, good grass and poor grass. Levin lost all count of time and had no idea whether it was late or early. A change began to come over his work which gave him intense satisfaction. There were moments when he forgot what he was doing, he mowed without effort and his line was almost as smooth and good as Titus's. But as soon as he began thinking what he was doing and trying to do better, he was at once conscious how hard the task was, and would mow badly.
>
> The longer Levin mowed, the oftener he experienced those moments of oblivion when it was not his arms which swung the scythe but the scythe seemed to mow of itself, a body full of life and consciousness of its own, and as though by magic, without a thought being given to it, the work did itself regularly and carefully. These were the most blessed moments.[1]

One need not be a Tolstoy to know of such joyous moments in life and to experience them "simply," or unconditionally.

There is also a conditional form of joy, for which we will use the term *satisfaction*. We experience this form of joy when we succeed in satisfying our desires. The distinction between joy in life and satisfaction is that the latter depends on both external and internal circumstances. Internal circumstances are the wishes and desires we cherish; external circumstances are the situations to which our desires are directed. Together they constitute the conditions for satisfaction.

Materialistic and Spiritual Views of Happiness

Ordinarily we use the word *happiness* to refer to the satisfaction of desires. Happiness in this sense is dependent on
circumstances: certain conditions must be fulfilled if we want
to be happy. Happiness depends on something that *brings*
happiness. It comes from outside us: "When you have finished school, you will feel better. When you have a good job/
partner/friends, you will be happy. When you are healthy
again/when you get along well with your children/when you
are free, you will be happy. Try to accomplish that!" While
there is something to be said for this type of ambition, it is
not the whole story. Moreover, it is misleading to suggest that
if we could only control our circumstances, we could attain
happiness for ourselves. True, this is an appealing notion—if
we put forth our best effort, we can have happiness, meaning
possessions, esteem, and power. It suggests that we are not
entirely powerless.

However, the implication of this view is that we can also
lose this kind of happiness, just as we can lose material possessions. Thus, this materialistic view of happiness is the basis
for a life dominated by anxiety, hope for gain, and fear of loss.
In addition, our desires can differ from those of others and
become a source of conflict. Finally, our desires themselves
can be unrealistic, so the attempt to fulfill them plunges us
into further unhappiness. Even if we succeed in satisfying our
desires, usually through much labor and pain, this happiness
is short-lived since it actually consists of the cessation of the
tension caused by unfulfilled desires.

When the moment of satisfaction passes, we must once
again continue the search for happiness. When we achieve that
which we expected to bring us happiness, it becomes apparent
sooner or later that the feeling of being happy does not last.
Once again, we begin to search for happiness in life or become
disappointed and more anxious; we no longer trust life. Our

attitude may change from searching for happiness to avoiding unhappiness. We now judge future circumstances primarily in light of the degree to which they can hurt us and make us unhappy. The basic motivation of our lives becomes the search for safety and protection, for invulnerability. Again and again, when we find that this search is fruitless, our fear increases until it turns into a fear of life. The world becomes one huge, threatening place in which even survival can become too great a task. Some people feel that the only way out is death.

The materialistic view of happiness is problematic not only because it does not fulfill our expectations in a lasting way but also because it severs our connection with our humaneness and thereby our joy in life. The experience of joy in life that belongs to us by nature becomes less frequent; we therefore attach less and less value to it and look for it less often. Because joy in life does not spring essentially from external circumstances, although we do search for happiness there, disappointment is heaped on disappointment.

In contrast to this materialistic view, there is a spiritual view of happiness, in which happiness is not viewed as a moment of satisfaction but as a moment of joy in life. This view does not look down on striving for satisfaction, but it rejects the high expectations that appear in the materialistic view, particularly the suggestion that satisfaction *is* joy in life or necessarily leads to joy in life. In the spiritual view, happiness is quite different from satisfaction. Perhaps, while we are preoccupied with searching for happiness by adapting our circumstances and our desires to each other, we look up for no reason at all at the big fluffy clouds drifting lazily across the blue sky, or we see a sparrow hopping about on the sidewalk. For just that one moment, our preoccupation is gone, and we experience reconciliation and joy in life—just for a moment, but possibly an intense moment because of the great contrast. We may then recognize that a leap of perception has occurred that places our search for happiness in another light. Perhaps this search is unmasked as fundamentally misleading, because at those moments we know that what we are searching for is something we already possess.

In our Western culture with its great material prosperity, we are well aware that favorable material circumstances are no guarantee of joy in life, as the old adage "Money cannot buy happiness" says. But even that insight often only leads us to search for happiness elsewhere, such as in social circumstances or even internal, or mental, states. In the latter case, we may see our desires and wishes as major causes of unhappiness. We want to liberate ourselves from them and search for ways to manipulate the mind to get what we want. Perhaps we think that the practice of spiritual disciplines can help us, but that is not how we can make our humaneness flourish because our basic attitude is still the same—if only we could attain what we desire or eliminate that which stands in our way, then we would be happy. The only merit of such attempts is that, in doing them, we can learn to see their inadequacy.

Moreover, the belief that the only way to achieve happiness is by manipulating our external or internal circumstances makes us vulnerable to manipulation; we become susceptible to promises of all kinds—realistic and unrealistic—related to material, social, psychological, and spiritual "success." If we believe that only riches or social status will make us happy, we are sometimes prepared to work ourselves to death and resort to practices that are less than decent, even to ourselves. If we believe that the destruction of our enemies will ultimately bring us happiness, then we will fight. If we see our minds or ourselves as the enemy, we will try to conquer the mind or destroy ourselves.

Many spiritual traditions say that we lose our humaneness by approaching ourselves and our world (including religion) from the materialistic view of happiness. The fruit we pick personally and communally from this view has a bitter taste. Although we continue to experience our humaneness at moments in spite of this, such moments quickly pass. Surmounting adversity or promoting our good fortune soon demands all our attention again. In light of this, such moments seem unrealistic and irrelevant. It is then difficult to imagine that they are the foundation of and the door to a completely different way of living.

The reason we have discussed the aspect of joy in life in some detail is that the same problem occurs in the other three aspects of our humaneness—courage in life, compassion, and clarity of mind. These three are unconditional as well; they are not related to certain circumstances but are independent of them. When we live from the perspective of our humaneness, then our compassion manifests itself freely and unconditionally whenever suffering appears: we quickly jump to someone's aid, not because we see it as our moral duty at that moment, but because we cannot do otherwise. If we see a toddler fall into the water, we run to pull him out. At that moment we are not at all concerned with moral duty. We have already pulled the child to safety without thinking about it. But if we are not in touch with our humaneness, we might easily come to believe that mercy is a matter of maintaining and propagating good morals. However, sermons on morality have seldom accomplished anything, certainly not in times of danger. At those times, it is only our fundamental humanity that can achieve anything.

When we no longer have courage in life, we quickly come to believe that toughness, perseverance, and persistence in the difficult struggle to achieve our goals and defy adversity is true courage. When we lose our clarity of mind, we come to see it as something vague that cannot compete with being well informed and having a great deal of knowledge. Or we regard it as presence of mind at best, which is useful for the promotion of our own interests; it is a form of cleverness that prevents the wool from being pulled over our eyes.

Humaneness, when we are no longer in touch with it, seems to be a beautiful utopia, good for chronic optimists or religious people. There is something to be said for this, because it is precisely in the great religious traditions that we find all kinds of indications and insights that refer to fundamental humanity. We will explore them in the first part of this book. The religious traditions also give instructions as to how this humaneness can be cultivated by means of certain disciplines, which we will discuss in the second part of this book. It is for this reason that our investigations into contemplative psychology lead us to consult the religious traditions; they prove to contain quite a bit of psychological insight. For some people, this book will therefore be a "religious" book; for others, it will be a book that discusses humaneness and its cultivation, which the Shambhala tradition calls *basic goodness*[2] and which those who reflect deeply about our culture sometimes call *spiritual humanism*.[3]

Humaneness is a universal human power that is not associated with a particular ideology or philosophy of life. We can discover it in our personal experience and make it flourish. The fruit of this flourishing within manifests itself in our actions and speech, which in turn affect our society and culture. It is that which is able to elevate our own existence and that of others. In the words of Sakyong Mipham, "It is what creates and sustains a good human society."[4]

Searching for or Bestowing Happiness?

It is a typically contemplative premise that joy in life, courage in life, compassion, and clarity of mind are qualities that do not come from outside but from within—qualities that we do not need to acquire but possess from birth. If so, does this mean that we should simply allow our external life situation to run its course, that we can afford to become passive and cease to care about our external circumstances? This is certainly not the implication, but to allow these four qualities to flourish, we do need to give up our self-deception, illusions, and unrealistic expectations as to what our situation in life can offer us in terms of joy in life. These stand in the way of our humaneness—a humaneness that is by nature (that is, unconditionally) involved with life and manifests itself in the form of a caring and understanding way of dealing with others and our external circumstances.

Importantly, the more our humaneness manifests itself, the stronger it becomes. Inasmuch as we are able to live from the perspective of our humaneness, we are able to become people who unconditionally *bestow* happiness, instead of people who *seek* happiness. Thus, we have not turned away from the world around us but have turned toward the world unconditionally, in a truly human way. Bringing about this turn of mind or conversion is the concern of the religious traditions, and contemplative psychology is concerned with the how and why of this turn of mind.

At present, most of us are seekers rather than bestowers of happiness. This is why specific external circumstances are still definitely relevant and cannot be ignored, for to the extent that we think our humaneness depends on specific circumstances and the satisfaction of our desires, we are no longer able to ignore those circumstances and desires. If we wish to cultivate our humaneness, we have to face the circumstances of our lives and examine how they play on our expectations and blind spots, because all of these have become the source, or focal points, of our fear of life. It is possible that we are right to change certain circumstances in our lives temporarily or perhaps permanently, as long as we cannot let go of our expectations of (and our hopes and fears about) them.

However, this is about giving a certain shape to our way of life—a shape that could be called a spiritual way of life, one that allows us space for exploring and penetrating our fear of life. To do so is both the manifestation and essence of courage in life as well. In this way, we restore our link to our humaneness. This process is quite different from attempting to turn away internally from or becoming insensitive to life. It is the opposite of fleeing from the realities of our existence into materialistic or spiritual fantasy worlds that please the imagination and seem to offer security. Rather, it is the creation of circumstances in which we can rediscover and cultivate our humaneness. In such circumstances, we discover not only that we are able to rise above ourselves but also how we can do this, how we can be at our best. The more we grow in our ability to do this, the more independent of our circumstances we become. Situations become less and less effective in destroying the manifestation of our humaneness; they become stepping-stones for its manifestation rather than focal points of our fear of life. Psychological factors play a role in this process of inner transformation, and we will examine these factors in the following chapters.

The Spiritual Way of Life

As already stated, moments of unconditional courage and joy in life exist just as much as moments when we are gripped by fear of life and depression. That we have these moments, that they are part of human existence, is beyond dispute. They are present in all cultures, but there are many different ideas as to what value we should attach to those moments when our humaneness manifests itself and what price we should be willing to pay for uncovering it. Such moments often disrupt our customary attitude toward life in such a radical way that they seem to be beyond our reach or control while simultaneously being part of our lives.

At the same time, we continue to long for these moments as long as we live—these moments of courage, kindness, and clarity of mind that can appear at any time and for any or no reason. Sometimes we wonder hesitantly whether it would be possible to live from the perspective of these moments, whether that is what some people do and why they inspire us. Perhaps we then even ask the question of why we do *not* live from the perspective of these moments and ask ourselves whether the obstacles to this can be removed. However, when we look back at these moments and the idea occurs to us, "If only it could always be this way for everyone," then often despair and so-called realism take over: "If that were possible, it would already be so, and because it is not, it apparently cannot be so." Maybe we are willing to acknowledge that such moments do occur, but we are unsure as to whether we can cultivate them. From the perspective of our usual attitude toward life, we tend to occupy ourselves with keeping our affairs in order. That in itself is already difficult and time consuming enough.

In every culture, however, there are traditions that apply themselves to cultivating our fundamental humanity with disciplines of action, speech, and the mind. How does this work? These disciplines first reveal the factors that smother our humaneness and then help us to eliminate them. For although we do not control our humaneness—we are not capable of manipulating or holding on to the moments at which it manifests itself—we do control the factors that cause it to recede, for we have created these factors ourselves. That is why the cultivation of inner flourishing is more a process of uncovering our humaneness by exposing and eliminating that which chokes it rather than directly cultivating the humaneness itself. Subsequently, we begin to (re)discover and trust our humanity. Finally, we begin to identify with it more and more and live from this perspective.

The desire to realize our humaneness fully and manifest it lies at the basis of the spiritual path. It is the origin of the religious traditions. The desire for a truly human life is universal, being an expression and proof of fundamental humanity. But the ways in which that desire acquires form in our lives are extremely varied—forms of searching that are wise and foolish, fruitful and sterile. Sometimes people leave the environment in which they grew up, searching for a more authentic existence. All great religious traditions have countless stories of people who have done this. Prince Siddhartha, who would later be known as the Buddha, fled his princely existence with all its comforts and ease when he was twenty-nine years old and already had a wife and child. Shocked by the painful realities of life that he saw when exploring the life outside his sheltered royal environment, he set off in search of a way of life that could awaken insight into the human existence in his heart. Although this was undoubtedly a drastic approach to the problem, he was not the only one to embark on such a course.

This approach is also abundantly present in the New Testament. A striking story is that of a rich young ruler who asked Jesus what he must do to inherit eternal life. When the ruler said that he had lived according to the commandments since he was a boy, Jesus replied, "You still lack one thing. Sell everything you have and give to the poor, and you will have treasure in heaven. Then come, follow me" (Luke 18:22). This is no small task, but one about which Jesus remarks, "I tell you the truth, no one who has left home or wife or brothers or parents or children for the sake of the kingdom of God will fail to receive many times as much in this age and, in the age to come, eternal life" (Luke 18:29–30).

Others do not break away from their current lives in a dramatic way but grow out of it slowly, because in one way or another, they have kept an ear open to the voice of truth. The life of Saint Augustine is a beautiful and—in all respects—modern example of this. It is actually a double example, because as a young man, he broke with the Christian tradition in which his mother had raised him. This break had to do with his desire to make it in the world, to acquire honor and fame by shining as an orator and generally respected intellectual. He believed this was the way to find true joy in life. He made the fortunate error of listening to a famous orator—Ambrose, the bishop of Milan:

And I studiously hearkened to him preaching to the people, not with the motive I should, but, as it were, trying to discover whether his eloquence came up to the fame thereof, or flowed fuller or lower than was asserted . . . and yet I was drawing nearer gradually and unconsciously. For although I took no trouble to learn what he spake, but only to hear how he spake (for that empty care alone remained to me, despairing of a way accessible for man to Thee), yet, together with the words which I prized, there came into my mind also the things about which I was careless; for I could not separate them. And whilst I opened my heart to admit "how skillfully he spake," there also entered with it, but gradually, "and how truly he spake!"[5]

Still others do not break physically with their surroundings or grow out of them as Augustine did; instead, they seem to grow more into those surroundings. They somehow know how to use their actual situation in life as a means for developing their humaneness. A familiar example from Buddhism is the legendary king Suchandra of Shambhala, who did not give up his kingship and its comforts but, having received instruction from the Buddha, took advantage of his position in the world as a spiritual path. He awakened in his subjects their own humaneness, and in that way an enlightened society was created. There are people who live a spiritual life in the midst of the world in our day and age as well. They are not necessarily people in high social positions, such as U Thant or Dag Hammarskjöld. Our own lives can be lived this way.

Throughout the centuries, people have sought and found ways of life that strengthen and support the spiritual path. Such a way belongs to all times and cultures. In some traditions, it has led to the development of monastic ways of life. In others, such as the Jewish and Protestant traditions, it is

practiced in everyday life, which is why such traditions have
no monasteries. There are also traditions, such as Hinduism,
Buddhism, and Catholicism, in which the spiritual journey
has been given form in both everyday and monastic life.

Regardless of how a spiritual way of life is lived and which
form it takes in a certain time or culture, it is always based on
the desire to uncover true humanity and on deep psychological
insight into the human mind and the ways in which humanity
can be developed. This insight is not so much something theoretical or philosophical, attainable only by learned minds, but
is a concrete type of understanding of human nature—both
our humaneness and into that about which we say, *Homo
sum; humani nil a me alienum puto* ("I am a human being;
nothing human is foreign to me").

In conclusion, perhaps a warning is in order here. Although
we are searching for the ways in which religious traditions
uncover humaneness, that is not to say that all existing religious traditions actually contribute to such discovery. There
is much that is ripe and green in this area, and it is also possible for existing traditions to degenerate. Traditions are maintained and passed on by people, and there is no guarantee that
every tradition currently offers an effective support for cultivating humanity. However, by practicing the disciplines of a
tradition and studying its insights, we can establish through
experience whether or not it helps to cultivate our inner flourishing and yields fruit in our words and deeds.

When we refer to religious traditions in the following chapters, we are referring only to those traditions that do reveal
our humaneness. Traditions with a different aim are not considered here because they do not offer relevant material for
the development of a contemplative psychology aimed at inner
flourishing and its results. If we are aware of this restriction,
we do not run the risk of forming too rosy an image of religious traditions or seeing them as unassailable authorities.
As history has taught us, they are not. However, it cannot be

denied that it is precisely in these traditions, more than any-where else, that valuable psychological insights and disciplines directed toward the cultivation of humaneness in our concrete existence are to be found. This is what we will examine in the following chapters.

PART ONE

Explorations

1

Contemplative Psychology

A s part of Western culture and its globalizing reach, we are perhaps not always aware that in the last half century it has developed into a distinctly psychological (or "psychologizing") culture. In fact, we now take for granted that much of our experience tends to be viewed from a psychological perspective in a way that may have been overlooked or not given such credence in the past. People think and speak in psychological terms much more often than they used to in order to express genuine understanding of their own human existence as well as to give an impression of understanding. We find it quite normal to speak to one another about our feelings and motivations, including the unconscious ones, and their effects on our behavior using terms that did not even exist before the last century. We have grown up with this.

Of course, the growth of psychology as a discipline has played a major role in this development. Our psychological vocabulary and the conceptual frameworks that we use in daily life have expanded tremendously due to the expansion and popularization of psychology, and we even have the term *pop psychology* to represent its acceptance by the masses. This growth has its pros and cons. On the plus side, we are able to discuss certain psychological issues in a much more nuanced way and with much more precision than we could a century ago. Yet this assumes that we are all familiar with the new, enlarged vocabulary, which is not always the case. On the negative side, it is not always clear what certain terms mean because they have not been clearly defined. Often, we have only a vague notion of what they signify and use them to communicate as best we can—true of psychologists as well as laypeople. Because of this, we run the risk of supporting psychological theories that are presented with a certain aplomb or surrounded with the aura of scholarship, even if we cannot link them to our own concrete experience. Theories can then begin to combine and function as an ideology, which leads us to try to bring our experiences into agreement with the theory rather than ensuring that the theory matches our feelings, emotions, thoughts, and perceptions. In fact, when we rely on theory to "know" ourselves, there is a danger that we may no longer be either open to or aware of our actual experience.

Entire generations in the West have grown up with the concept of humanity proposed by Sigmund Freud, and they learned to interpret their experiences by means of this theoretical framework. Many Freudian ideas, such as unconscious impulses and the Oedipus complex, have made their way into popular culture. Even without having studied psychology, people are familiar with these theories, which are now taken for granted in our society. In fact, psychological interest is subject to fashion. Some topics are front-page news in psychological journals for a decade or so, only to disappear and sometimes be entirely forgotten. For instance, research into personality types was popular up until the middle of the twentieth century. Then research into motivation was popular for a while. With the advent of the computer, interest has shifted to the human being as an "information processing system." In any case, the presence of psychology is a fact in modern society. Whether we like it or not, this is how things are.

All of this, of course, leads to the question: Is contemplative psychology, which is central to this book, not itself an expression of the psychologizing tendencies in our culture?

In a certain sense it is, since it arises from the question of how we can communicate about basic human themes—such as how we concretely experience and give shape to being human—with people who have begun to think more about these themes. Contemplative psychology is necessarily rooted in this type of "psychology-mindedness," while inquiring into how we can understand and speak about spiritual development and all that is related to it.

It is a paradox in our culture that, in spite of the developments in psychology, the precise topics that concern humanity are thrust into the background. We consider the satisfaction of material and emotional needs and desires of paramount importance. This, in turn, strongly determines the direction in which the sciences, including psychology, develop. In a standard psychology text, there are a number of themes that we will not necessarily encounter or that may be noted as historical sidebars. For example, theories as to the nature of the mind, consciousness, and experience are rarely offered. Self-knowledge, clarity of mind, compassion, courage, and how they can be attained are not discussed in these texts. Notwithstanding the advent of positive psychology and the contemporary interest in mindfulness, which has brought some demonstrated changes to the academic presentation of the subject as reflected in introductory textbooks. In general, topics such as how we relate and respond to life are relegated in part to the realm of philosophy and in part to self-help literature and magazines. Scientific psychology has little to do with it.

Yet there exists—in our own culture as well as elsewhere—another tradition in which these fundamental topics do receive full attention: the tradition of the contemplative life. The definition of the term *contemplative life* was touched on in the introduction to this book. We will examine it in more detail in the following chapters. For the time being, let us say that this term refers to a specific, disciplined way of life. *Discipline* is a word that easily scares us. But here we are concerned with the practice of a gentle and intelligent discipline that is directed at cultivating humaneness—within both ourselves and others. This discipline is based on an understanding of human nature and awakens such understanding.

In most cultures, the contemplative life is discussed in a religious context, which does not always make it easy for some people. This is particularly so when the terms of the religion in question hardly or no longer speak to us *because* we have begun to think so much in psychological terms. A religious vocabulary quickly gives us the impression of being old-fashioned, vague, unrealistic, or excessively moralistic. Many people are no longer immediately inclined to lend an ear to these great religious traditions for the answers to vital questions.

Yet it is precisely within these traditions that one can find psychological insight into the human mind and the experience of reality. Earlier studies actually showed that many religious traditions do include a contemplative psychology, one that can clarify the nature of the mind and spiritual development and the function of spiritual disciplines.[1] William James, considered the founder of modern psychology and writing in the early nineteenth century, was the first to acknowledge the psychological insights of many religious traditions. However, because of the historical split between psychology and philosophy, as well as the changing role of religion in society, it has become difficult to see a relationship between our human psychology and traditions that promote spiritual development. In fact, even the concept of contemplative psychology may, for some readers, seem like an oxymoron. So, what do I mean by this term? I define it as a psychology that can clarify the nature of the mind and human experience, as well as provide guidance for spiritual development and understanding of spiritual disciplines.

Expressing this knowledge in terms of contemplative psychology is like pouring old wine into new wineskins. It is a wine we had almost forgotten was stored in the cellar, a very special wine of high quality and immense, wholesome power—the wine of spiritual development. The new wineskins represent a psychological conceptual framework. This is a rather risky way of expressing it. We could easily read into this interpretation that modern Western psychology is able to survey and clarify the nature of the contemplative life by means of its own conceptual frameworks. Many psychologists have approached spirituality in this way—certainly not without results, as the work of people like Carl Jung, Abraham Maslow, Eugen Drewermann, Ken Wilber, and many others who work in the field of the psychology of religion demonstrates. Nonetheless, as we shall see later, this approach has its limitations.

It is for this reason that we will follow a completely different—one might say reversed—approach in this book. We will begin by looking at the psychological ideas that have been developed and maintained by the contemplative traditions from the premise that these traditions have something to contribute to our understanding of the human mind and experience: they contain insights that are of great importance to humankind. That is why it is important that we first listen to what these traditions have to say. In this way, I will show how the psychological approach inherent in the great contemplative traditions themselves will become visible. Thus, we will not explore spirituality from the perspective of existing psychological frameworks but will examine the frameworks and ways of thinking within the religious traditions themselves. This will provide us with a unique psychology—a contemplative one.

Unfortunately, the distrust between psychologists and those involved in contemplative and spiritual traditions is so great at times that they do not want to delve into each other's conceptual framework. This distrust is not completely without grounds. Every now and then, both psychologists and religious people have developed and propagated the most absurd, fantastic, and even harmful theories about people. Errors are and will be made on both sides. A critical stance with regard to both psychology and religion is necessary. However, a critical stance does not mean shying away from being willing to search for the valuable psychological insights within the religions. Psychological insights include everything that relates to the human mind—motivations, emotions, cognition, actions and speech, language and communication— and, perhaps most radically, how all of these facets influence spiritual growth, the inner flourishing of courage, wisdom, and joy in life. It is these spiritual qualities that are prominent in contemplative psychology. A critical stance toward religion also requires not shying away from acknowledging the human qualities and virtues valued in the traditions, separate from the structural and belief system that have historically framed those human attributes.

Interestingly, another tradition also has a connection to the contemplative approach: art. Like the scientific and religious traditions, this tradition attempts in its own way to explore and clarify human experience. We could, of course, view art as a purely aesthetic matter, but it also involves trying to make something visible. Whether this occurs through the visual arts, music, or literature, there is an aspect to the process besides the aesthetic one: a truth-seeking aspect. In one way or another, the artist attempts to make something clear, to arouse and communicate a certain perspective, a certain kind of experience in which something is revealed so that the audience looks at things in a different way, even if just for a moment. This is an important motivation for the artist. Art reveals or clarifies something. Thus, it is not amazing to find that in many cultures art is practiced in connection with religion. Perhaps "searching for truth" seems too grand a phrase for this discipline, but art does involve a form of research in this direction. In this sense, it is a tradition that in its own way seeks and contains insights into the nature of human experience. Who knows the psychological significance (and effect) of form and color better than the visual artist? Who knows the effect that sounds and tones have on our state of mind better than the composer? No sensory psychologist can match them. With respect to literature, one of the founders of scientific psychology in the Netherlands, Hubertus Duijker, used to say that it would be very valuable for psychologists to read the novels of Marcel Proust.

In all cultures we find the three main traditions: the religious or spiritual tradition, the scientific tradition, and the artistic tradition. Although they are all very different and follow very different approaches, they also have something in common: the desire to explain in one way or another what it is to be human. In this sense, these three traditions have a common psychological root.

Conventional and Contemplative Psychology

Before we look more closely at what contemplative psychology has to say on the topic of humaneness and spiritual growth, it will be useful to compare a few points between it and the familiar scientific psychology. This can help illustrate the ways in which contemplative psychology is different from what we normally think of as "psychology," for our general view of this discipline has been strongly colored by the scientific aspect.

Of course, the various facets of scientific psychology do not form one coherent whole. So many theories and conceptual frameworks have been developed in the last hundred years that today we could almost say there are as many psychological opinions as there are psychologists. Psychology has become a very extensive science with many fields and subdisciplines, such as social psychology, child psychology, educational psychology, clinical psychology, positive psychology, and research psychology. Many kinds of different approaches have also arisen, of which behavioral psychology,

depth psychology, cognitive psychology, and neuropsychology are the most familiar. All in all, it has not become any
less complicated, since one theory sometimes denies precisely
what another theory confirms. Psychologists of various subdisciplines often have little use for one another. For example,
cognitive psychologists usually want little to do with depth
psychologists and vice versa. Some psychologists, like many
laypeople, drift eclectically from one conceptual framework
to another, depending on the problem with which they are
confronted. Others adhere to one framework as if it were an
article of faith, even if the main defects of this framework can
be demonstrated. At the same time, many psychologists regret
the fact that their science is not a clearly unified discipline.

The Plasticity of the Human Mind

There is a minority of psychologists who see the large number of psychologies as the inevitable result of the plasticity of
the human mind itself. This view is to be found among those
involved in phenomenological and existential work and in
forms of cognitive psychotherapy. These psychologists accept
rather than deplore the large number of approaches within the
discipline. In their view, the human mind is capable, to a certain degree, of creating its own patterns, and the task of psychology is to chart these patterns. Inevitably, this chart must
constantly be updated because people change psychologically,
both individually and collectively. This is why more than one
type of psychology is necessary. But although each of the psychological theories contains a number of useful insights, these
insights cannot be integrated into a single theory that is not a
source of contention.

According to this view of psychology, plasticity (the freedom to shape one's psychological existence) and rigidity (lack
of that freedom) also exist in an interesting relationship: people have the ability to change themselves and, simultaneously,

to deny themselves this opportunity by forming habits. Simply put, to a certain degree, we have the freedom to form our own minds and the freedom to imprison ourselves within the mind, to limit our psychological space. Cultural anthropological research has demonstrated that this freedom is much greater than we normally think. In fact, the great diversity and rigidity of cultures and forms of society illustrate the extent of this freedom.

Contemplative traditions emphasize the idea of the plasticity of the human mind but also recognize the rigidity of human beings. According to these traditions, people almost always use their freedom to form certain egocentric habits in which, once formed, they are imprisoned. In the contemplative psychology of Buddhism, these patterns are called *samskaras*, or mental conditionings, that together form our egocentric motivations and give direction to our actions.[2] In essence, samskaras are mental habits that are continually practiced and thereby become ruts into which we fall. Once formed, it is difficult to change these ruts: they become psychological patterns.

However, habits develop not only in individual's minds but also in disciplines such as psychology and in entire cultures, since these also arise out of the human mind. When a group or collective becomes so convinced of the apparent inevitability of the formed patterns, then they are viewed as absolute truths and easily become part of a concept of humanity: "That's how human beings are." This concept of humanity subsequently influences the way in which people raise their children, thus closing the circle. When psychologists study and describe people or a particular group of people, they find patterns that conform to their concept of humanity, even though the conclusion may be expressed as, "It has been scientifically confirmed . . ." Within this vicious circle, it is difficult to unravel which is the cause and which is the effect.

Contemplative psychology explores our concept of humanity and focuses on identifying the mental habits or patterns that are destructive and blinding in our lives. This includes exploring how these habits are allowed to become even more ingrained, how to prevent this from occurring, and how to let go of them. Inasmuch as a mental habit causes a certain behavior, that behavior ceases when the mental habit does. Contemplative living is therefore concerned with uncovering the basic mental freedom of human beings so they are no longer imprisoned by self-made patterns. This is not so much for the sake of some theoretical ideal of freedom or some psychotherapeutic ideal of health, but to open the mental space in which the Holy Spirit, the Buddha-nature, Allah, Yahweh, Brahma, or whatever a particular tradition calls it can transform our lives. In the terminology of contemplative psychology, the contemplative life is directed toward "opening a mental space" in which our humaneness can flourish. Within this space, the mind is governed by something other than the patterns that conventional psychology often implicitly holds to be valid for humankind. In this contemplative development, freedom and health are not a goal but a kind of bonus. People who travel the contemplative path may no longer be described or explained satisfactorily by conventional psychological jargon.

Having said that, it is also true that we are at an interesting point in the history of psychology. The impact of the mindfulness movement, for example, has resulted in terms such as *attunement, presence,* and *nowness* becoming part of the psychological lexicon, at least for a small number of subdisciplines. However, it is still early days to know how broad and enduring an impact this will have on conventional psychology's view of humanity.

In the meantime, let us look to the contemplative traditions to help us navigate this terrain, since they have used their own psychological concepts, while embracing the basic plasticity or freedom of the human mind to study the extent of that freedom. It is because of this plasticity that something like a spiritual path exists. Being on the path can even be compared with molding the mind in a number of ways. We will discuss this in the next chapter.

The Objectivity of Research

The difference of opinion on the plasticity of the mind is one of the causes of the tension between much (but not all) of scientific psychology and religion. There are other causes for this tension. One such cause, as suggested earlier, is the fact that psychology as we know it in Western culture has disassociated itself from religion. In one respect, this disassociation was linked with the abandonment of the Christian concept of humanity in relation to an omnipotent God; because of this, a number of new concepts of humanity—that is, new definitions of the object of psychological study—were developed. Not surprisingly, these new concepts deliberately left out the spiritual dimension.[3] However, this break between psychology and religion also allowed for the development of new methods for studying human life. A new methodology arose in terms of how to acquire reliable knowledge with regard to human functioning. This methodology specifies an approach known as the *empirical method* of research. It was originally used in the natural sciences and over time has come to be applied to psychological research.

The empirical method is quite different from the approaches used by the contemplative traditions for the development of insight into people. The essence of the empirical method is that it attempts to discover patterns between psychological phenomena that are *intersubjective observable*—those that can be observed by everyone by using the senses, either with or without the help of technologically refined tools. So that which is studied is independent of the researcher. In practice, this means that the researcher must endeavor to design and conduct research in such a way that the outcome is in no way influenced by their personal attitudes and subjective experiences. No matter who conducts the research, if it is conducted correctly, the results are always (or should always be) the same. Only then can the results be regarded as objective facts. When scientific psychology studies religious phenomena, it makes use of the empirical method. In that way, it has made an important contribution to the development of the psychology of religion; for example, it has increased our insight into the causal relationships between religious and other (psychological) phenomena.

Yet this methodology has certain limitations within scientific psychology. There is a sizable field that the empirical method of research must leave out—the field of one's own mental or inner life—because it is not directly accessible by other researchers. According to empirical psychology, this field is not independent of the researcher and therefore not open to empirical research. At the same time, it is precisely this field with which the contemplative traditions are concerned. The advantage of empiricism's objectivity is countered by the loss in another domain—the domain of the mind; the world as experienced subjectively by human beings falls outside its range of possible research. At best we can see a correlation between (mental) experience and the brain, but the experience itself cannot be observed by the researcher. Disengaged from the domain of the mind, the remaining domains of speech and actions are cast in an artificial and distorted light. Of course, philosophers of science and scientific psychologists are aware of this but can see no possible solution. The dilemma entails the question of how mental phenomena can be studied without damaging the scientific, objective nature of the method of study. In contemplative psychology, this dilemma is formulated somewhat differently, phrased in terms that also direct us toward a certain solution. Let us take a closer look at this point.

Research in the First and Third Person

As stated earlier, it is characteristic of the empirical method that it can be used only for the study of phenomena that are accessible to all researchers. In practical terms, this means that psychological research is restricted to research in the third person, meaning someone other than the researcher is its object of study. The researcher studies the other. This type of study is characteristic of academic research psychology, which is why it is usually used to study subjects' behavior and speech, since that is what we can see of others. This is its field of study.

But there is yet another, quite large field—that of mental experience, or mental phenomena, which is not accessible in the third person. This mental field is only directly accessible by the person involved, requiring research in the first person, or self-examination. After all, I can experience what is going on in *my* mind but not what is going on in someone else's.

If we wish to study the mental field, we can no longer use the empirical, third-person approach. We must use a first-person approach, a form of self-examination in which our own subjective experience (including our thoughts and emotions) is the object of study.

In contrast to scientific traditions, study in the first person is central to contemplative traditions. For this reason, many traditions have refined instructions at their disposal so this first-person form of study may be conducted in a thorough and reliable manner. In other words, these traditions feature a first-person methodology.

At the beginning of the twentieth century, scientific psychology rejected introspection as a method of research, giving primacy to research in the third person. Of course, it is possible to learn (and sometimes also to conjecture by means of analogies) something of what goes on in the minds of others,

but again, we cannot see directly what is happening in someone else's mind like we can in our own. Moreover, what others
tell us about their minds or what we conjecture about them
is not always reliable. Distortion is possible when someone
attempts to express what is going on within themselves. For
example, in attempting to give expression to our feelings, language itself can fail. It is also possible for us to think that we
are saying what is going on inside ourselves, whereas this is
not the case. Finally, we can refuse to say what we think and
choose to say something else instead.

This unreliability is the reason the student of scientific
psychology is reserved about research in which so-called
self-reports are used as data. There is no guarantee that the
subjects (can or will) give an accurate account of their mental
field. Late nineteenth-century introspective psychologists like
Wilhelm Wundt, Oswald Külpe, and Edward B. Titchener
attempted to teach people to be accurate, but these attempts
yielded few or no results. They led only to a conviction in
scientific psychology that stands to this day: reliable introspective research is suspect, if not impossible.

This conviction has led to a parting of the ways within psychology. On one hand, it has led to the development of what
we now call *scientific psychology*—a psychology based on the
empirical method of research. This discipline attempts to clarify our thinking about our experience by testing our thoughts
(theories) against our experience. On the other hand, it has led
to forms of psychology that bear traces of the old psychology
of consciousness that Wilhelm Wundt tried to develop. These
disciplines attempt to clarify our experience by transforming
our consciousness and our way of thinking. Examples are
clinical psychology and many forms of psychotherapy. We
will return to these two forms of clarification extensively in
chapters 4 and 6.

When we consider psychology has developed into two main
approaches, it is interesting to note that according to many

contemplative traditions, human beings possess a mental dis-cernment (or "discriminating awareness") that allows them to clarify their experience. They have the capacity to distinguish between illusion and reality, self-deception and truth. From the contemplative perspective, this discriminating awareness does not usually function adequately, unless it is cultivated. It can be trained in such a way that we are able to view our own mental domain clearly and recognize patterns in it. Simply put, these traditions claim that we can explore and know our own minds! On the basis of this, we can also learn to identify the causal connections between what we think, say, and do. Contemplative traditions claim to have the methods for such identification. We will investigate them in detail in the second part of this book. These methods have been tested and refined by generations of practitioners and are effective if we train ourselves in them. Just as the training of our intellectual or conceptual powers requires time, so does the training of our discriminating awareness.

What is the nature of this training? First of all, its purpose is different from that of academic psychology. One could say that academic psychology aims at acquiring insight by collect-ing information about human functioning. Contemplative psy-chology, however, aims at acquiring insight by bringing about a transformation of human functioning. It is, to use Adrian van Kaam's terms, primarily a *formative science*, whereas aca-demic psychology is primarily an *informative science*.[4] Con-templative psychology is not directed exclusively at collecting knowledge in the form of information but also at cultivating wisdom. Therefore, it is concerned with the transformation of the one who acquires knowledge, the "knower," rather than collecting knowledge that may or may not be used to help transform others in some way; for example, using acquired knowledge to help shape future best-practice treatments of mental illness. However, we should be careful not to reject the collecting of knowledge or information in this idea of a *formative spirituality* as suggested by van Kaam. He did not reject it, and neither do I. Within a contemplative psychology, collecting information acquires a different function: the intellectual knowledge or information acquired has a transforming effect on the knower if it is taken into account and studied. This transformation refers specifically to the change in one's own mind toward what we have called humaneness. So once again we see the first-person approach, which in some way reverses the basis for study and acquiring knowledge. The methods for transformation have been proven effective by experience, and on that basis, further study has been undertaken.

The central idea behind this is, of course, that ignorance and mental blindness do not always arise from a lack of knowledge per se but because things escape our awareness or confuse us. If the mind is not clear, the result is a faulty or incorrect way of perceiving and thinking about the world and its people, including ourselves. This, in turn, leads to all kinds of confusing and conflicting emotions, which then dim our clarity of mind.

Further, because our state of mind also determines our experience of reality, we can say that contemplative psychology is concerned with clarifying our experience of reality. Spiritual traditions have developed special methods for this purpose—methods that are entirely different from those used in empirical psychology. They are directed at discovering and freeing ourselves from confusion and ignorance and will be covered in detail in chapter 4.

These methods are extremely varied, both within as well as between the various spiritual traditions. A factor common to all, however, is that they involve cultivating a clarity of mind that frees us from confusion, ignorance, and self-centeredness. Such methods include disciplines like meditation, contemplation, and some forms of prayer. Together, they are meant to clarify confusion and are based on an analysis of the nature of ignorance, what I have elsewhere called an *anepistemology*, a theory about not knowing or ignorance.[5] These methods form the "hard core" of the contemplative life.

There are also many other spiritual disciplines, since in principle, *all* activities can be used toward this aim when practiced in the context of a spiritual discipline. The emphasis then shifts from what we do to how we do it. Suppose that as a spiritual disciple you have been assigned the task of trimming the hedge or cleaning the hall every morning. What is important is not that the results be perfect but that you cultivate your clarity of mind while performing the task. The test for this is, of course, whether the hedge is trimmed neatly or the hall is clean. If you are a practiced gardener, capable of trimming a hedge on automatic pilot and able to daydream during this task, then trimming the hedge is not per se the most helpful discipline with which to begin. This example demonstrates that contemplative methods are not determined by their external form but by the internal function that they have on the mind of the practitioner.

As we have seen, the empirical methods of scientific psychology can be defined in terms of actions that are visible to everyone: the researcher posits a hypothesis about certain causal relationships in reality; conducts an experiment (whether in a laboratory or outside it); manipulates the object of research in a certain way; notes the effects; and tests whether or not they support the hypothesis. In contrast, the methods of first-person research in the contemplative traditions consist of internal (mental) activity, such as systematically directing one's attention, observing patterns of thought, and in that way acquiring firsthand insight into the workings of the mind. Thus, the activity involved is visible only to the researcher performing it and not to others. It involves a first-person approach—a form of systematic exploration carried out in the hiddenness of one's own mind. That does not mean, however, that the results of such explorations are wholly subjective and lack all objectivity or reliability, because the results can be compared with those of other first-person researchers. That can lead to the same kind of objectivity that experienced judges of wine share with each other, even though the tasting itself is completely a first-person event. This is the kind of research in which contemplative traditions specialize; that is why we can call contemplative psychology a first-person science of mind.

The Concept of Humanity in Contemplative Psychology

Scientific psychology and contemplative psychology differ from each other on another essential point other than their methods of research: their concepts of humanity. "Concept of humanity" refers to the idea and collection of views that arise when we ask ourselves what the term *human being* means. The idea of humanity is not innocuous or a purely abstract philosophy; each of us holds such an idea. We all form a concept of people and respond from the perspective of that concept. Our idea of humanity therefore determines the way in which we relate to people, including researchers to their research participants. To a certain degree, concepts of humanity indicate the direction that scientific research can or should take since they function as a kind of presupposition.

Human Beings as Objects

The concepts of humanity that we find in scientific psychology are closely linked with the third-person approach, meaning they are not based on self-investigation but on what the researcher sees people do and hears them say. The human being is a third party, the other, an object of study. This concept of humanity is a scientific version of the "concept of the other."

Much of the psychological knowledge we use every day is also based on what we (believe we) see in the people around us. In the way we usually think about people—people are often present as third persons, as objects. Other people are the objects of our projected expectations, desires, thoughts, emotions, hopes, and fears—in short, the objects of our way of thinking and our emotional life. Together, our thoughts and emotions are the mental phenomena that lead to the formation of a certain concept of humanity, and in turn, this concept functions as a starting point for our attempts to increase our understanding of human nature. Thus, the concept of humanity suggests the direction in which we should look if we want to have a better understanding of human behavior.

However, because such a concept arises from our own mental processes, our view of humanity can be skewed, if not sometimes incorrect and even detrimental to the flourishing of our humaneness. It can lead us to see what we hope or are afraid to see, which can create a self-generating feedback loop. For example, our concept of humanity can be useful if we want to justify our behavior to others: "Because people behave the way they do, that is how they are; therefore, it makes sense for me to respond in the way I do."

Of course, others have their own ideas about us. We are third persons to others, objects for their expectations. In this third-person approach, it is useful to know what ideas others have about us because these ideas determine the behavior they direct toward us. If we know what those ideas are, then we can better judge whether our expectations about them can be fulfilled. Thus, we all function as objects for one another, objects of our mutual expectations, whether realistic or not. Our everyday psychology consists of the art of gauging one another's expectations and gearing them toward each other. Actually, we cannot speak of "knowledge" at this point with regard to our everyday psychology because we do not yet know whether the concepts that we hold about others and that others hold about us are correct. This requires systematic study, in which scientific psychology specializes.

Our concept of humanity directs our world—the psychological private politics, which is frequently politics of "enlightened self-interest" directed at the satisfaction of our personal
desires. I use *enlightened* here in the sense of mutually respect-
ing (working around) each other's self-interest or ego.

We may take this third-person perspective one step further: Not only can we attempt to gauge the ideas that others
have about us, but we can also identify ourselves with these
ideas. We then see ourselves through the eyes of others, as it
were, for whom we exist as third persons. This generates a
form of *indirect self-knowledge*—indirect because the knowledge is secondhand, received from others about ourselves,
third-person knowledge. From the perspective of this indirect
self-knowledge, we have become objects to ourselves. This indirect self-knowledge exists independently of the way in which
we directly experience ourselves as subjects. That is why our
direct experience of ourselves can contradict our indirect
self-knowledge, causing an inner conflict. Sometimes it seems
like we have to enter into a kind of negotiating process with
ourselves to achieve a good relationship with ourselves. But
there are also times when this indirect self-knowledge can help
us to clarify our direct experience of ourselves. Much of psychotherapy is based on this.

Human Beings as Subjects

The concepts of humanity that we find in contemplative psychology and some forms of psychotherapy have a different
origin than those we find in scientific or third-person psychology. In the former, concepts of humanity arise from the way in
which people experience themselves. Here, the human being in
the first person is central, and in this case, the understanding
of human nature is based on *direct self-knowledge*, meaning
knowledge that springs from direct perception of ourselves,
or self-experience. This form of self-knowledge is firsthand,

first-person knowledge based not on something we heard from others but on direct observation. It is not so much linked to concepts or thinking about ourselves but rather it's based on getting to know ourselves by perceiving ourselves again and again. It is knowledge in the sense of "being acquainted with." Therefore, this kind of knowledge is known both as perceptual knowledge and first-person knowledge (see chapter 4). Here again, however, we cannot speak simply of "knowledge" because we do not know whether our self-experience, our perceptual knowledge, is biased or not. This is why systematic exploration of our own minds, in which the contemplative traditions specialize, is necessary.

Direct self-knowledge consists of the knowledge of our personal experience. Much of what we personally experience, however, is not as unique as we often think. Other people frequently experience the same personal things. Thus, direct self-knowledge could well contain first-person knowledge of universally human phenomena. Love and anger, for example, are emotions we all know from firsthand experience, and we are familiar with them as first-person phenomena. We assume that they are also universally human phenomena and that other people have had similar personal experiences. Thus, our individual self-knowledge at times extends beyond ourselves. It broadens our knowledge of others, but this is an indirect, or a kind of empathic, knowledge. It is a form of *indirect* first-person knowledge in which we see others as if they are us. The knowledge of people is, in this case, an extrapolation of our direct self-knowledge.

Obviously, direct and indirect forms of knowledge, both of others and ourselves, interact to shape and direct our concept of humanity. They also function to shape our *self-concept*— that is, the totality of the ideas and views that we have formed about ourselves. This concept of ourselves, especially where it refers to universally human phenomena within us, again offers the basis for the development of a concept of humanity. At the same time, both our direct and our indirect knowledge of others acquires shape in the concept of the other; that concept also forms the basis for our concept of humanity. Practically speaking, then, there are two sources for the development of our concept of humanity: our direct first-person knowledge and our direct third-person knowledge. Over time, we can change, refine, and deepen our understanding of ourselves and others through self-knowledge, so our concept of humanity will reflect that change, refinement, or fuller understanding.

Two Asymmetrical Concepts of Humanity

As we have seen, because of the third-person approach used in conventional scientific and everyday psychology, the concept of humanity is usually formed on the basis of direct third-person knowledge. This knowledge also shapes our self-concept by means of indirect self-knowledge, through which we internalize ideas about ourselves based on what others say about us. In contrast, in contemplative psychology, the concept of humanity is formed to a large degree on the basis of our experience of ourselves and the direct first-person knowledge derived from that experience. This first-person knowledge is also the basis for the indirect, or empathic, knowing of others when universal human themes and experiences are addressed.

However, because the way in which we experience ourselves directly and the way in which we experience others directly are basically different, it is not really surprising that the concepts of humankind that arise from both sources are also very different. The mind—our way of thinking and our emotional life—has a very important place in the way we experience ourselves. Of course, others also have an important place in our minds, but that place is fundamentally different from the place that we ourselves occupy; we do not know them as we know ourselves. We know they have their own way of thinking as well, but that is not part of our direct experience. Other people have a place in our way of thinking and experience of reality just as we also have a place in their way of thinking, but their way of thinking and experience of reality still does not take place in us.

This asymmetry explains why, if we think and speak about people, we often have ideas that are very different from the ideas we have when we think and speak about ourselves. If we talk about people, they are objects for us, whereas we ourselves are subjects. For example, if we are regularly disappointed in what we expect of other people, or if they do not satisfy our emotional needs, we easily develop a negative concept of humanity. It takes little effort then to speak about people as a whole negatively and with contempt. But usually this does not include ourselves or the person to whom we are speaking about "people"! Contrarily, if others fulfill our expectations, then a positive concept of humanity is more easily fostered. At the same time, we know that our self-experience and concept of ourselves influences our concept of humanity positively or negatively as well, on any given day, let alone how we relate to others.

The Concept of Humanity as a Challenge

Fundamentally, our concept of humanity is an important factor in our attitude toward life. The spiritual traditions are aware of this and explore how realistic our concept of humanity is. What if our expectations about people, including ourselves, stem from a lack of understanding and egocentricity? Will we not often then be disappointed by people and ourselves? And will our disappointment not be expressed in actions that will in turn disappoint others and confirm within them a negative concept of humanity?

Our concept of humanity, whether positive or negative, bears traces of our own expectations. It tells us something about ourselves, about the place we give to others in our way of thinking and our emotional life. It is this phenomenon—more so than the so-called truth of a concept of humanity—with which the contemplative traditions are concerned. For example, when someone strongly believes and asserts that people are basically good or created in the image of God, third-person psychological research (see, for example, the extensive study by Matthieu Ricard) has shown that this belief correlates with more social, caring behavior in those who hold that belief.[6] From a contemplative psychological point of view, that fact is more important than the presumed truth of the falsehood of this belief. In terms of creating a culture of humaneness, it would therefore be helpful if people strongly believed in the basic goodness of others. Maybe we could even claim that the humanizing effect of this strong belief shows that it resonates with our human nature and therefore must be true.

From this point of view, it makes sense to study thoroughly our expectations of ourselves and others and the effect of those expectations on our concept of humanity. A belief in people's basis goodness should not be dismissed as a naive attempt to deny human callousness; in the moment, it can actually function as an appeal to locate, examine, and free ourselves from our own heartlessness, egocentricity, and unrealistic expectations.

The contemplative traditions are premised on the possibility that our experience of ourselves can reveal a glimpse of something fundamental about ourselves and, by extension, about human nature. This opens us to a different perspective on people, one that the spiritual traditions endeavor to cultivate. Thus, we can learn to experience ourselves and the other not exclusively as an object—the object of our expectations and needs—but as a subject, a being within whom we can recognize, beyond our shortsightedness and callousness, fundamental humanity. When we tap into this, we can actually experience the other as much as possible as a first person—that is, as we experience ourselves. We are able to identify with the other. A feeling of relatedness and fundamental connection begins to color our experience of the other and our concept of humanity. The degree to which we are capable of this is also the degree to which we are capable of empathy, of loving our neighbor as ourselves. In concrete terms, this amounts to a deep change in our attitude toward life and our concept of humanity. According to some contemplative traditions, this way of experiencing can even develop into something that seems like telepathy.

Thus, in living contemplatively, the examination of our own humaneness does not remain confined to ourselves: it leads to the ability and readiness to recognize the humaneness of our fellow human beings as well. This is neither a theoretical matter nor a matter of good intentions; in fact, having good intentions is not enough. We need to practice contemplative disciplines that uncover our own humaneness, something we may even scarcely believe in at times. Subsequently, we must also practice disciplines that open our eyes to the humaneness of others and teach us to approach them as we would ourselves—as beings who are as kind and sensitive as we are, although they too are dominated by blindness; egocentricity; aggression; fear of life; and disappointment in people, themselves, and possibly life in general. Nearly all the great spiritual traditions provide such disciplines.

Humaneness and the Concept of Humanity

Is it possible to let go of our unrealistic expectations and the concept of humanity that arises from them? Is it too much to ask for a development in this direction? Certainly, we have all developed a reasonably solid concept of humanity that, in our view, is based on years of experience with people. However, there is a gateway for the development of a concept of humanity based on humaneness, and that gateway can be found within a human being in the first person, that is, in our experience of ourselves.

Our experience of ourselves contains aspects that we sometimes find difficult to recognize in others. In fact, we sometimes become aware of these aspects precisely because we are unable to recognize them in others. When someone treats us in a way that we consider (correctly or not) callous or shortsighted, we simultaneously experience our own (injured) kindness and insight and vice versa. We are not robots but people, and people are only able to recognize callousness and suffering because they are sensitive beings. It is because people have a sense of justice that they are able to recognize injustice. Even when we do something that others consider depraved, we often cannot deny we are trying to attain some good, albeit in a clumsy or shortsighted way. Even then we try to make the best of it; we do not mean any harm. And when we do mean harm and set out to hurt others intentionally, the fact that we know how to do so also indicates that we are aware of what is beneficial. That awareness is an unconditional part of us, present in good moments as well as bad. The desire to cause chaos, confusion, and suffering implies that we are cognizant of harmony, clarity, and happiness, and the opposite is also true. We can only recognize our own moments of heartlessness because we do have compassionate hearts. We are aware of both sides through experience: in addition to our most negative and destructive moments, we also have moments of kindness, happiness, tenderness and devotion, appreciation, love and compassion, as well as of genuine insight and understanding. Such moments are not accidental or coincidental but, in spite of all the negativity that we experience within ourselves, are a part of our being, even though they may last only for a short time and we may fail to act on them in the moment. When we examine ourselves, it is very difficult, if not impossible, to completely deny the existence of such moments of compassion, kindness, and so forth. Transformation comes when they become incorporated into our concept of ourselves *and* our concept of humanity.

However, it is possible that we banish moments of genuine concern and understanding from our consciousness too easily when they do not fit in with the concepts of ourselves and humanity that we already have. Perhaps we have formed a very negative concept of ourselves on the basis of negative indirect self-knowledge or of seeing our own egotism. However, the moments when we are *aware* of our own callousness and shortsightedness are actually moments of compassion and insight. Unfortunately, we often are so overwhelmed by recognizing our callousness and shortsightedness that we cannot feel any joy in the fact that at least we have recognized them. Still, that is the basis for spiritual growth. Our lack of humaneness and the disappointment when we seem to fail can overshadow our moments of insight and compassion. Our confidence in our humaneness can gradually fade, and ultimately, we may no longer believe that we possess it. We become our own enemy and fear this enemy. Our attempts to deal with this enemy acquire the form of an increasingly bitter inner struggle. Even if this struggle takes on religious clothing (*armor* would be a better word if we are talking about our "heroic" struggle against our negativity!), it leads only to self-destruction. Our spiritual health is in danger. This is not the path to which genuine spiritual traditions point. That path begins with a renewed and frank look at who or what we are at this very moment. There is room for what we have called our negative and positive aspects in this examination. We turn back to our experience of ourselves and explore it with the help of the contemplative disciplines. In the words of Pema Chödrön, "you start where you are."[7]

Unlike the concept of humanity in scientific psychology, which stems from the third person, the concept of humanity in contemplative psychology and much of psychotherapy stems from the first person, from our experience of ourselves. This is why, in the concept of humanity in third-person psychology, all of those mental phenomena that are so important in our self-experience and determine our lives almost never come up for consideration. In contemplative psychology, these phenomena—the personal experience of our own love and hate, suffering and joy, insight and confusion—have a central place, for they are directly linked to the inner flourishing of our humaneness.

Concepts of Humanity: Correct or Effective?

The problem with concepts of humanity is that one cannot prove whether a certain concept is correct or not; one can only note its effects in what one does and does not do. Thus, although these concepts have arisen through experience with people, they have transcended and separated from such experience and acquired the status of universal ideas which— together with related concepts, such as those of self, the world, and God—play a large role in our world of thought. They have become, to use a philosophical term, *metaphysical* notions. At the same time, however, they do guide our actions, influencing our behavior and the way in which we interpret and assess behavior and situations.

The contemplative traditions have always had an eye for the psychological consequences of these concepts. As already mentioned, these traditions are interested not so much in whether such concepts of humanity are correct as in the consequences that the belief in their correctness have for contemplative growth. And there are definite consequences. Together with our concepts of the world and God (in some traditions), they determine our attitude toward and experience of reality.

Scientific psychology maintains certain concepts of humanity as starting points—concepts that follow naturally from its third-person form of research. The most well known are the utilitarian and hedonistic concepts of humanity. According to the *utilitarian concept of humanity*, a person seeks profit and avoids loss: all thoughts, words, and actions are ultimately guided by striving for what one wants and avoiding or destroying what one does not want. According to the *hedonistic concept of humanity*, people are pleasure-seekers: human beings seek out what gives pleasure and avoid whatever causes suffering. It is ultimately this that guides all one's action. This concept of humanity is found in behaviorist and modern cognitive psychology as well as in Freud's depth psychology. The problem with these concepts is that they are presented as the explanation for *all* human action. In itself, striving for profit or pleasure is a very human activity, people do so quite often. Whether the psychology is conventional or contemplative, it must also recognize and acknowledge this striving—but it is something else to claim that all human actions at any time can be explained by this striving.

Utilitarian and hedonistic concepts of humanity also play a large role in everyday psychology. We could characterize them as materialistic concepts of humanity. In materialistic approaches, all aspects of life are viewed as if they were material goods that we can grasp, reject, or destroy. If well-being, wisdom, love, hate, suffering, health, youth, age, and so on are viewed as similar to material goods of one kind or another, we attempt either to acquire and hold on to them or to avoid and destroy them as we do with material goods. We are then, as discussed in the introduction to this book, attempting to apply a strategy on a level at which it does not work. This is, of course, a source of suffering. We cannot grasp and hoard our youth, nor can we cut suffering into pieces and destroy it.

As stated earlier, concepts of humanity are metaphysical notions, and as such, they cannot be refuted by facts. This can be illustrated by means of the hedonistic concept of humanity. From the perspective of this concept, even the contemplative life can be interpreted as being motivated by the search for pleasure and avoidance of suffering. Suppose that Jane has chosen the contemplative life because she believes it can help her find the truth (whatever that may be). A hedonistic concept of humanity does not admit of such a motivation and will instead explain her choice as arising from the fact that she finds it pleasant—it satisfies her. From Jane's perspective, however, other factors come into play. After all, there are times when the contemplative life does not appeal to her at all, and moreover, she maintains that seeking pleasure is not her first priority. She is not interested in that at all; her concern is to find wisdom, to find truth. But hedonist psychologists are not to be put off by one obstacle; they can continue to maintain that Jane has chosen to seek truth because she likes it. Jane can then explain that her basic motivation for practicing the contemplative life has much more to do with the discovery that her life and the lives of others are dominated by a spiritual blindness and callousness—a blindness and callousness that may be "comfortable" (which is a word the hedonists like to hear) but at the same time causes us to be completely unrealistic. She can add that she is motivated by the desire for truth even if it causes her pain. The hedonist psychologists will then say, "We know all about it. We call it *delayed need satisfaction*. Ultimately, you assume that the truth will be pleasant; otherwise, you would not seek it. You are not a masochist, I hope?" And Jane, somewhat hurt, will lash out, "My search is unconditional! It is not tied to hopes and fears, pleasure or suffering, profit or loss!" But the hedonistic interpretation leaves no room for the authenticity of a power like the search for truth as a way of experiencing. This power is constantly reinterpreted as the search for pleasure and the avoidance of suffering, and its stated aim is viewed as a form of self-deception.

We could tell the same story, replacing the hedonists with utilitarian psychologists, who assume that John seeks the truth because he believes it will benefit him. If John should say, "I want to seek the truth even if I am hurt by it," the utilitarian psychologists could still maintain that he is so perverse and confused that he sees profit in loss.

No real dialogue takes place here because the starting points do not share any common ground. Nevertheless, these starting points play a role in the dialogue between psychologies based on a utilitarian or hedonistic view on one hand and contemplative psychology on the other. From the contemplative point of view, utilitarian and hedonistic psychologies are profane or materialistic; they are based on a concept of humanity that allows no room for a spiritual or contemplative dimension as an authentic power. Therefore, the difference between the contemplative traditions and academic psychology lies not only in the method of investigation—first person or third person—but also in the materialistic concept of humanity versus a spiritual one. The materialistic concept of humanity impoverishes our human existence, and adhering to it prevents us from seeing the relativity of this concept of humanity and from freeing ourselves from it.

Concepts of Humanity as Gauges

Concepts of humanity have an entirely different function within the contemplative traditions. Here, they do not function as theoretical presuppositions but as gauges for the development of the mentality of people on the Way. Contemplative concepts of humanity are also not fixed notions but change in relation to one's contemplative development. The concept of humanity that we have now is a creation and therefore an expression of the mind as it is now. It concurs with a certain phase in our experience of ourselves and of reality. Thus, the contemplative life is concerned with becoming conscious of these concepts of humanity, recognizing them, and transforming them so that our humaneness can flourish. Its concern is not to provide a more correct concept of humanity or a new ideology but to offer concepts of humanity that awaken a concrete experience of our humaneness within us. That experience itself is not a theory or a presupposition.

It is inevitable on the contemplative path that we come face-to-face with aspects of ourselves that are callous and short-sighted. If we should be asked at that moment what kind of concept of humanity we have, it would in all likelihood be relatively negative, or at least mixed. Rather than constituting a problem, acknowledging such a concept is a necessary stage on the Path: there must be room to recognize and study negativity. After all, negativity is a part of us.

Because it is a stage, however, we do not see our negative concept of humanity as absolute. If we did, we would certainly become depressed. Because it is relative, something that we can see and let go of in a broader perspective, viewing our negativity (sin, inhumanity, or whatever we want to call it) is a step—as inspiring as it is painful—along the contemplative way. When we find the courage to see our negativity clearly, we simultaneously have the ability to face that negativity. Apparently, this clarity of mind is also a part of us. We do not have hearts of stone, even though we may think so at times. Is it not precisely because we are gentle of heart that harshness hurts us? Is the discovery of our confusion and shortsightedness not the manifestation of clarity and broad-mindedness? From that point of view, our negative self-concept and concept of humanity end up in a broader context, thereby losing their depressing characteristics without forcing us to deny our negativity. Thus, an entirely different, much more nuanced self-experience arises that also changes our concept of humanity into a more positive one: we discover that we can deal with our negativity in a productive way, that it is not our destiny but a challenge. At this stage, we discover that it is, as Buddhism expresses it, like manure: it has a ghastly smell, but it is fertile—it is useful to spread over the field of the *bodhi* (the enlightened state of mind).[8] In Christian terms, we could say that the farmer who works this field is created in the image of God. This positive view of our humanity is now brought into the foreground. So, the concept of humanity that is progressively formed along the contemplative way is based on concrete experience, experience that frees us from the negative concept of humanity that we often initially perceive as our inevitable destiny.

The Value of Dialogue

We have seen that contemplative psychologies and the psychologies with which we are familiar (both the scientific and everyday versions) differ from each other on fundamental points. This is exactly why contemplative psychologies have something to say to us. They offer their psychological insights and their own methods of research. Perhaps one contemplative tradition has developed its psychological insights somewhat more than another, and one places more emphasis on these insights than another, but in all cases, we find universal insights into human experience and the human mind—insights that nowadays are called psychological. This is not surprising because, although there are major differences in the theology of the great religions, religions are always practiced by human beings. Whatever the culture or period into which people are born, they all have two eyes and two hands. They all have minds. Thus, there is a broad, common ground: all people must deal with such fundamental concerns as fear of life and joy in life, compassion and callousness, insight and ignorance. Greed, jealousy, and aggression, as well as their opposites, exist among people of all cultures. The circumstances and people toward which these emotions and attitudes are directed are obviously different, but the profane or materialistic way of being exists in other cultures just as it does in our own. And it hurts. It is for this reason that all great world religions attempt to transform or liberate that way of being. This is also why the contemplative way of life can be found in all cultures.

All contemplative psychologies help us to understand what happens to an individual along the Way and how to watch out for pitfalls and dead ends. They provide a close look at human beings from the first-person perspective (see chapter 3). We will explore how the profane, egocentric mentality and the accompanying psychology arises and reinforces itself. How do people get out of touch with their humaneness and maintain that disconnection from day to day or even moment to moment? How do we do this and why?

Of course, we could avoid these practical questions, for example, by placing the rise of the profane mentality in a historical context. Then it becomes something that happened in the past and against which we are now powerless to fight. Formulated in Christian terms, people were driven out of Paradise when they fell into sin. Such a historical interpretation then immediately compels additional ones—for example, that about two thousand years ago, Jesus took away the sin of humankind. We also find these kinds of historical interpretations in other religions.

Yet these interpretations do not affect the core that is important to those who live a contemplative life. They do not affect our personal and daily experiences in life; they are ideologies rather than instruments we can use to find traces of our egocentric experience of reality and liberate ourselves from them. This is why the contemplative life puts more emphasis on a psychological interpretation. For example, within the Christian tradition, one can view the Fall as something that takes place each and every moment again and again and, in principle, can also be undone each and every moment. From this point of view, the Kingdom of God is not something far away from us but something that we tend to hold at a great distance again and again. When we are capable of allowing Christ into our hearts or of discovering Christ, then we can work with our sin; our hearts then become so spacious that they are capable of taking up our sin. This is a Christian formulation of this problem, but the same theme can be expressed just as well in terms of other religions. This has been clearly revealed by interreligious dialogue in recent years.

Stated in contemplative psychological terms, our fundamental humanity is never actually absent but can be made to flourish, and that which obscures it—our negativity—is not only not fundamental but can also be overcome. This is the concern of the practice of every spiritual discipline. It is the foundation of the contemplative way, and we encounter it, although in other terms, in a great many traditions.

With the notion that such flourishing is possible, the contemplative traditions knowingly fly directly in the face of the profane concept of humanity found in materialistic psychology. They also oppose the depressing and destructive view of people that sees the fulfillment of human happiness in the satisfaction of desires. This is why the contemplative traditions are provocative as well as valuable partners for the dialogue with conventional psychology.

Of course, contemplative insights are often embedded in a religious way of thought and terminology. For example, the Christian tradition states that people are made in the image of God, whereas the Mahayana Buddhist tradition asserts that people possess Buddha-nature. Without further explanation, such statements can often lead to misunderstanding among regular psychologists and laypeople. This is why a dialogue between theology and contemplative psychology is also needed. Such a dialogue can help us to see through worn or seemingly inaccessible theological and religious packaging. We can discover whether certain religious concepts and statements of faith (still) function with respect to cultivating the flourishing within, and if so, how.

In the dialogue with theology, however, we must not forget that contemplative psychology, like all psychology, is *anthropocentric* (centered on humans), whereas theology is obviously *theocentric* (centered on God). A "theocentric psychology" does not exist; it is a contradiction in terms. Contemplative psychology does deal with people and their minds, which includes people who may experience their reality from a theo-centric perspective. Let us immediately recognize that the term *anthropocentric* must not be confused with the term *egocentric*. Contemplative psychology is not an egocentric psychology, but it is a psychology that studies our egocentrism and offers various means for transforming it. What this means will be discussed in the following chapter.

2

Perceiving Reality and the Metaphor of the Way

The previous chapter frequently referred to *the Way*. The Way, or the Path, is a universal metaphor encountered again and again in the great world religions. The term *journey* is used to indicate actual progress along the Way. In this chapter, we will examine what this metaphor has to tell us and how it can help us understand the psychological work and transformative outcomes of contemplative practice. We will first look at a number of fundamental aspects included in the meaning of the metaphor, as well as what appears to be the essence of the Way: the constantly changing perception of reality. Finally, we will look at the limits suggested by the metaphor of the Way.

Aspects of the Metaphor of the Way

What do we mean when we say "the Way"? How does it function as a metaphor, and what does it represent? Why is the use of this metaphor so widespread? The Way is a powerful expression; first, it serves to capture the fact that the contemplative life, or spirituality itself, has to do with our development as human beings in a certain direction. The contemplative traditions point to this direction, claiming they can show us the Way in a literal sense. Second, the metaphor suggests movement and travel as a continually changing perspective on the landscape. We will discuss this suggestion later in the chapter in terms of the "changing perception of reality." Third, the metaphor also suggests that there are stages along the way, and that it is possible, if not necessary, to obtain guidance and guides. We will return to this idea in the chapters that follow. Finally, the idea of a way suggests a certain constraint: a way is bounded by sides, and we can wander from the path or stay on it. The two sides also suggest that we can speak of a double-sided development.

With regard to the first point, we may ask to what the notion of direction refers. Some say that life itself is a journey, regardless of whether we belong to a religious tradition or not. Isn't our passage from the cradle to the grave a journey? The contemplative traditions, of course, do not deny this, but their message refers to yet another journey that we as humans can make—a journey whose beginning and end are different from those of our biologically determined journey through time. From the contemplative perspective, a life's journey can lead in two fundamentally different directions—either one in which we become entangled in the grip of callousness, shortsightedness, and fear of life, or one in which kindness and insight, joy in life and wisdom, increasingly guide us.

The essence of this message of two possible life directions is that we need not, or possibly should not, leave the direction and progress of this journey entirely to chance. Moreover, we are required to navigate the realities of life—birth; sickness; old age; death; interaction with our environment, one another, and ourselves. One Way can make us gentle rather than callous, does not compel us to stick our heads in the sand out of fear, and makes us more realistic and honest. This is a hopeful message. In the following chapters, we will consider from various perspectives whether this message is realistic or not.

The Viability of the Way

From the perspective of the Way, development toward compassion and wisdom in life has to do with the development of a basic attitude to life as a whole—inclusive of both its adversity and its prosperity, both its happiness and its sorrow. It has to do with the creation or discovery of a certain mental space, a fundamental "magnanimity" or mental openness that gives insight. Because it includes relating to the realities of our life situation, it ennobles us and our fellow beings.

That it is actually possible to uncover such a space in our concrete existence and continue to develop it is the inspiration for the contemplative life. Basically, this inspiration can arise neither from what we see as a projected, faraway, final goal nor from our ever-changing circumstances in life but from each step we actually take along the Way. Such steps show us that the Way is actually viable and that the obstacles we encounter can be overcome and incorporated as part of the journey. Thus, the metaphor of traveling along the Way does not refer, as is sometimes thought, to a life in which the satisfaction of needs is delayed to the future. For the promise of future rewards is simply not a strong enough motivation for bringing about a real transformation. Moreover, it is easy for us to ignore ourselves in the present if we are fixed on a certain future goal. We tend to dream about that goal and do not keep in touch with our actual situation in life or ourselves as we are. Instead, we dream about ourselves as we would like to be. So even though the Way leads to a realization or fulfillment, reconciliation, liberation, or whatever the tradition calls it, in practice that final goal does not function as the fundamental source of inspiration. More radically, the inspiration lies in the sense of progress that we make in the way we deal with our everyday circumstances, both good and bad—that is, how we apply the methods and practices, and develop insights in relation to our lived experiences.

This kind of inspiration does not need to be understood in religious terms. After all, it has to do with the development of something that belongs to being human. In contemplative psychological terms, we could describe this development as a liberation from all of those attitudes and views that cause us to be hard-hearted, defensive, and blind to the realities of our lives and to reality as a whole. This development is central to the great religions and thus is also the focus in the practice of the contemplative life in both its monastic and its secular forms.

We will return later to the degree to which such a development is a matter of human action or grace. Here, we will focus only on the fact that all spiritual disciplines of the contemplative life (the mental exercises, the performance of work and study) are practiced to give our fundamental humanity space to flourish and to cultivate its expression in words and deeds. The idea of the Way actually inspires us to remember that people are capable of developing these ways, as evidenced in all times and cultures, and that it involves application and effort.

The Borders of the Way

The metaphor of the Way also includes the idea of certain borders or constraints. After all, a path has two sides that serve as borders on the left and right. In contemplative thought, these borders point to the contemplative practices that place certain restrictions on us, a certain form of discipline that influences the cultivation of both the mind and actions. With respect to the mind, it is chiefly the development of insight into life or wisdom that is involved; with respect to actions, it is the cultivation of mercy, compassion, kindness, and love. *Mercy* and *compassion* refer here not only to feelings but also to actual mercy, that is, mercy in speech and actions. Thus, we might interpret the left- and right-hand sides of the Way as the "side of insight" and the "side of loving-kindness and compassion" respectively.

This interpretation also emphasizes that in our actual progress along the Way, there is simultaneous growth in insight and mercy. We cannot travel the contemplative path without having these two sides. We need them both to stay on course. In concrete terms, growth in genuine insight is accompanied by growth in our dedication to our fellow human beings, and conversely, genuine caring is bound to give us insight. The reason for this is simply that caring turns us toward reality; we are open to seeing everything more clearly and turning toward rather than away or wishing to keep reality at a safe distance. The converse is also true—insight leads to understanding, and understanding leads to loving care and compassion. It has been said that to understand everything is to forgive everything. It is striking that we find both aspects continually emphasized in the great religious traditions—but not as opposites. We cannot practice one without the other.

Yet some people view insight and loving care as opposites and even sometimes pitted against each other, as if they were two distinct ways: a purely "mental" way of finding insight and, in contrast, a practical way of caring, loving thy neighbor, and charity. Sometimes both ways are linked with the idea of a vertical religiosity (directed toward God) and a horizontal one (directed toward human beings). Social action (working toward a better world) is then viewed as distinct from—and therefore placed on a plane other than—the transformation of our profane perception of reality. At most, the practitioner is urged to balance these two dimensions. But the image of two perpendicular dimensions suggests a false opposition. The lines are not perpendicular but parallel. Many years ago, the famous Dutch theologian Harry Kuitert made a number of comments well worth our consideration on the danger of the Christian tradition going off the rails if it ignored "the fundamental question of the perspective in which that work of making our world worth living in is to be placed."[1]

It is this pairing of insight and loving-kindness that makes us capable of actually dealing with situations when we must courageously intervene, even if the intervention is painful to the other or to ourselves. If we attempt to cultivate both aspects independently of each other, we run the risk of developing shortsighted care as well as callous insight. When we act out of shortsighted care, or *blind compassion* as it is called in the Buddhist tradition, we often only help people go from bad to worse. We may behave in a friendly and tolerant way, but we do so at the wrong moments, with the result that we cause rather than prevent suffering. While callous insight may help us to see more clearly the shortcomings, sins, and other negative things in ourselves and others, we are not capable of dealing with them in a caring, compassionate way that leads to their amelioration. We can, in fact, become enmeshed in an increasingly aggressive struggle against evil in ourselves and others. Insight without compassion is like a sharp sword wielded by an uncompassionate hand.

Thus, even though loving care and insight develop simultaneously just as the two sides of a path run parallel, there is still a difference between them. Insight is something that grows within us and, in a certain sense, is concealed from others. Conversely, the growth of caring or compassion is visible to others. It is through this visible growth that it is possible to perceive indirectly whether the inner flourishing of insight is real or imaginary—a tree is known by its fruit. Effective charity and care are the visible fruits of genuine insight as part of a flourishing within.

The Way as a Changing Perception of Reality

Another aspect of the metaphor of the Way is that it entails a continually changing perspective on the landscape. Of course, it is not only our perspective that changes. The landscape itself changes, whether we are traveling or not. Here, the

"landscape" is a metaphor for the events in our lives, the continually changing situations in which we find ourselves. Thus,
we have two sorts of changeability: the (external) changeability of our concrete situation in life and the (inner) changeability of our shifting perspective on it.

The contemplative traditions are primarily concerned with
the inner shifting perspective on our situation in life, for this
perspective determines how we perceive the events of our lives.
Moreover, this perspective and the way in which it shifts differ
with every individual. Two people involved in the same event
each experience it in their own way. We know all of this from
our daily lives, although we still do not know how consequen-
tial this fact is from moment to moment.

If we now look at what actually "travels along the Way,"
we could say that it is our perception of reality. This concept
is a basic notion of contemplative psychology. What makes the
term *perception of reality* so useful is the fact that the word
perception highlights the subjective side of what is happening,
while the word *reality* emphasizes its objective side. It gives a
good indication that what we perceive as real is subjective but
is experienced as objective. On closer inspection, the reality
in which we live is actually reality as we perceive it personally. This reality is relative to us, although in terms of our
daily lives, we regularly lose sight of this fact. We perceive
our situation as if it were not relative but absolute in the sense
of being objective and independent of us. This is why, instead
of using *perception of reality*, we could also use terms like
relative, subjective, or *personal* (in the sense of *individual*)
reality. The articulation and communication of our personal
reality to others may give rise to an *intersubjective* perception
of reality that people share; however, it remains dependent on
the individual and, in that sense, relative.

For many people, including philosophers and psychologists,
the story ends here. They view the unmistakable relativity of
our perception of reality as a fact that cannot be tampered

with. Their final conclusion is, "All perception is interpreted experience." In other words, the fact that we live in a *relative reality* has become an absolute given, an indisputable fact. At most, we can attempt to understand one another's relative realities to some degree, to grasp them by means of what is called *hermeneutics*, the science of explanation and interpretation. However, the possibility of a stance or, better yet, a mental space within which our perception of relative reality is completely exposed so that its relativity is visible to us is rarely acknowledged as a possible experience. As a consequence, the possibility of training in mental development that would allow us to recognize and see through this relativity is not acknowledged either.

This, too, is a crucial difference between the contemplative traditions and the discipline of psychology. The former not only acknowledge this relativity but also assert that humans possess and are able to develop a discriminating awareness that allows them to discover and completely eliminate the blinding effect of this relativity. For the contemplative traditions, this relativity is not an absolute given to which we should resign ourselves but a factual characteristic of the blinded individual. Many disciplines of the contemplative life are therefore directed at developing a clarity of mind that enables us to discover where and when this relativity happens and how to free ourselves from it. Thus, the recognition of relativity neither leads to a "worldly" despondency nor remains an intellectual relativism. Rather, it is an incitement to travel along the contemplative way.

Perception of Reality along Our Course of Life

Let us attempt to make this rather abstract concept of perception of reality more concrete by means of some examples that look at an earlier phase in life—childhood. If we look back at our perception of reality when we were children (in as much as we remember it), certain aspects gave our perception a sense of reality—trusted and familiar (though not necessarily always pleasant) aspects that acted as buttresses for our childish perceptions: the way our house smelled; certain corners in the room where we played; the open door to the garden; special objects such as the large vase with sunflowers on the dresser; our mother's box of buttons; the bear we took to bed; and last but not least, our parents, the sound of their voices, the way they moved and held our hand. All of those were immediately surrounded by the physical building with the sidewalk as a boundary beyond which we were not allowed to go by ourselves.

Together, these aspects formed the reality in which we lived. Some of them were so important to us that our reality would have collapsed if they had disappeared, so they also formed the object of our anxieties and delights, our hopes and fears. If Mommy or Daddy stayed away too long, we were scared they might never return. Then we felt that our existence was threatened. Or we could not sleep if our teddy bear was missing. All these certainties and uncertainties formed the world that we perceived then as reality: our childish perception of reality.

Let us look at our perception of reality on the basis of a classic North American example. As children, most of us believed in Santa Claus. This produced a certain perception of reality around Christmas. Everything was permeated by it and directed toward it. This perception no longer exists for us because we no longer believe in Santa Claus. We are no longer impressed by him because we see that he is simply a man dressed in a costume. Our awareness of what reality is—that is, what is real and not real—has changed. The person dressed in a costume is more real to us now than Santa Claus is. In this respect, at least, we have become more realistic, and this can be seen in our behavior toward the man in the beard when we no longer play the game with him.

The question asked by contemplative psychology is, how many Santa Clauses have we held on to in a metaphorical sense? Perhaps we still view every day as December 25, with illusions that are different but just as powerful as those that played a role in our childish perceptions of reality surrounding that date. For example, what illusions might we hold about birth, parenting, society, sickness, old age, and death? Nor should we forget illusions about ourselves. Even if we are academically trained psychologists, theologians, or philosophers, there is no guarantee that we do not have all kinds of illusions—as taken-for-granted perceptions—in our daily personal and professional lives. These illusions determine our perception of reality with all their emotional reactions and the behaviors that follow in their wake.

In any case, we know that our childhood world is gone. We no longer live in that world. Yet when that world did exist, it was absolute reality for us. If we look back now, we realize that it was a relative reality—relative to our mode of perception as children. The elements to which we clung to maintain our sense of reality have lost their function. A teddy bear no longer comforts us, and our mother's hand has long been replaced by other buttresses. When we look back to puberty or young adulthood, we see that the buttressing elements, the building blocks of our perception of reality, have been changing constantly. Those realities were relative as well.

Of course, we have not yet reached the end of this development: what we perceive as reality now will be gone in the course of time. There will be other aspects from which we will derive our sense of reality and orientation. The reality in which we live from day to day now is also relative to the way of experiencing that is peculiar to us now. The problem is that it is difficult for us to see at this time exactly where that relativity is, how extensive it is, and how pervasive its hold on us is.

The Perception of Reality along the Contemplative Way

Why are the preceding examples significant? Because the contemplative traditions are primarily interested in the development of our perception of reality. But their interest does not involve so much the transformation of childish perception into a more mature form. As suggested by the idea of the Way, we can travel in two directions: our perception of reality can develop in a direction that makes us wilt mentally—one that makes us callous and defensive, increases our shortsightedness and fear of life and thereby causes endless suffering for us and our fellow human beings—or in the opposite direction—the direction of internal flourishing within which the visible fruits in our speech and actions are those that the contemplative traditions seek to ripen. When we go in the latter direction, either within or outside the context of a religious tradition, we find ourselves on the Way of the contemplative life.

In contemplative terms, this concerns the transformation of our profane perception of reality into a sacred one—a development to which many traditions refer as a (continuing) conversion or transformation. This conversion is also characterized as the transformation of a materialistic attitude toward life into a spiritual one. In more philosophical terms, we can refer to "appearance" and "reality" or, as Jacques Lacan does in many of his works, to the imaginary (*l'imaginaire*) and the real (*le réel*).[2] The nature of appearance is to present itself as reality. The contemplative transformation concerns freeing ourselves from holding appearances or the imaginary—fictions, self-deception, and illusions for reality—by learning to see them for what they are.

Another philosophical and contemplative formulation is one that uses the terms *relative reality* (the relative) and *absolute reality* (the absolute). Progress along the Way means that we learn to recognize our relative reality as it is and begin to live more and more within absolute reality. In psychological terms, we speak of the "egocentric perception of reality" and the "egoless perception of reality," but we use these terms in a contemplative sense as well; we can see our egocentric perception of reality for what it really is only from an egoless perspective.

These pairs of terms can easily lead us to believe that we must abandon the one and embrace the other. But we do not, in fact, go anywhere. Nor, in the contemplative sense, do these pairs refer to two different places or actual realities. They do not form an opposition but are rather each other's complement; they mirror each other in the same sense that the separate terms of conceptual pairs like pleasure and pain entail each other in Jacques Derrida's thinking.[3] Thus, concepts such as the absolute and the relative, appearance and reality, are themselves relative concepts, as the Madhyamaka philosophy of Buddhism also asserts.[4] This is a typical contemplative insight, and it is therefore important to know what these concepts refer to on the experiential level. A typical contemplative twist is that the moment when we no longer see our relative reality as absolute but on the spot for what it is (as relative!) *is* the perception of absolute reality. It means that our perception of reality, which initially appeared to be absolute reality, later turns out to be relative. We are clear minded. If we hold our relative reality to be absolute, we live in confusion. Thus, these pairs of terms refer not to two different realities, one deeper than the other and hidden *behind* the other, but to one and the same reality viewed from two different perspectives—a confused one and a clear one.

Yet whatever terms we use for the mental transformation to which the contemplative traditions are directed, they always refer to a change in our perception of the concrete events in our lives, a change that leads to the flourishing of our fundamental humanity. Thus, the image of stages that follow one another, suggested by the metaphor of the Way, represents a sequential experiencing of reality that carries us further and further away from what chokes our joy in life toward compassion and clarity of mind.

Such a development is, of course, no small matter. After all, our perception of reality does include *all* aspects of our lives. Our emotional life; our way of thinking; our expectations and memories; our mental values; our concepts of ourselves, humanity, the world, and God—all these internal aspects are just as much a part of our development as our external circumstances in life. And because we mistakenly perceive our relative reality as real, letting go of it seems like letting go of reality itself—a form of mental suicide that can only lead to our downfall or psychosis. This is why we often prefer to change our external circumstances rather than our way of experiencing them. For example, we tend to destroy or acquire the objects of our aggression or greed rather than freeing ourselves from our aggression or greed. This often seems the only possible choice to make and can cause us to adhere to certain ways of experiencing even though we may rationally know better and understand that these ways are harmful to us or others. However, the power or motivation to let go of a destructive way of experiencing reality often escapes us precisely because we cannot recognize its illusory, relative nature.

As stated above, the contemplative traditions are directed primarily at a transformation of our perception of reality and, based on that, a transformation of reality. These directions are both distinct and connected. The more transparent our perspective on (our) reality becomes, the more mental freedom we have to work with our circumstances. Within that freedom lies an element of increasing selflessness because our desires and interests have also become more transparent. In this way, more room is created for a less compulsive and more open way of working with our circumstances in life. This also means that our contemplative development is increasingly less determined by our external circumstances and more by how much open-mindedness and mental freedom we have attained.

This selfless openness unlocks possibilities, but possibilities for what? The answer is possibilities for changing something in our perceived reality for the well-being of all. Thus, the transformation of our perception of reality manifests itself and bears fruit in the world as involvement.

This involvement is not governed by social preconceptions or political ideology that tell us what to do but by clarity of mind and loving care. Involvement, because it is based on that clarity and care, implies being free from fixating on what we want and don't want for ourselves from the world. Or, as Christians often say (based on John 15:19): the less we are *of* the world, the more we can be *in* the world, and do something good *for* the world. This does not detract from the fact that circumstances in life, especially in the contemplative development toward this openness, can be helpful as well as harmful. We cannot close our eyes to this fact, and the contemplative traditions do not do so. Just as a mother does not attempt to force her newborn baby to walk, neither does a competent mentor (immediately) ask the impossible from a new student. It is considerations such as these that determine the concrete form of guidance along the Way. But the development at which the Way points is ultimately one that leads to an unconditional wisdom in life and loving care—a form of wisdom and compassion that can manifest itself freely and that is *continually active regardless of the circumstances.*

The Stream of Experience

We will examine what the contemplative psychological aspects of a profane or spiritual perception of reality are and look at how one can develop from the other in the next chapter. These issues are of fundamental importance. Because we speak and act *from the perspective of* as well as *within* our perception of reality, the effects are far-reaching, both for ourselves and for our fellow human beings and surroundings. But before we take this up, we must ask a very practical question: How does our continually shifting perception of reality—whether it is profane, spiritual, or something in between—actually come into being from moment to moment?

Within the contemplative traditions, the answer to this question is not informed by theology or philosophy but by a psychological insight that has been acquired through the practice of observing the mind. It begins with a concrete observation: the form or content of our perception of reality arises through the confluence of six sources of experience. Of these six sources, five are linked to our senses, which together provide us with the stream of *sensory experience*. The sixth source, which we could call our mind or psyche, supplies the stream of our *mental experience*.

All our sensual experiences—what we hear, see, smell, taste, or touch physically—combine from moment to moment with our mental experience, meaning what we think, find, feel, and desire; our hopes and fears, fantasies, and imagination; and everything else that we can conceive and goes through our minds. The six streams of experience constantly merge together into our perception of reality of the moment without our being aware of the precise contribution of each source. In this way, an imagined reality arises that we do not recognize as imagined. For example, if we hear the *sound* of a car, we often have the *perception* of a car going by. Although we only hear the sound of a car, we mentally augment that sound with the image of a car. A mental image can be so strong that when, for example, we recognize the noise typical of a truck, it is as if we actually see that truck go by, whereas we actually experience only the sound of its engine. In the same way, the mental stream can be mixed with the sensual streams without our knowledge. In the words of Marcel Proust:

> Even the simple act which we describe as "seeing someone we know" is, to some extent, an intellectual

process. We pack the physical outline of the creature we see with all the ideas we have already formed
about him, and in the complete picture of him which
we compose in our minds those ideas have certainly
the principal place. In the end they come to fill out
so completely the curve of his cheeks, to follow so
exactly the line of his nose, they blend so harmoni-
ously in the sound of his voice that these seem to be
no more than a transparent envelope, so that each
time we see the face or hear the voice it is our own
ideas of him which we recognize and to which we
listen.[5]

We can gain a good view of the stream of mental events if
we keep the sensual stream of experience constant—for example, if we perform a monotonous physical task or sit still, so
that the situation of our body and senses is more or less constant. All that moves is our stream of thoughts, allowing us
the opportunity to see this stream more or less in vacuo. We
can learn something from this—namely, what our mind constantly produces and how that contributes to establishing our
perception of reality. The possibility of learning in this way
is also the basis of many contemplative disciplines or mental
practices. We will return to this in chapters 7 and 8.

A Metaphor: The Film of Experience

The meaning of the term *perception of reality* can also be
clarified through the metaphor of a movie. When we watch
a movie, we see a visual stream of images and almost constantly hear a stream of voices and sound, including music.
The more we become involved and are caught up in the movie
(assuming it is a well-made film that appeals to us), the less
we distinguish those streams from one another, which is what

allows a reality to unfold that engrosses us for an hour and a half. During the making of the movie, the director consciously distinguishes between these streams of experience. The director's art consists of allowing these streams to flow together in such a way that they present the viewer with a perception of reality. The director knows that, with the addition of a certain kind of music, the image of an old car driving slowly down a shaded lane toward a lonely, abandoned house can be the opening of either a comedy or a horror movie. That skill allows us to forget that we are sitting in a large room with other people, listening to noises and watching moving pictures. The director switches off a certain kind of discriminating awareness within us, and as viewers, we are all too prepared to go along because we want to get our money's worth—we want to be caught up. It is because movie directors make use of *their* discriminating awareness that they are able to control *ours*. They know the mental effects that the viewer attaches to the visual and auditory impressions offered, and they know how to combine them in such a way that the viewer experiences them as reality.

Our six sources or streams of experience operate in approximately the same way. Our sensual experience—that which we collect through our senses—flows together and combines with givens from a mental source. In contrast to the production of a movie, however, we are simultaneously the director and the audience. Moreover, the production and the observation of the product take place at more or less the same moment. The movie is not fabricated beforehand in a studio but is more or less improvised on the spot with the material on hand. The director (the mind) in this case operates so inconspicuously and quickly that we are seldom aware of its activity. We are much too caught up or captured by our self-created perception of reality to see the activities of the mind. We lack the space or distance (Greek: *anachorese*) that allows us to see the

director in action. Concretely, the mindfulness or discriminating awareness (see chapter 8) that is needed for this does
not function.

The Stream of Thoughts as Internal Reporter

Although we lack the distance characteristic of open awareness when we are caught up in our perception of reality, there
may be another kind of distance at work: an intellectual or
conceptual one. This distance does not necessarily bring
openness but often serves to bind us even more firmly to our
mental stream. I am referring here to a distance created by
this inner voice that usually provides a running commentary
on everything we undergo. It is as if an internal reporter is at
work, telling us and "explaining" to us what we see, hear, and
experience. A contemporary term used in psychotherapy for
this is *self-talk*. To continue with the metaphor of the movie,
we experience our reality as a documentary or news program
that in fact uses a voice-over or subtitles to explain our experiences from a distant position.

This internal reporter is familiar to all of us. It is almost
always speaking: it informs, evaluates, warns, and lectures; it
admonishes and encourages us. All of this often occurs with
an urgency that implies it is guarding our interests. It is active
not only with respect to the situation in which we actually find
ourselves but also with respect to situations in which we do *not*
find ourselves—situations that are both possible and impossible, in the future and in the past. This so-called reporter is, of
course, a metaphor for the inner commentary that takes the
form of a stream of often highly emotional thoughts that fills
the mind from early in the morning until late at night and even
our dreams. It is this stream of thoughts to which Proust refers
as those ideas "which we recognize and to which we listen."

The distance that our mental stream appears to take in
the form of an internal reporter with regard to our actual

experience is specious because, regardless of the content of our commentary, *it is part of our situation of this moment*. Even though this commentary is about our actual situation (see chapter 4), it is also part of our total stream of experience and colors it. In the guise of apparently distanced subtitles about our subsequent experiences, it gives our perception of reality its subjective character. It is on the basis of this commentary that a certain situation can be irritating to one person while it brings joy to another. If our running commentary about someone is aggressive, then we believe we see an enemy; if it is friendly, then we believe we see a friend. Consequently, we also believe that the enemy or friend exists outside us and has an objective existence from her own side. However, since one individual's friend can be another's enemy, the existence of that person as a friend or enemy in themselves is not as objective as it seems. To put it even more strongly, matters are not settled once and for all in our own experiences. We are continually occupied with making adjustments. For example, when we believe we recognize someone from a distance, the history that we have had with that person comes to mind, and we experience the person in that context. We approach the person from the perspective of that context in which she is a friend or an enemy. For us, that person is who we think she is. If the person comes closer and turns out to be someone else, then our perception of the reality of that same person—the one now in front of us—shifts again.

Direct Self-Knowledge

The preceding examples are familiar enough, but it actually becomes more difficult to determine the influence that our commentary has on our experience if we look at ourselves; it is easier to see how this commentary influences our experience of someone from our surroundings. We also have an internal commentary (whether well-documented or not) that causes us to see and deal with ourselves in a certain way. But are we who we think we are? If so, then we can never be mistaken about ourselves. If not, how do we determine whether, when, and to what degree we are mistaken? This question is relevant because the answer determines the way in which we relate to ourselves. Shall we ask others and involve them in our self-examination? That could be risky: "I think I'm like this, but you think I'm like that. I think you simply cannot see me in any way other than the way in which I think you see me." The ensuing discussion could go on into the wee hours of the morning, the goal being to build a common intersubjective perception of reality in which our concept of ourselves and our concepts of others acquire an acceptable place.

But have we ever looked at ourselves, at the activity of the mind, directly? Or have we only thought and speculated about ourselves and identified ourselves with the results of those speculations—in other words, identified who we *thought* we were? Have we examined the reporter—our stream of thoughts—itself rather than listened to the commentary and allowed ourselves to be swept along with the stream?

How True Is Our Perception of Reality?

It becomes even more difficult if we attempt to trace the influence of our stream of thoughts on the totality of our experience. What is our relationship to reality as a whole? How true is our perception of reality from moment to moment? Do we perceive reality as friend or foe, as threatening or benevolent, as workable or overwhelming? Is it corrupt or sacred, and how real is this kind of experience? Does our perception of reality tell us something about reality or about ourselves and our way of experiencing? Or does it say something about both at the same time and to what extent? Although we are groping in the dark, these questions are important because our perception of reality affects our speech and actions, our concrete working with the world and our fellow human beings.

The point that the contemplative traditions never tire of emphasizing is that we do not actually know the precise area and depth of our blindness or darkness. We do experience moments at which we (perhaps briefly) become aware of some aspect of our blindness: moments at which we "wake up" to our self-deception. There is no guarantee, however, that we will not immediately become submerged in a new illusion. Nor do we know just how many illusions we have in progress. However, from the perspective of the contemplative traditions, we *are* able to cultivate that waking up, thereby becoming more familiar with that typically human discernment—to wake up in a space in which we have a clear view of the nature of our perception of reality. It is precisely that capacity that the contemplative traditions systematically attempt to cultivate.

These traditions view the nature of the unenlightened individual as that of a blind person in the sense that the individual believes in the reality of his own self-created perception of reality. This perception is taken to be an absolute rather than the relative one it is. When perception is taken as an absolute, a truth, people do not see the possibility of—let alone the need for—freeing themselves from it. Perhaps only those few, usually unsolicited, moments that briefly reveal something of that relativity (moments that form the basis of what we will discuss later within the framework of conversion or transformation) allow someone to see this possibility.

In short, our perception of reality is permeated by an unknown degree of blindness, confusion, or (if you wish) self-deception. Blindness is one of *the* major contemplative themes. Thus, contemplative traditions make use of various terms such as *darkness, confusion, blindness,* and *ignorance,* as well as their opposites: *light, clarity of mind,* and *insight.*

For example, the Tenach (the Old Testament) of the Jewish tradition speaks of opening one's eyes. In the New Testament, Paul prays for the enlightenment of "the eyes of your understanding" (Ephesians 1:18). Islam praises Allah as "He who blesses you, and his angels, to bring you forth from the shadows into the light" (Sura 33:43). The Hindu tradition speaks of the "third eye" opening. The Buddhist sutras refer to the rousing of mental discrimination and awareness with the phrase "the opening of the eye of Wisdom."[6] That light or open eye makes us see the degree to which our perception of reality is our own misleading creation.

Guidance

A mentally open eye is obviously essential for the one who is guiding people along the contemplative way—a theme we will discuss in greater detail in the chapters that follow. In contemplative guidance, a guide or mentor engages us with great care and wisdom in creating a space in which we are able to let go of the apparently necessary but illusory buttresses of our perception of reality without being overwhelmed by panic or fear. This letting go cannot always be done without some uneasiness, but it can be done in such a way that we do not lose our nerve entirely.

It is cruel to ask a little child who, in her own perception of reality, sees her mother's place in her life as absolute and is unable to relativize it to any degree: "Do you know that there will come a time when your mother will not be with you anymore?" We would never do that while raising a child; it would only make her fearful and increase the tendency to hold on more frantically to what she thinks is there. Instead, we guide children in such a way that they gradually outgrow their childhood world and create space for other elements so that a more adult perception of reality gradually develops. Indeed, a degree of openness is often lost if, while parenting, we absolutize our *own* perception of reality and believe we must introduce our children to it as well.

With respect to care, however, a knowledgeable guide along the contemplative way takes up their task much as good parents do with their children. In this instance, however, the goal is not to replace one perception of reality with another, but to expose the student's relative reality and make it transparent.

It is important to note that such a development is not solely dependent on the guide. It is only natural that, in shifting our perception of reality, we might encounter moments where a total collapse does occur, an internal breakdown or a *contritio cordis*. Then it might be better for our guide to offer a (temporary) buttress to make the *contritio* bearable. This buttress can prevent us from fleeing and becoming enmeshed in defensiveness, and it can help promote growth in realism and compassion. We will return to this in chapter 10.

The Hazards of the Metaphor of the Way

Finally, something must also be said about the hazards involved in the metaphor of the Way. The imagery of this metaphor is so strong that we may be tempted to absolutize the metaphor itself. It would be easy to allow it to function as a new buttress in our spiritual perception of reality. For this reason, we will now discuss its weak points.

One weakness of the metaphor is that it suggests that the Way has a starting point and an end to which it leads. There is a linearity in this that cannot always be found in our experience. So, the metaphor could encourage too strict a view of the sequential stages: "What stage am I in now? Let me consult my guide or the literature of my tradition." This occurs among practitioners in many traditions and arises from the desire to acquire certainty, to find a new buttress for our perception of reality at that moment, and possibly to evaluate ourselves through comparison with others. When we do this, we no longer look openly at the whole of our experience but only at the aspects that we think are relevant for comparison. This actually impedes further progress along the Way.

The metaphor also suggests something that resembles our Western faith in the idea of progress or advancement. However, from the contemplative perspective, the Way is not analogous with ideas such as climbing the social ladder or having a successful career. Although many traditions make use of such imagery (for example, climbing Mount Carmel or ascending the ladder of the Benedictine tradition), they also stress that this ascension must occur *humiliando*, or "through (the practice of) humility." The practitioner experiences journeying along the Way more as a descent. Practitioners in the Buddhist tradition sometimes say that one travels along the spiritual way walking backward. This idea of a reversed direction and the sense of going backward rather than forward arise because, as we journey along the Way, we progressively acquire a better view of our egocentrism and blindness that frustrates our naive ideas and ambitions for self-improvement (if not self-advancement). Traveling on the Way is similar to removing ourselves further from what we have naively set as our ideals and subsequently projected onto the Way as our goals.

We might find that our ideals and expectations quickly develop into new buttresses, thereby becoming obstacles to contemplative development. Our ideas about the goal (enlightenment, perfection, or fulfillment) can become a new theme on which and by which we model and measure everything around us. When this occurs, as it inevitably will, we are no longer free to look openly at ourselves because we may see things that do not fit in with our travel plans and destination. In the Christian tradition, André Louf expresses it this way: "Obedience, self-discipline, even prayer—these can all be directed away from the living God and become subordinated to an ideal of perfection that in essence barely differs from a secular ethics."[7] This expresses the tendency to climb the ladder of spiritual ambition and success. In the Buddhist tradition, Chögyam Trungpa introduced a term for this branching away or perversion of spirituality: *spiritual materialism*.[8] It is a provocative term, especially since we tend to view spirituality and a materialistic attitude as irreconcilable opposites—which they are. Yet that does not prevent us from perverting authentic spirituality by viewing it materialistically as something we must draw toward ourselves to enrich or "save" ourselves. When this occurs, we have arrived at (or reinforce) the utilitarian mentality (see chapter 1) in which we allow our lives to be led by striving for that which we see as advantageous. We make our decisions on the basis of an analysis of profit and loss: there must be some "spiritual" profit.

It is easy for spiritual ambition to float along in the wake of the materialistic approach to spirituality. The metaphor of the Way appears to allow room for it, which is one of its weak points in addition to the linearity already discussed. We could view the contemplative way as a racetrack where it is possible to win honor and wonderful prizes. Spiritual ambition and the resulting spiritual pride play a role not only at the beginning but also along the whole length of the Way. There are moments when some insight about the Way as our perception of reality dawns on us. At times, we might not resist the temptation to display the insight we have developed like a feather in our cap. At other times, we do not do so openly but tuck that insight away in a little box. In moments when no one is watching, we open the box so we can savor its contents. This is how we feed our spiritual pride.

When we begin to perceive our pride about our progress, we may initially be somewhat shocked. But the more often we see it, the more it begins to rouse our sense of humor: all that spiritual pretentiousness is so naive and childish. At the same time, we begin to see the seriousness of our situation:

it is risky to feed our spiritual pride for it causes the flourishing within to wilt. We then slowly outgrow our tendency to
exalt ourselves and develop a natural and true humility, one
that arises not out of feelings of guilt or self-reproach but out
of self-knowledge. This self-knowledge is the awareness that
the fruits of our contemplative practices are *in* us but not *of*
us. That is, they are real, but we do not possess them. It is
not surprising that the contemplative traditions include many
remedies to alleviate the development of spiritual pride.

Lastly, the metaphor of the Way suggests that we are concerned with a road that has already been paved. This is because
how we think of a road in our day and age is very different
from how people thought of a road when this metaphor first
arose. In the not-so-distant past, there were almost no roads as
we know them today. Going on a journey meant putting oneself in danger. It also meant leaving a familiar neighborhood
without any certainty of ever seeing it again. It was impossible
to obtain a reliable or detailed map or preview of the road,
and information about what lay in the direct future was gathered day by day. The metaphor of the Way does not express
this aspect of uncertainty and risk as well as metaphors such
as a journey and mountain climbing, which are used in the
tradition of the Carmelites and others. The contemplative life
or spiritual growth is a risky business because it amounts to a
departure from our familiar, conventional perception of reality. And with regard to the traveling instructions the traditions
give, without modern streetlights, they only illuminate the
Way a little beyond what lies directly before us at every step.
Or, as it is expressed in Psalm 119:105, "Your word is a lamp
for my feet and a light for my path."

3

The Development of Ego

A central theme in the psychology of the contemplative life is the restlessness within our own hearts, which arises from uncertainty about our existence and is compounded by our ignorance as to who or what we are. In a variety of ways, the contemplative traditions state that this restlessness is connected to an egocentric mental attitude that makes it impossible for our humaneness to flourish. This suggests that there is something wrong with what we usually call the "I" or ego in our experience of reality.

This chapter will acquaint us with the many aspects included in this theme. Before we go into more detail as to the contemplative meaning of the term *ego* and how ego develops, we will first define it roughly by contrasting it with a related concept—namely, self-experience. The latter term refers to all those phenomena that occur, as we said in chapter 1, in the first person—phenomena that are not directly visible to others because they occur in our internal landscape. Everything and anything is to be found there: our thoughts, emotions, expectations, memories, dreams, impressions, perceptions, images, and anything else we can think of. Also, our "I," or ego, as it is viewed in contemplative psychology, is to be found there. It lives in this mental domain, as do the accompanying phenomena such as self-image, self-love, and self-hate.

Thus, the contemplative psychological term *self-experience* refers to a mental domain within which our "I," as well as other mental and emotional phenomena, is present. In this domain, the "I" can be present to a greater or lesser degree at different times; it also influences our self-experience. As we will see, it can even be absent from our self-experience. Thus, the term *self-experience* is much broader and certainly not the same as the experience of "I." When we speak of self-experience, we do not mean something like "I-experience" or "I-awareness" but the experience of our mental domain, with everything that occurs within it from moment to moment.

According to the contemplative traditions, both our self-experience and our experience of our surroundings include many blind spots that result from ego. These blind spots are why we live our lives in a way that brings immeasurable psychological and social suffering. What is at stake here, therefore, is no small matter. Fundamentally, despite what we actually imagine to be the case, we do not know ourselves, and what is more, we are seldom aware of this fact. This is a form of a blind spot. As a result of this ignorance, we regularly travel in directions that can cause harm to ourselves and our surroundings, often without being aware of it. These directions can also lead to a destructive darkness or even sometimes a fear of life; this can cause some people to seek mental ease by escaping into fantasy worlds and dreamlike states. Even if these states were somehow about wisdom, goodness, and spiritual flourishing (as we saw in the last chapter, for example), by projecting an ideal, faraway goal onto the spiritual path, they would still obscure our vision because we cannot live on dreams. They cause us to wither spiritually. When confronted by reality, dreams can often make us more fearful and callous. In this chapter, we will study the nature and cause of the blind spots in our self-experience.

Before we begin, we must return for a moment to what we discussed in the previous chapter: our experience of reality, which includes all our self-experience. After all, we are part of reality. We have seen that our experience of reality is neither completely objective nor completely subjective. Nor is it invariable. It is actually similar to any living organism, something that grows and flourishes but can also calcify or die off, with all life and flexibility ebbing out of it. "Reality" is in a state of constant change. This does not mean only that certain situations appear in and disappear from our lives but also and foremost that the way in which we experience our situation in life is constantly changing. It is true that our childhood toys have disappeared from our lives, but that is not the primary concern of contemplative psychology. We are concerned with the shift that causes our childhood toys to have another *experiential value* when we look at them today. That shift has to do with the development of a continually changing perspective of what may well be the same world of phenomena.

As stated above, there is an aspect of blindness to our experience of reality. Actually, a more appropriate word would be *darkness*. A well-known contemplative metaphor is that, like caterpillars, we spin a protective mental cocoon to ward off the naked experience of reality. We begin to live within its seemingly safe but actually oppressive limitations. Not much light penetrates this cocoon, but at least the situation is orderly—because it *is* limited. In any case, we have the feeling that we know where we are. However, when this cocoon is damaged or even touched, panic often arises within. We become aware that the world is larger (perhaps much larger and possibly dizzyingly so) than our cocoon. Then our awareness of living in the cocoon may arise and, with that, the sense that we have no influence whatsoever on the larger world. Since this cocoon is actually spun by our fear of life, we experience the choice between either confronting and in some way going through that fear or succumbing to it and letting our humaneness or inner flourishing slowly die. Encased tightly within the cocoon, our ability to make contact with, or even simply anticipate that which is outside, is compromised. As a result, we cannot give way to and dance with the wind like a vulnerable butterfly but must hope that the cocoon, spun onto a twig in the shelter of a leaf, can withstand the gusts of wind. The only possibility for self-preservation appears to be in strengthening the threads of the cocoon. In concrete terms, this means that we begin to spin new threads of thought to keep our personal reality intact and inhabitable.

If we wanted to use a philosophical term, we could say that our self-conceived and self-centered reality is *solipsistic*, meaning that "my experience of reality only (*solus*) exists as long as I myself (*ipse*) exist." In other words, it is born and dies with us. Not only our friends and enemies, what we like and what we loathe, come and go with us, but our entire experience of reality, including our self-experience, appears and disappears with us. This is why we, like the contemplative traditions, cannot avoid the psychological question of who the creator or what the creative power of this solipsistic world is. After all, we suffer under (and in) this restrictive cocoon that gradually deadens our joy in life. How did it come into existence and why? What do we mean when we say that we have created it ourselves? How, in concrete terms, does that work? What is the psychological process that leads to it?

A Contemplative View of Ego

Before we give a more concrete psychological analysis of ego, we will look more closely at how this concept is commonly used in a spiritual context. First, we must understand that the term *ego* is not the same as the personal pronoun "I" that people use to refer to themselves. The use of this pronoun does not imply that the speaker has an ego. Conversely, the fact that some languages do not even have the pronoun "I" does not imply that the speakers of these languages do not have egos.

In a spiritual context, the concept of ego (although it is often indicated by other terms) refers to a certain mentality—an egocentric or egotistic mentality. This mentality is considered to be the cause of spiritual blindness and lack of human kindness and must therefore be overcome. Ego is what prompts each of us to create, defend, and enlarge our own realm of influence. This ego sees self-exaltation as self-development and impulsiveness as spontaneity; it confuses the power to fulfill our desires with freedom. This is why many traditions speak of the spiritual path as "transcending ego." Some Christian traditions even use the phrase "crucifying ego." Ego is the hardened sinner, the center of our self-conceit and our egotism. Hindu traditions speak of *jivanmukta*, the "liberation (*mukta*) of ego (*jiva*)"; the transcendence of the false self; and the discovery of the true Self (Brahman). Buddhism speaks of the realization of egolessness (*anatman*) and seeing through the illusion of ego (*atman*). The Hasidic tradition of Judaism considers *bittul*, the "erasing of the self," to be a condition for the highest *unio mystica*, the "highest spiritual realization."[1] These egocentric tendencies result in judging everything in relation to either satisfying or not satisfying what would make "me" happy, important, influential, powerful, right, or whatever it might be in any given situation.

Is it really possible for us to free ourselves from our egocentric experience of reality? According to the contemplative traditions, even though we tend to miss them, we do have egoless moments of experience in which the internal commentary run by our ego with all its projected images and fantasies about reality is silent for a moment. Then something else may be brought forth or revealed. Augustine captured this brilliantly in a famous conversation he had with his mother:

> We were saying, then, If to any man the tumult of the flesh were silenced,—silenced the phantasies of earth, waters, and air,—silenced, too, the poles; yea, the very soul be silenced to herself, and go beyond herself by not thinking of herself,—silenced fancies

and imaginary revelations, every tongue, and every sign, and whatsoever exists bypassing away. . . . If this could be sustained, and other visions of a far different kind be withdrawn, and this one ravish, and absorb, and envelope its beholder amid these inward joys, so that his life might be eternally like that one moment of knowledge which we now sighed after, were not this "Enter thou into the joy of Thy Lord"? [2]

The moment at which our internal commentary ceases and all conceptualizations, meaning conceptual frameworks within which we define ourselves and our reality, sink into nothingness is given many different names: nakedness, liberation, enlightenment, openness, truth, wholeness. From the perspective of ego, such moments are associated with its own death and destruction. For example, the mystical tradition of Islam calls the fulfillment of the spiritual journey *fanaa*, which literally means "destruction." In Buddhism it is said, "The attainment of enlightenment from ego's point of view is extreme death, the death of self, the death of me and mine, the death of the watcher. It is the ultimate and final disappointment." [3] In the Zen tradition, enlightenment is also called *taishi*, the Great Death. [4] A well-known Zen poem puts it this way:

Die while you live,
be completely dead,
then do as you wish,
all is well.

The last two lines of this poem are interesting because they demonstrate that these "moments of death" of ego are also associated with joy in life, or to put it more strongly, they are the only moments when we are truly alive. In Buddhist terms, the moments of egolessness are at the same time the moments in which Buddha-nature is able to unfold and permeate our lives. This double-sidedness is encountered again and again in contemplative traditions. For example, in Vajrayana Buddhism, it is evident in images where the enlightened state is depicted as a naked royal individual or couple dancing on a corpse—the corpse of ego. It is also through the destruction of ego that the purified Muslim "becomes so concentrated on God that 'He becomes the ear with which he hears, the eye with which he sees, the tongue with which he speaks, the heart with which he observes', as expressed in a well-known *hadith kudsi*."[5] And then there is the familiar double-sided passage from the Bible that proclaims the liberation from ego not simply as a possibility but as a fact: "I have been crucified with Christ and I no longer live, but Christ lives in me" (Galatians 2:20). In Christian terms, we could say that these moments create room for the activity of the Holy Spirit.

But people know of these things outside of religious traditions as well. In the eighth elegy of *The Duino Elegies*, Rainer Maria Rilke expressed the double-sidedness between *we* (his italics!)—that is, our conventional me or ego—and the space of the flourishing within as follows:

> *We*'ve never possessed, not for a day,
> the clear space in front of us, in which flowers
> constantly open. We have the world with us, always,
> never that unnamed place which is no place: the pure,
> undefined air we breathe and intimately
> *know* and never yearn for. A really young child
> can get lost in that silence, must be shaken
> back to itself. Or, someone dies and *becomes* this.[6]

On one hand, this double-sidedness presents ego as something negative, for this term refers to the psychological basis of self-centeredness and egoism. Ego is the culprit, the basis of our nonenlightened mentality and the cause of blindness, fear,

and strife. As such, it chokes the flourishing of our humaneness, and we have to fight it. On the other hand, according to
many contemplative traditions, ego is not some kind of entity
or something tangible and concrete against which we can and
must fight. Rather, it is more like a state of mind, a bad daydream from which we must try to awaken ourselves. In fact,
there is no point in fighting it. There is no culprit.

Psychotherapeutic and Contemplative Views of Ego

The preceding section has already shown that the contemplative meaning of the term *ego* is very different from the meaning it is given in clinical psychology and psychotherapy. There
it is often stated that a person must have a strong ego to be
able to function in a healthy way. The concept of ego is then
linked with the idea that one must be able to have confidence
in oneself, confidence that one has the right to exist.

The contemplative traditions also speak of this type of confidence in a positive sense, but they do not use the term *ego* for it.
Why not? Because these traditions state that at its core this confidence is a confidence in the fundamental ground of our existence. Simply put, it is a confidence in ourselves as human beings
and in our truly humane qualities. This kind of self-confidence
is very different from what the contemplative traditions call
ego. There the term refers precisely to what undermines our
self-confidence and our acceptance of ourselves. It is the expression of a lack of self-existing confidence; that is, the absence of
a confidence that does not have to prove itself.

It is necessary to remember this difference in meaning when
we speak of ego in the contemplative sense. It would be misleading to say that in contemplative development one must
first build up a strong ego before one is able to begin the spiritual process of letting go of this ego. In this statement, the
term *ego*, which is used twice, refers to two different things.
The first time it refers to ego as it is defined in psychotherapy

and the second time as it defined in the contemplative traditions. The strong ego sometimes discussed by psychotherapy
is *not* the ego of the contemplative traditions. If that were the
case, this statement would mean that it is healthy to develop a
strong measure of selfishness, blindness, arrogance, and fear
of life before we can begin the process of letting go of them.
This is something that neither psychotherapy nor contemplative psychology aims to encourage. Or else the statement
would mean that we first have to develop a strong dose of
confidence in our own humaneness and then let go of this
confidence. This, again, is certainly not the direction in which
the contemplative traditions or psychotherapy want to lead us.

Thus, the meanings of *ego* in both traditions are almost diametrically opposed to each other, even though in some forms
of psychotherapy[7] and anthropology[8] that take spirituality
into account, we find ideas concerning ego that lie very close
to its contemplative interpretation.

The reason that some contemplative traditions say ego must
be transcended, crucified, or humbled is not so much moral as
psychological. Ego must be transcended or let go, not because
it is necessarily *bad* (such a moral judgment is of no help to
anyone) but because it is psychologically destructive. The cultivation of ego does not lead to a flourishing of our fundamental
humanity but instead chokes it. The mental attitude that considers self-exaltation to be self-development does, after all, rest
on the notion that we must try to be on top of things and build a
strong position for ourselves so we can remain in control of life,
including our emotions and even for ourselves—yes, for our
cursed ego! When we attempt to travel along a spiritual path
with this attitude, then a bitter battle can take place within us
in which we, for the sake of spiritual development, manipulate
ourselves with the threat of hell and damnation. Such a battle,
whether raged in the mundane or spiritual domains, is nothing but an attempt to control ourselves by subjugating or even
destroying the parts of ourselves we reject or despise.

Ego and Egolessness

Where do ego and the egocentric experience of reality that accompanies it come from? Do contemplative traditions have answers to that question—answers that, psychologically speaking, are somewhat more precise and informative than a reference to the Fall or related theological concepts? It appears so. We will trace the origin and development of ego step-by-step, not by thinking about it but by trying to look as openly as we can at our self-experience and the mind. We will thus follow in the footsteps of the practitioners of the contemplative traditions, those who have thoroughly examined and searched the mind by means of meditative disciplines.

What do we actually see when we look at the mind? As we discussed in chapter 2, there is continuous activity in the form of a running commentary or subtitles, a stream of thoughts, that more or less randomly merges with our sensory stream of experience. This is how our solipsistic experience of reality arises.

This stream of thoughts creates a mental world consisting entirely of thoughts with all their emotional coloring. If we look at it more closely, we can see that in that mental world, there is someone who plays the lead, a person who answers to the name "I." When we examine the contents of our thoughts, we frequently encounter this "I." We often think about ourselves; ourselves and others; ourselves and the world around us; ourselves and our past, present, and future; ourselves and our bodies and minds. Almost all aspects of our experience can be reflected in our stream of thoughts and, as a reflection, can be related to thoughts about "me." It is when this egocentric stream of thoughts merges with our sensory experience that our egocentric experience of reality arises.

Thus, it is not only the cocoon woven by the threads of our thoughts that can obscure our view. The egocentric structure of our way of thinking also works in a biased way, adding a measure of confusion to the mix. This confusion has far-reaching

consequences because the "I" or ego, which plays such a prominent role in our thinking, offers a fixed reference point to which
we are very attached—not necessarily because it is pleasant
(after all, we can think negatively about ourselves) but because
it offers security and familiarity. We would not miss it for the
world. We would even be willing to give our lives or take the
lives of others for it, fighting with fire and sword if necessary.
As we will see, it is the basis of our aggression and greed.

We are so used to and attached to this egocentric way of
thinking that we find it inconceivable that the "I" should play
no part in our experience of ourselves. What would remain of
our way of thinking and emotional life if this leading character turned out to be an actor that plays a role in the first scene
of our lives only to disappear for the rest of the play? Would
we die, cease to exist? Could we still function, or would
the words of Paul ("I no longer live, but Christ lives in me")
become meaningful to us? To answer this in contemplative
terms, when we give up our egocentric thinking, it is no longer
ego but humaneness that lives in our self-experience.

This is not necessarily as huge a leap as it may seem, nor is
it an abstract idea or an elevated experience beyond our reach.
In fact, in addition to habitual and almost ongoing egocentric moments of experience, we also have moments in which
our egocentric experience is absent. Yet something concrete
is involved here, although it is not easy to express because
it is so subtle. It is something we can easily pass by without
noticing. Perhaps an example can clarify matters. Suppose
we are doing something that requires our attention, such as
playing the piano or painting a cupboard. If we are really
into it, completely absorbed in what we are doing, we forget
ourselves—for as long as we are doing this particular activity,
we are not preoccupied with ourselves or with the question of
whether we are good at playing or painting. It is not ourselves
but the situation or the activity that directs our actions and
observations. Jean-Paul Sartre wrote:

> In fact, I am then immersed in the world of objects;
> they constitute the unity of my consciousnesses [that
> is, moments of consciousness], which present them-
> selves with values, attractive and repulsive qualities,
> but *I*, I have disappeared, I have been annihilated.
> There is no place for *me* on this level, and this does
> not prove to be coincidental, a momentary lack of
> attention, but the very structure of consciousness.[9]

Phenomenological psychologists say that we "coincide" with our actions at such moments. Contemplative psychologists say that in this situation the mental separation between the action and the one who carries it out is absent. In Buddhist psychology, this way of experiencing is called *threefold purity*: the mental (and psychological) separation between the actor, the action, and that which is acted on does not (yet or no longer) play a role in one's experience.

Tolstoy described this experience clearly when he said it was the effectiveness and flexibility with which people are able to function and the absence of uncertainty that together characterize these moments of experience (see page 7). Then, as he wrote, "the scythe seemed to mow of itself." Such blessed moments are well known to musicians, moments when the music seems to take us over. The notes on the score, our understanding of music, our concentration, our hands on the keyboard, and our awareness all work together in an effective unity. It is not "we" who make the music, but all of these components together. This is why it is called "not doing" (Chinese: *wu wei*) in the contemplative tradition of Taoism. This is being in harmony with the Way, or the Tao. In fact, "we" would only get in the way. If "we" were part of the music unfolding, "we" would only fret about a certain passage coming up, worried that we would not get through it without making a mistake. Or, if things went well, we might pat ourselves on the back and thereby lose contact with the keyboard. In the same way, the surface of a cupboard, the thickness of the paint, the stiffness of the brush—our awareness of and experience with these qualities determine how we paint. "We" are outside of this; at most, we sit and watch, but we do nothing.

Then the moment occurs when this clear, efficacious, intelligent unity of conscious experiencing and acting breaks down; suddenly we are overcome by self-consciousness, and then the fear that we may have lost control of the situation may arise. We panic, thinking that we have not paid attention to ourselves. We fear we have lost sight of ourselves. When this panic seizes us, we may ask ourselves, "Where am I?" or "How am I doing?"

Many contemplative traditions stress that there is something abrupt about this return moment of ego-centered consciousness, that it is a fracture of some sort—or even an infraction—that seems to occur involuntarily. In the first instance, the fracture is not much more than a feeble awareness of this versus that, a psychological dualism of "me here" and "that there." This is the conception of a reference point, something we could possibly hang on to or identify ourselves with. It is the birth, or rather the conception, of ego that occurs here, the starting point of the development of ego. Let us look at this development in more detail.

A Contemplative Psychological View of Ego

Contemplative psychology is concerned with the question of how the initial mental movement we just described develops further into our egocentric experience of reality. In Christian traditions, the origin of ego and an egocentric experience of reality is usually spoken of in terms of the Fall and being driven out of Paradise. Of course, these are typically religious and theological concepts, but they also have a contemplative psychological interpretation. For example, we can say that the Fall refers to the origin of the egocentric experience of reality, which is the result of a certain movement of the mind. What kind of movement is that? In answering that question, it turns out that the Buddhist tradition offers a valuable contribution. We can describe the development of ego in terms of four subsequent mental movements.

Let us begin, however, with exploring the state of mind that exists *before* the development of ego takes place. Before any of these mental movements occur, there is total openness. In this open space, all phenomena interact with one another according to their own natures, with a certain equality and without commentary or the illusion of distance created by a mental reporter; this situation was described in the earlier examples of playing the piano or painting a cupboard. As we know, almost all contemplative traditions have a way to point out these moments of openness. From the Buddhist tradition, this openness is likened to "a spacious hall where there is room to dance about, where there is no danger of knocking things over or tripping over things, for there is completely open space. We *are* this space, we are *one* with it, with *vidya*, intelligence and openness."[10] We all have these moments of openness— moments that, from ego's perspective, are unfathomable and threaten chaos, but that, from their own perspective, are as clear as water, true and full of joy. These moments form the underlying basis on which, by not recognizing them for what they are, the development of ego takes place.

The Dualistic Split

The first movement is that in which our mind reflects back to itself, withdrawing into itself and thereby separating itself from all the appearances that manifest themselves in the open space of experience. Through this one mental movement arises the duality of "I" and "the other" in our experience. It is the starting point of the development of ego in the contemplative sense of the word. Psychologically, it can be characterized as a moment of mental constriction or drawing back. But why do we draw back?

What has happened? Chögyam Trungpa, from the Tibetan Buddhist tradition, captures the subjective nature of this moment:

> Nothing has happened, as a matter of fact. We just became too active in that space. Because it is spacious, it brings inspiration to dance about; but our dance became a bit too active, we began to spin more than was necessary to express that space. At this point we became *self*-conscious, conscious that "I" am dancing in space. At such a point, space is no longer space as such. It becomes solid. Instead of being one with the space, we feel space as a separate entity, as tangible. This is the first experience of duality—space and I.[11]

Carried away by our own energy—of dancing, of playing the piano—the fear suddenly arises that "I" have lost control. Fear is a poor adviser. In fact, we do not realize that we never actually had control in the way we thought we did, that we will never be able to have that kind of control, and that we do not need it in order to live, to dance. However, the idea of control and the fear of its loss has taken hold, and we proceed mentally along a road that is disastrous and a dead end in all respects, since this ego is not the basis of our existence but the creation of our fear and contraction. This fear does not trust the nature of the fundamentally open space, which is nothing other than the state of total openness of mind. But now the open space is experienced as something obscure, as an area external to "I."[12] It is because of this that we are then compelled to begin to look for something to hold on to.

Ego Identification

There is nothing to hold on to in this open space, and this reinforces our fear. We engage in a sometimes-frantic search for something to hold on to, which in itself becomes a huge and never-ending task at which we must continually work. We have the feeling that in order to be, we must be *someone*. But who? It is as if we must create and prove our existence as "I." Existing—just being, being a creature—is not enough; it is too spacious. Of course, our continuous attempts to find or create something to hold on to actually become something to hold on to. Therefore, these attempts form the second step in the development of ego. They are directed at giving substance to the as yet abstract and naked "I."

This occurs in a subsequent mental movement that divides the field of our experience into "what I am" or "what belongs to me" on one hand and "what I am not" or "what does not belong to me" on the other. Expressed more concretely, after making the dualistic split, the mind moves to identify with certain phenomena and call them "I," while identifying other phenomena as "not-I." However, these identifications are shifting or changing every moment, which is why we see that what we call "I" is continually changing. For example, one moment we identify ourselves with the body, as when we say, "I fell down." The next moment we identify ourselves with the feeling of pain that we had when we fell and say, "I hurt myself." At another moment, we identify ourselves with a certain emotion, such as when we say, "I am angry that I hurt myself." Are the one who fell down and the one who is hurt and the one who is angry about it the same "I" or not? If you say, "I fell down," then it is actually your body that falls down, but it is not your body that is angry about it.

We are not consistent with our identifications; for example, we do not even identify ourselves with our emotions all the time. Sometimes we see them as things outside of us, such as when we say, "I was overcome by grief." In a certain sense, the emotions have then become part of the world around us, and our "I" withdraws to another point. This point can be the body, sensations, perceptions, thoughts themselves, or the consciousness. Thus, the scope of ego varies: it expands and contracts according to the situation. As a result, we can appreciate that the meaning of the word *I*—that to which this word refers—shifts continually. It is not something fixed or solid, for at each moment, the actual substance or content of ego is something different again.

Because we execute this mental movement of ego identification very quickly in each moment of experience, a certain continuity and stability is suggested—the feeling is present that this "I" is always there and is something fixed, even though it is never the same. We could compare it to walking on ice floes: we cannot stay on one floe too long because it will sink; we have to jump across to another floe quickly to maintain the illusion of firm ground under our feet. In the same way, this mental movement creates an illusion of firm ground, even though it is the quick jumping from one identification to another that creates this illusion.

In our experience of reality, the first two mental movements—the dualistic split and ego identification—together constitute the appearance of ego as an entity or object. Around it lies the phenomenal world, which is then equally experienced as a collection of objects or things. We can refer to these two movements together as *object formation*, or the mental move that causes the "I" to appear as an object or a thing amid other objects. In Western philosophy and psychology, this particular thing is often referred to as "the subject." But this subject is quite different from the notion of subject that contemplative psychology uses and was discussed in chapter 1 under the heading "Human Beings as Subjects."

The metaphor of swimming in an ocean might clarify both of these first movements further. The first movement can be compared with a swimmer, who in the vast and fathomless ocean, is suddenly struck by panic that she might drown. That first movement of panic triggers a second move; the swimmer grabs a piece of driftwood floating nearby. When we find ourselves in the vast and fathomless ocean of experience and suddenly doubt we can swim, however, we grab what we *think* is a piece of driftwood. However, what we are actually grasping is one of our own limbs, which makes swimming extremely difficult. Grabbing hold of ourselves, we "discover" that we can indeed barely swim. This only feeds our fear and causes us to tighten our hold on ourselves. We will not drown, however, because we actually can swim. By letting go of the driftwood (the limb) for a moment to get a better hold on it, we might become aware of our situation and realize that we can swim, that we do not need something to hold on to, and that our fear was groundless. But it is also possible that we believe we have been very clever in quickly finding a more convenient hold on our "driftwood" and have managed to save ourselves once more! We have once again succeeded in continuing to float, thanks to the driftwood and our clever-ness in taking advantage of it.

Here the continually renewed hold on the driftwood is, of course, a metaphor for the ongoing creation of ego. It clarifies that ego is sustained only as a mental activity. The swimmer is the mind which, when it is directed toward the development of ego, grabs hold of itself, creating the illusion of having some-thing to hang on to. The ocean represents the phenomenal world, and the (nonexistent) driftwood represents ego. This second mental movement of the mind grasping itself is almost on an instinctive level. In Buddhist contemplative psychology, the result of this movement is often called *sahaja atmagraha* in Sanskrit, translated as "impulsive ego grasping," or "coemergent ego grasping." Here, coemergent (*sahaja*) refers to the simultaneous appearance of the fearful "me" grasping (*atmagraha*) and the unknown other, which is the vast ocean of experience that seems to appear around "me."

In contemplative psychology, mind as subject and experi-ence as object are not two established entities; they are the result of the ongoing mental activity of dividing the open space into "me here" and "that there." We could also characterize this mental movement as one that turns all fleeting internal and external phenomena into entities that are perceived by another entity—"me." This entity should be protected against what (the mind thinks) it fears and provided with what (the mind thinks) it wants.

Dressing Up Ego

In this phase, ego is still unstable and naked. Thus, the third mental movement is one in which we "dress up" this naked ego. How do we do this? The mind generates an enormous amount of mental activity in the shape of a continual stream of thoughts about ourselves in relation to what we see as not being ourselves—a kind of internal administrative process in which we keep track of who we are and how we are doing. This administrative process consists of the internal dialogue that we carry on with ourselves (see chapter 2). Even though we do not do it out loud, is it not true that we often talk to ourselves? We admonish and encourage ourselves, explain things to ourselves, and form many opinions about ourselves. It is not clear whether in this process we are the ones who listen to this internal dialogue or the ones who speak. We experience a kind of mental division, as if there were two of us within. Why should we say something to ourselves if the person who speaks is also the person who listens? We already know what we will hear, so there is no real need to do so.

However, from the perspective of our struggle toward a stable ego, it is literally and figuratively necessary for us to fill the open space with something that we seem able to hold on to: a running commentary. This commentary seems to define and explain the world and our place in it, which is why the maintenance of this internal administration, or bookkeeping about ourselves, seems useful, if not necessary. Who would we be without it? Would we be at all without it?

At the same time, this commentary actually creates a world: our ego-centered experience of reality. With the help of this commentary, which serves as a conceptual garb to cover the nakedness of ego, we begin to dress up our ego with all kinds of ideas—ideas about ourselves. We have a wide range of ideas available and a great deal of freedom in selecting from them. There are as many ideas as we or others can think up about ourselves: accurate ideas, foolish ideas; happy and discouraging ideas; ideas that are superficial, deep, philosophical, psychological, and social; ideas borrowed from our personal history or our expectations of the future. In short, we dress up our naked ego with a definition of who we (think we) are. We then form what we called in chapter 1 a self-concept or self-image. We can now understand better that our self-concept functions to contain the information about ourselves that is registered in our internal ledger system. We come to rely on this ledger system, as it seems to offer us a certain security, a structure, and a feeling of having an overall picture of things.

Ego Identification with the Concept of Self

Finally, there is a fourth, very ingenious and subtle mental movement in the development of ego, which now is no longer naked. This movement serves to increase ego's stability—or to go back to our metaphor, it increases the buoyancy of the driftwood that we seem to depend on for the survival of "me."

The third movement introduced a new phenomenon into our world of experience: our self-concept, a mental construction that we are able, with periodic mental bookkeeping, to keep relatively stable. This self-concept is now part of our stream of experience. Why then, in our search for a stable idea as to who or what we are, should we not identify with this construction? The fourth mental movement is just that: it is another movement of ego identification, which we discussed earlier but now takes our self-concept as the object with which to identify. That is, we identify ourselves (our ego) with our self-concept. From this moment on, we are who we *think* we are. In Buddhist contemplative psychology, the result of these last two movements is called *vikalpita atmagraha* ("conceptual ego grasping" or "acquired ego"). We now believe that our concept of ourselves *is* ourselves. It is from this position that we now deal with the world around us; even the world around *us* becomes the world as we think it to be.

We must not view these movements as mental activity that occurs only once in our lives, after which we are irrevocably trapped in one dualistic experience of reality. In contemplative psychology, these movements that create our ego-centered experience of reality are viewed as a fairly ongoing activity that recurs in almost every moment of experience. The mental movements are actually very swift, usually unnoticed, and as a rule, habitual. Nonetheless, they can be detected and released through the practice of meditation.

In sum, these four movements show us in what sense ego is not a thing, as we usually think of it, but a mental activity that through its continuity provides the illusion of permanence. In Buddhism, this activity is often compared with the circle of light that we see when swinging a torch around. We think we see an entity, but that is not what it is. Our mind has to keep swinging the torch of ego around in order to maintain it. Note that because ego is an ongoing activity, I have not used an article in front of it—I do not speak of *the* ego but of ego. Lastly, we should not equate ego with the body. Self-preservation, our attempt to maintain our ego, is not the same as protecting and preserving the body. This is proved by the fact that people sometimes damage their own health in order to defend or aggrandize their ego, resulting in all kinds of abuse of the body. Even when the distinction between the body as a physical entity and ego is made, the mind tends to conceive of ego as analogous to the body in some way—as an entity in its own right, or a homunculus, a little human being that exists somewhere and is the owner and boss of both a body and a mind. The mind even allows this homunculus to claim the right to use and misuse its body to fulfill its ambitions. According to the contemplative psychology of most spiritual traditions, however, the body is viewed as the precious basis for walking the spiritual path. Therefore, we should take good care of it.

The Callousness and Vulnerability of Ego

At last, on the basis of the four mental movements, we now think we know who we are. It is registered in our mental ledger! The ledger contains ego's version of our self-knowledge, or the indirect knowledge of ourselves that we discussed in chapter 1. It is an impressive mental achievement, but one that has taken us far away from the open space of which Augustine and many others of the contemplative traditions spoke. Expressed in stronger terms, ego, which has arisen as a result of the four mental movements, conceals the entrance to that open space in which ego's illusory nature would be revealed. This leads to what we will discuss in the next chapter: perceptual confusion and, in turn, suffering.

Moreover, at the moment we identify or equate our self-concept with ourselves, a new kind of vulnerability arises—perhaps *irritability* is a better word—because whoever now affects our self-concept affects "us." If our mental ledger contains the entry, "I am a patient and charming person," and we hear someone (perhaps behind our back) say, "You have to watch out for him. He always goes off the deep end. He's bad news," then not only is our self-concept hurt, but we also feel hurt personally: "we" are hurt. We can brood on it for days, intent on revenge at one moment, anxious at others. We become so lost within ourselves that we do not notice the summer wind that makes the poppies in the garden flutter or our friend's cheerful, affectionate glance inviting us to enjoy this moment together.

If we further elaborate and modify the self-concept with which we identify, then ultimately all aspects of our world of experience are related to it in one way or another. Almost nothing can happen or be said without our self-concept, and thus ourselves, being at stake. Everything refers back to us—whether for good or bad, as something that confirms or something that hurts. Our egocentric experience of reality has become fact.

On this basis, the range of the egocentric experience of reality can continually expand. Ego can act as a web, continually spreading out over the field of our experience, more and more of which comes under the domain of ego. The psychological field that we feel we must control to safeguard our ego becomes bigger and bigger. This also has an effect on our speech and actions. Now we can be open and unselfish only as long as our ego is not at stake, as long as it feels little or no threat. In other words, our fundamental humanity becomes constricted and may only manifest itself (sometimes only partially) under certain conditions—and those times and conditions are dictated by ego. Moments in which we rise above ourselves may become rare, even though there is a great deal above which we must rise. Sadly, if not painfully, our fundamental humanity has become "conditional humanity." If, for example, we have the idea that, to avoid feeling threatened, we must have fifty thousand dollars in our savings account, and we are fixed on this idea for our security in the world and peace of mind, then our generosity and willingness to give to a good cause may be compromised; generosity may manifest itself only when that condition (fifty thousand dollars in the bank) is met. Likewise, we may find that in protecting our self-concept, we are only able to extend friendship and care to people if our ego is not threatened in any way. The development and hold ego has over us chokes the hidden flourishing of our fundamental humanity. As a consequence, the development of the fruits of that fundamental humanity, such as kindness and compassion, are thwarted before they can manifest in our speech and actions.

Imprisoned in Ego

Ego, the development of which we have described, is like a structure erected within our hearts. No one may enter. We ourselves do not really know why it is like this. Nor do we necessarily know what is behind the walls of this defensive structure or even whether there *is* something behind or beyond it to be found. We may be confused as to whether the structure protects our joy in life and gentleness or whether it confines our fear of life so we are not too troubled by our circumstances. Is it possible, as many contemplative traditions maintain, that the same open space resides behind the walls of ego as that space in which we lived before the structure of ego was erected? Could it be otherwise? Whatever the case may be, the development of ego is directed at building an impregnable fortress to which others are seldom admitted and then only when blessed with our permission.

There is another side to the closed nature of our ego, the impenetrableness of this mental structure—it is impossible to just will our way out of it. The stronger and more invulnerable ego becomes, the more it becomes like a prison for our fundamental humanity. This is an inadvertent and certainly not consciously desired side effect of the development of ego: we have imprisoned the fundamental open ground of who we are. Inevitably when we live at ego's will, we feel deeply dissatisfied since we can never secure the conditions of happiness ego craves and demands. Nor can we see that this situation is one of our own mental making, that we have allowed our illusory ego to drive us. We—that is, our undisciplined and fearful mind—have caused this imprisonment ourselves; this is our own personal "fall." As already stated with the metaphor of the cocoon, the impenetrability of ego only causes us to feel separateness as if it is true. Of course, we are provided with the psychological comfort of having our own interpretation for every possible situation in life, which secures our position and seemingly renders ego harmless, or at least interested only in our best interests. However, the atmosphere within this structure is particularly stale and dark, like a room without a window. Fundamentally, we suffer greatly because of this.

Obviously, the concrete form of ego varies in every person since we each construct it with our own mental material. The complexity of each structure varies as well. Some people maintain a small house, and because it is so small, it is easy to build it out of concrete. Other designs include huge palaces with tall, splendid towers that reach high into the heavens and extensive additions that take up a lot of space—in short, constructions that are very impressive but also very vulnerable. Extra measures are necessary to guard against collapse and possible intruders. Guards must be employed to watch the gates of such structures so no one enters and throws everything into confusion or steals the valuables. In all cases, we have to understand that ego and our egocentric thoughts isolate us from direct naked experience. Proust expressed it this way:

> And then my thoughts, did they not form a similar sort of hiding place, in the depths of which I felt that I could bury myself and remain invisible even when I was looking at what went on outside? When I saw any external object, my consciousness that I was seeing it would remain between me and it, enclosing it in a slender, incorporeal outline which prevented me from ever coming directly in contact with the material form; for it would volatilize itself in some way before I could touch it, just as an incandescent body which is moved toward something wet, never actually touches moisture, since it is always preceded, itself, by a zone of evaporation.[13]

Buried deep in the fortification of ego resides an intense longing for open space, playfulness, and freedom. We have not entirely forgotten the spaciousness and openness of our fundamental humanity. This desire is our natural and original desire to see life (and ourselves) flourish—Thomas Aquinas called this the *desiderium naturale,* the "natural desire." However, now that our separation has become a psychological fact, this desire manifests itself as a wish to unite with our world because we suspect that the space and freedom we want are to be found outside ourselves. Thus, simultaneously with the rise of ego, there is the desire to undo this separation. Desire for unity and believing we can find it outside ourselves increases our restlessness within the split. It motivates us to make many attempts to break out or resolve this split in some way. These attempts go in two directions—either external or internal.

In one direction, we attempt to change or even destroy our concrete everyday situation—a different job, partner, or environment. We tend to think that there is something in our surroundings that must change for our original warmth in life to be restored—that warmth that we suspect always exists even though we do not know where to find it.

In the other direction, we attempt to change or destroy our ego: we search for another concept of ourselves, another state of being, and try to become someone else. However, in whatever direction we go, these attempts are fundamentally ineffective because at each moment they recreate again and again the dualistic experience of reality of ego. The result of these attempts is the opposite of our aim: The battle against "this" or "that" only intensifies our preoccupation with and belief in their existence. As a consequence, our sense of imprisonment and pain intensifies, often into an aggressive, defensive attitude toward life.

The Development of Egocentric Emotionality

Thus, even though the blueprint of ego differs for every person, it is still based on universal psychological principles. We have described a number of those principles in terms of mental movements that lead to a more or less solid ego. But there is more. These movements also form the basis for the development of an egocentric emotionality. How does this work?

Let us return for a moment to the process of ego identification within the development of ego. In the process of ego development, we tend to identify ourselves (our ego) with both external and internal phenomena. Sometimes we identify ourselves with our bodies and at other times we do not; sometimes we identify ourselves with our emotions and sometimes we do not. The same happens with our perceptions, ideas, or consciousness. But in all of these cases, a dualistic experience of reality emerges within which ego is defined as a sort of entity over or against its world.

We can think about it this way: things can attract or repel one another or move alongside one another without exerting any influence on each other. Analogous to this, between the "I" conceived as an entity and the other things—internal and external phenomena—a game of attraction, repulsion, or indifference begins. It is as if ego approaches every situation with the questions: Shall I draw this toward me, repel it, or ignore it? Is this situation important to me because I can get something out of it, is it repulsive to me because I am threatened by it, or is it not important to me at all? Stated in psychological terms, with the appearance of ego in our self-experience, three fundamental responses—greed, aggression, and indifference—come into play with respect to the phenomena with which ego engages. In Buddhism, these three emotions are the basic emotions of a mentality within which the illusion of ego is present. They are called *kleshas* ("poisons") because they poison the mind. Like a veil, they obscure our humanity and suppress its manifestation in word and deed. Contemplative psychology calls them "egocentric emotions." As mentioned before, in the Abrahamic religions, these emotions are the demons that follow on the heels of the devil. The Greek word for "devil" is *diabolos*, which is related to the verb *diaballein* ("splitting into" or "creating discord"). This is very close to the Buddhist notion of the dualistic split that makes us see the world in terms of "I" and "other" and makes us suffer. No wonder we can never step on the devil's tail, as he is not an entity but a way of seeing! Obviously, all contemplative traditions have their own, often detailed classifications of egocentric emotions, as well as their own terminology. They describe the egocentric emotionality of the profane mentality that obscures and frustrates our altruistic or—as we call them in contemplative psychology—egoless emotions, like love, compassion, dedication, and loyalty.

It is important to note that emotions (and thoughts, as we shall see in chapter 4) are always directed at something. We call this the intentional nature of emotions—this means emotions have an object. Thus, a person or situation can be the object or target of our aggression or passion. However, we do not always identify with our emotions and ideas: "I was carried away by my emotions. The idea just came to me . . ." At that moment, we perceive our emotions (and ideas) as external to us; belonging to the world outside our ego, they have become objects to us. Therefore, emotions not only have an object but they can also be objects themselves.

When we conceive of an emotion as an object, our self-experience once again undergoes a dualistic split, a further fragmentation and complication: there is "me here" and "my emotion there." It is on this basis that the question can arise as to what we think of our egocentric emotion, how we must react to it. Thus, a further layer of egocentric emotions may reveal themselves: "Shall I foster my egocentric emotion, fight it, or ignore it?" At this moment, emotions about emotions arise. We are all familiar with this internal fragmentation and complication: "I enjoyed my burst of anger"; "It angered me that I desired them so." These mental movements by which we make internal phenomena objects of other internal phenomena (emotions about emotions, ideas about ideas, ideas about emotions, and vice versa) open up far-reaching perspectives for the building of ego. We can complicate our mental lives—our way of thinking, our emotional world—as much as we want or are able to.

We are dealing here with the phenomenon of conflicting levels of emotions. At times we like becoming angry, and at times we are angry precisely because we enjoy something. We become a mass of contradictions. Apparently, the emotional life is not a simple affair but includes emotions about emotions about emotions. We can always add to that; there are even times when we are irritated by something but have forgotten what it was. We can experience regret for this later on, although we also feel it to be childish, and so it goes. In this way, we can develop very complex emotional lives and ways of thinking with more or less fixed patterns of emotional reactions toward other emotions. At times those patterns of reaction are so automatic and quick that the original emotional response may no longer even penetrate our consciousness. This is the way we gradually become lost in the structure of ego, self-absorbed and focused inward. Our ledger system can become hopelessly confused. At a given moment, if we feel a certain dissatisfaction with ourselves, we may no longer remember its source. This dissatisfaction is the final, visible, exterior wall of ego. We suffer because of it and wonder if we should do something about it; maybe we consider whether or not it is time for psychotherapy. And yes, it might well be!

Moreover, psychological research has proven that people who possess a rich vocabulary and conceptual framework (and can therefore use a more detailed mental ledger system) have a greater range of emotions as well. This means there is also a connection between our conceptual framework and the emotions that we can distinguish. Therefore, with the help of this conceptual framework and because of the possibility of viewing emotions as the object of other emotions and ideas, we can create very elaborate emotional lives. We can also identify with this and include it in our self-concept. We might even be somewhat proud of our nuanced emotionality and our ability to maintain order over such a demanding matter.

As you read this, you may feel that there is something almost denigrating in the way I have talked about the emotional life. This would be incorrect, because something important is involved: the development of ego's emotionality, or the development in the emotional relationships between ego and its environment. But allowing ourselves to be intimidated or guided by it would be going too far. On balance, this development is the result of an unfortunate turn of mind, a *metanoia* ("conversion") in the wrong direction that distorts the emotional energy of our humaneness into egocentric emotions and thus chokes any mental flourishing.

In other words, there are real tears and crocodile tears—tears that we shed out of compassion and tears that we shed because our ego is hurt. Saint Augustine went so far as to wonder whether the latter are tears of real grief. When he lost his mother, he wondered whether his tears were not an expression of a certain spiritual immaturity, of the desire to hold on to a piece of ego's territory of which his mother was a part, so that the flood of tears welled up more out of self-pity than out of love for his mother. He wondered whether, by shedding tears out of frustrated self-interest, he did not harm himself and others. Later he cried freely out of love and compassion for his mother, because of her minor sins and the life that she had led. Those tears, he wrote, were completely different from the ones he had shed earlier.

Thus, in the contemplative traditions, we also see a strong interest in emotion because ego's emotionality is a fertile area. Ultimately, all egocentric emotions, although they are distorted, contain the energy of our humaneness. The mental movements that lead to the rise of ego can also bring our emotional energy and humaneness under ego's control. When this happens, our altruistic emotions shrink and narrow down to egocentric emotions. The energy of care is perverted into self-preservation and dedication into self-interest. Love shrinks to self-love, unconditional joy in life turns into the satisfaction of desires, equanimity is transformed into indifference, inspiration becomes ambition, power becomes high-handedness, and freedom becomes imprisonment. This is how the emotionality of the egocentric mentality arises.

First-Person Psychology and Ego Psychology

The development of ego not only leads to a cessation, or at least a minimization, in our experience of our humaneness; we find that way of living to be a normal, human state of affairs. Living at ego's beck and call also has consequences on the level of actions and speech, impeding our fundamental humanity from becoming visible to others as well. On the level of speech, we tend to maintain our position as "I" and, if possible, strengthen it by doing some advertising for ourselves. For example, we make some slighting remark about others, satisfying our ambition and jealousy in order to extend our own little kingdom. Our egocentric mentality is also expressed in actions: taking things that are not ours, creating situations by which we please our ego, destroying that which does not satisfy us or threatens us. And so, we slip into various egocentric patterns of behavior—patterns through which we and others suffer. Perhaps in our interaction with people we have acquired the idea that, when protecting our ego, it is better to strike the first blow. In new situations, we immediately tend to assert and display ourselves, to dominate the situation. Or perhaps we are of the opinion that we can best protect the ego by going through life in as inconspicuous a way as possible so no one will take aim at us. These behavioral patterns are the externally visible, bitter fruits of our internal attitude. They can be so deeply ingrained that they persist, even if we have lost faith in their effectiveness as protectors of our ego. That is why the contemplative traditions not only provide mental disciplines directed at recognizing and letting go of the mental movements that create and maintain the illusion of ego but also offer disciplines directed at transforming actions and speech. We will focus on this in the second part of this volume.

From the perspective of ego, the egocentric mentality, emotionality, and ways of functioning in speech and action that follow, are self-evident. The approach to the discipline of psychology that arises from this perspective is a sort of "ego psychology," according to which certain emotions are self-evident: "a human being is a creature that . . ." followed by a catalog of the basic qualities of the egocentric mentality that portrays the human being as a selfish creature that seeks satisfaction, personal comfort, and the fulfillment of its wishes. However, this apparently obvious and therefore appealing psychology is not harmless. Based on a concept of humanity in which self-interest is the main motivation, it works its way through to our personal as well as our social lives, reinforcing each other. From this perspective of humanity, Queen Beatrix of the Netherlands best stated it in 1992: "Egoism is seen as the most normal thing in the world. As a social power it has indeed brought us to material progress. But a society whose only standards for human actions are self-interest, usefulness and economic efficiency will fall apart."[14]

A psychology that accepts and elevates egocentrism to the position of the true nature of the human being describes well the psychology of the profane human being. Such ego psychology is a valuable source for contemplative study. However, its perspective is very different from the first-person psychology that we encounter in the broader understanding of the contemplative traditions we are exploring. Here, ego psychology is viewed as unknowingly describing processes and structures, not of the human mind as such but of the deluded human mind only. Therefore, there is no motivation to explore ego and how it forms and functions. For first-person psychology, such exploration into our ordinary ego-centered experience is the way to recover the humaneness that has become obscured and, in some ways, lost to us.

Thus, we can see that the human being in the first person is central in contemplative psychology—a psychology that has the egoless, open space of experience rather than the ego as its starting point. It may be described more correctly as an egoless psychology that studies both the phenomena of ego in our self-experience and the dynamics of its disappearance. This is why the psychology that we encounter in the contemplative traditions is so different from conventional psychology, which is not only largely a third-person psychology but also mostly ego psychology.

It is not only because the contemplative traditions are directed at transcending ego (and its psychology) that their psychologies are distinct from conventional psychology. The first-person perspective also leads to a distinctive view of the nature and function of the human mind and knowledge. As a result, it also has its own psychology about thinking, experience, and awareness, which is the foundation of the contemplative disciplines themselves. Before we examine the contemplative disciplines in the second part of this book, we will look more closely at this psychology of mind and knowledge in the next chapter.

4

Mind and Knowledge in Contemplative Psychology

In the previous chapters, we used a number of terms like *experience, thinking, stream of thoughts*, and *discernment* somewhat loosely as well as differently from how we might normally use them. This follows from the typical first-person perspective of contemplative psychology. Before we look at how the contemplative disciplines work with the mind in the second part of this book, we should clarify the use of these terms in this psychology, for all these terms are related to aspects of the mind. They are also related to the question of knowledge. Clarifying these terms can help us to see what is understood by *mind* and *knowledge* in contemplative psychology.

In our ordinary use of language, terms such as *mind, understanding, consciousness*, and *insight* are somewhat vague. The concept of mind is certainly used somewhat casually. It is difficult to lay one's finger on what is meant by the term. We use it in various ways in everyday life: "He changed his mind." "Let this mind be in you" (Phil. 2:5). "Care for the mind and body." "She kept it in mind." *Merriam-Webster's Collegiate Dictionary* lists nine different meanings:

1. recollection, memory; 2a. the element or complex of elements in an individual that feels, perceives,

thinks, wills, and esp. reasons; 2b. the conscious mental events and capabilities in an organism; 2c. the organized conscious and unconscious adaptive mental activity of an organism; 3. intention, desire; 4. the normal or healthy condition of the mental faculties; 5. opinion, view; 6. disposition, mood; 7a. a person or group embodying mental qualities; 7b. intellectual ability; 8. Christian science: god; 9. a conscious substratum or factor in the universe.

In short, the term is too multifaceted to be reduced to one comprehensive definition.

The results of modern academic psychology are hardly more helpful. In this psychology, the use of the term *mind* or *psyche* was—amazingly enough—almost taboo until recently. During the first decades of the twentieth century, the term disappeared from the psychological vocabulary. This was a direct consequence of the rise of the third-person orientation of empirical psychology, which emphasized the perspective that it is impossible to observe other people's minds. Therefore, we cannot do third-person research on the mind.

Theological and religious interpretations of these terms do not offer any kind of concrete or agreed understanding of them either. We do find discussions about the human soul and the mind, and there is extensive theoretical discussion about connections between the soul, the intuition, the intellect, the mind, and so on. However, the emphasis in theology is not so much on the contemplative psychological dimension but on the construction of a consistent theology. Answers to the practical issue of how we, as practitioners of a spiritual path, can work with the mental domain and the experience of reality that arises from it are not discussed. With an emphasis on theological consistency, it could be said that many religious traditions have actually lost their contemplative psychology—which is what this book is seeking to address.

We can, of course, find answers in psychotherapy, but the questions in that field are posed with an entirely different aim, directed not at spiritual liberation but at the resolution of psychological problems. Even positive psychology, developed by Martin Seligman and with its focus on the development of authentic happiness, only touches on one (important) theme of contemplative psychology—the theme of well-being or happiness.[1] We discussed this in the introduction to this book. Positive psychology does not claim, however, to be necessarily relevant for those who practice contemplative disciplines.

The approaches to religion from the field of depth psychology have provided us with suggestions for a more psychological interpretation of terms that often appear to have only a theological connotation. Examples can be found, for instance, in the works of Carl Jung and Eugen Drewermann. The latter, in the spirit of Jung, said, "I believe that in psychotherapy many experiences are awakened and many levels of human experience are addressed that are originally religious. People usually don't interpret it that way and the Church often refuses to see it like that."[2]

Even though depth psychology can open our eyes to a more psychological point of view, there is the risk of importing a terminology that is essentially alien to the contemplative tradition. Because of this, depth psychology can obscure precisely what contemplative psychology has to offer us. This danger looms large, especially with respect to those non-Western or non-Christian religions that are rich with contemplative psychological insights. The particular danger here is that we may believe that the insights of other religions confirm our own existing psychological conceptual framework. The contemplative psychological insights that do not fit into that framework are easily overlooked or considered to be irrelevant. Jung's foreword to *The Tibetan Book of the Dead* is a typical example of this,[3] as John Reynolds pointed out.[4]

It is therefore wise to take a different step first—to show what particular kind of psychological interpretation the contemplative traditions employ with respect to terms such as *mind*, *consciousness*, *thinking*, *knowing*, and *experiencing*. We need to ask the contemplative traditions, how do the practitioners of contemplative disciplines use these terms? What does the practice of these disciplines actually do with, to, or in the mind? What do practitioners *see* when they focus their attention on the mind by means of these disciplines? Just as we have already seen in our discussion of the term *ego*, in answering these questions, contemplative psychology appears to give these terms different definitions than we, or contemporary academic psychology and psychotherapy, usually do.

Mind in Contemplative Psychology

In the previous chapters, we used the term *mental domain* a number of times. This term gives a first clue as to what contemplative psychology understands by the concept of mind. We also saw that contemplative psychology is primarily a first-person field, meaning that according to this psychology, the mental domain can be experienced. We can "experience" or "see" the mind's activities. The mind is thus not a domain about which we can only think, speculate, and imagine—as if it were the other side of the moon. We can see our mental activity and experience it immediately and consciously.

We have also used the terms *thinking* and *stream of thoughts* in a broad sense. Everything that occurs within us— what we think, imagine, remember, feel, hope, and fear—is found within this thought-stream. And with all its turbulence, rationality, and irrationality, it is not something separate from experience but constitutes a part of it. Our stream of thoughts, or thinking, flows next to the stream of sensory experience. They merge together to form what we have called our experience of reality.

What else has arisen in the previous chapters that is relevant for the question of what *mind* means in contemplative psychology? In chapter 2, we discussed the contemplative view that people have at their disposal a kind of internal capacity for perception, that is, that they are in a position to clearly see the movement of their minds. In this context, we spoke of the "enlightened eyes of our understanding" (Ephesians 1:18) and the "eye of wisdom."[5] We speak of the "mind's eye" in ordinary language as well. The word *eye* is, of course, a metaphor for an aspect of the mind. Which aspect? It has something to do with mindfulness, with awareness or consciousness.

We now have three terms relating to our mind: thinking, experience, and consciousness/awareness. We will analyze the contemplative psychological meanings of these terms more closely, starting with the relationship between thinking and experience.

The Relationship between Thought and Experience

The contemplative view is grounded in the belief that our thinking—the movement of the mind, our stream of thoughts with all its ideas, emotions, and desires—can be experienced in a way that deviates from the approaches of both academic and everyday psychology. As discussed in the previous chapter, these psychologies rely on the view that thinking is something that more or less stands separate from experience. The view that thoughts and experience are two separate phenomena is widespread in Western philosophy. This idea rests on the apparent distance that our internal commentary seems to take with respect to our experience. Here is a metaphor that characterizes this view. We often have the feeling that our (stream of) thoughts occur "backstage," as if this thinking, separated from the theater of our experience, leaves experience undisturbed.[6] We then look on it as an activity that is carried out in a kind of private space. On stage we have our world of experience (about which we have thoughts), and backstage we have our thoughts. Within the contemplative psychological perspective, in which thinking is something that can be experienced, thinking no longer stands in the wings. Rather, what we experience through our senses and our thoughts about what we experience both happen on stage.

This metaphor indicates not only that thinking is seen as something to be experienced but also that there is a reciprocal relationship between thinking and experience: we can think about our experiences *and* experience our thoughts. This is a key point in contemplative psychology.

Consciousness

Let us now look at the contemplative psychological term *consciousness*. We have seen that we can be conscious or unconscious of our thoughts. Sometimes we notice that we are thinking, and at other times we are so lost in thought that we do not even know that we are thinking. Our mind's eye closes. Mentally, we are asleep; we have been daydreaming, drowned in our stream of thoughts. Afterward, when we come to our senses again, most of what we thought about has been forgotten. We may remember that we thought of an errand we had to run, and the last link in the chain of thoughts, such as a memory of someone from third grade, may still be vivid in our minds but we no longer know how we arrived at that thought.

However, our mind's eye can close to more than our stream of thoughts. The same phenomenon also arises when we speak, act, or perceive with our senses. We may be doing something—perhaps talking out loud to ourselves—and not notice we are doing it. It is as if we are on automatic pilot. For example, we might be following our usual route to work, and when we arrive, we realize that although we managed to do so unscathed, we cannot remember how. Our senses were obviously working—nothing happened to us—but we were not conscious of the route we took. We were absentminded (an interesting word that expresses this phenomenon well). We were not "there." Instead, we were carried along unconsciously by the stream of our sensory experience. This is different from, if not the opposite of, what we discussed earlier about being fully present in an activity.

What does this phenomenon say about the mind? We can describe it briefly as follows: We are obviously capable of experiencing our sensory and mental stream consciously or unconsciously. Here a new phrase has come into our analysis of mind: "being (un)conscious." This reflects the fact that the term *consciousness* in contemplative psychology refers to a quality of experience or perception. Its use is linguistically similar to terms like *nakedness, happiness, eagerness,* and so on. Therefore, consciousness does not refer to a mental faculty or region. This is why we will avoid using of a phrase like "the unconscious," which suggests a specific area in the mind of which we are not conscious. Instead, we will use the neologism *unconsciousness* as shorthand for the "absence of the quality of consciousness." We will also use related terminology such as "(lack of) mindfulness," "mindlessness," and "(lack of) awareness" in the same way. When discussing the mental disciplines in chapters 7 and 8, we will introduce mindfulness and awareness as two aspects of the quality of consciousness.

Going back to our metaphor of a play, *unconsciousness* refers to the moments when the audience dozes off during the performance or when it only has attention for the star and does not pay any attention to the other players. Shakespeare wrote, "All the world's a stage, / And all the men and women merely players." But what kind of play would it be if we—simultaneously the audience and the players—sat in the theater and dozed off? Or did we come to the performance in the first place hoping that there would be seats comfortable enough for us to take a nap? The contemplative traditions have quite a bit to say about this, and the practice of the mental disciplines have everything to do with it.

Experience and Consciousness

We have seen that we can experience things both consciously and unconsciously, and that this applies to both the mental and the sensory domains. We find this view not only in the contemplative traditions but also in the old European psychology of consciousness developed by Wilhelm Wundt. We will not go into the latter in detail, but some connections in vocabulary are worth mentioning.

In modern psychology, the experience of events in the sensory domain are often referred to as *perception*. The connection with consciousness is that perception is selective; not all impressions that we undergo receive the same amount of attention. Here a mental process called "selective attention" plays a role. Moreover, the phenomenon that people can direct their attention to something subconsciously—that is, without being yet aware of it—is as well known to empirical psychology as it is to the driver who reaches her destination automatically. So-called anticipation can be experienced in traffic. To notice something consciously and to perceive something are two different mental events in modern psychology.

In Wundt's early psychology of consciousness, this distinction was also made vis-à-vis the mental domain. Wundt used the term *apperception* to refer to the directing of the attention to psychological content. In his view, "psychological content" could be both an element from our stream of thoughts and an element of perception—an element derived from the stream of sensory perception. Perceptions also counted as mental content. If we direct our apperception to thoughts or perceptions, they then lie within what Wundt calls the "focus of vision" (*Blickpunkt*) and are conscious. What falls outside this focus lies in the "field of vision" (*Blickfeld*) of which we are only vaguely aware. Blickfeld and Blickpunkt together determine the range and focus of our awareness or apperception. We are not aware of whatever thoughts or perceptions lie beyond them. In short, Wundt's term lends itself well to what we mean by the "conscious perception" of mental content. Also, according to Wundt, perception itself can, but need not, be conscious.

It is interesting that Wundt's terminology is closely related to that found in Buddhist contemplative psychology. Here, noticing mental content is called *manovijnana*. *Vijnana* can be translated as "consciousness," and *manas*, of which *mano* is a declension, as "mind" or "the mental." Manovijnana is therefore a moment of consciousness that has mental content as its object. In this psychology, we can be aware of sensory perceptions only as *mental events*. At that moment of awareness, they lie within the range of manovijnana, of apperception. We will not continue with these connections. For those who wish to explore Buddhist psychology more deeply, David Ross Komito's *Nagarjuna's "Seventy Stanzas"* offers a good introduction,[7] as does book six of Jamgön Kongtrul's *Treasury of Knowledge*.[8] Bhikkhu Bodhi offers a more detailed exposition in his *Comprehensive Manual of Abhidhamma*.[9]

To return to our main theme, what is actually meant by "(un)conscious experience"? We have already seen an example of unconscious experience of sensory phenomena: we can see, hear, or do something, such as driving to work, without paying attention. Conscious experience is the opposite; we notice the stream of our experience. We are not absent but present.

However, there is also the (un)conscious experience of the mind, mental domain. Let us look at two situations familiar to all of us: We can be in thought, and we can see our thoughts. If we are "in thought" and carried along by the stream, we often do not notice that we are thinking. We then live in our world of thoughts, which we experience at that moment as reality. We undergo all kinds of imaginary joys and sorrows.

At such moments, we have an unconscious experiencing of our thinking.

When we awaken from our stream of thoughts, we notice that we were thinking, and we often see only the tail end of the stream. At that moment, we have what we can call a conscious experiencing of our thinking. That is, we no longer experience our thoughts as reality but truly as thoughts. Practically speaking, there are all kinds of gradations between conscious and unconscious experiencing of our thoughts. They can be completely transparent, so we see them for what they are— merely thoughts. Sometimes they are a veil of clouds that colors our experiences. And often they are like a thick fog that obscures our view completely, so we live entirely in our world of thoughts. We can describe it by saying our consciousness has a degree of clarity. However, we can just as well say that this clarity is a quality of our experiencing: phenomena are continually experienced more or less consciously. This applies to the experiencing of both sensory and mental phenomena.

Two Aspects of Consciousness

With respect to the function of consciousness, two closely connected aspects are generally distinguished from each other within the contemplative traditions: one static and the other dynamic.

The first aspect is indicated by terms such as *mindfulness, attention, concentration,* and *one-pointedness.* It is the ability to direct our attention to something and keep it there. It is the opposite of absentmindedness or a restless, chaotic state of mind that moves from one object to another. This aspect confers a certain stability and precision to our way of experiencing; mindfulness counteracts the tendency to jump from one thing to another. It creates space for us to recognize the details of our actual situation. Thus, many contemplative traditions emphasize that the cultivation of mindfulness is also the development of a certain mental calm. We are not talking of a spasmodic, forced form of mindfulness, but of mindfulness that finds its natural resting place in itself. Stability, precision, and rest are all indications of this aspect of consciousness. We will discuss how the contemplative disciplines can help us develop this aspect in chapter 7.

The first, stabilizing aspect of consciousness is the basis for the development of the second dynamic aspect, which we described in previous chapters with the term *discernment*. This aspect is a discriminating awareness that offers an overview of and insight into the coherence of phenomena (both mental and sensory) that surface in the stream of our experience. This aspect is the mobile, dynamic quality of consciousness. It has a quality of inquisitiveness or interest—not an intellectual inquisitiveness but one like that displayed by young children for what they see around them; a child looks around with an open mind and in a carefree way. Therefore, this aspect of consciousness is also indicated by terms such as *open-mindedness* or *clarity of mind*. It is an intelligent, alert openness that is unhindered by biases, preoccupations, or prejudice—in short, a way of being aware that is free from fixation on our conventional experience of reality, with its running commentary in the form of our ego-centered stream of thoughts. The thought-stream need not be absent for this. On the contrary, because this alert intelligence is not inhibited or caught by our stream of thoughts, it can perceive its effect on our experience of reality most clearly. This kind of discriminating awareness gives us knowledge and insight, and it is cultivated by the practice of the contemplative disciplines of insight (see chapter 8).

An image sometimes used for this aspect of being conscious is that of a bird—an eagle or a *garuda*—that glides through the air with great ease and stability, almost without moving its wings, and therefore has a perfect view of the world of phenomena. This image represents those moments when our awareness is free from fixation.

Such moments sometimes arise spontaneously when the intensity of our experience is great, as in stirring moments. Our perception then changes as a result of an extremely energetic alertness. At these times, we experience more things more quickly than is the case when our consciousness is conditioned by our stream of thoughts. It is as if time stops or slows to a crawl. Filmmakers are acquainted with this: They attempt to awaken the suggestion of intensity by using slow motion, for example, for certain events such as an accident, a first embrace, or a death scene. Directors thus appeal to what we recognize from our own experience of intense situations—situations in which our consciousness is torn loose and flies free. Because of that, it is often capable of briefly seeing the smallest details of a situation with an unbelievable clarity. It is due to this ability that people have sometimes been able to save lives: seeing a car bearing down on her toddler in slow motion, a mother is somehow able to get to the child and pull him out of the way.

This discriminating awareness, which is free from all inhibition or fixation, is an unconditioned awareness. It constitutes the seed as well as the fruit of what the contemplative traditions seek to cultivate (see chapter 8). This awareness, when cultivated fully has been given many names: enlightenment, fulfillment, abyss, death, eternal life, surrender, and so on (see chapter 3). Whatever name we give it, these moments of intense, unconditioned awareness are when the mind's eye opens—initially, perhaps only for an instant. These moments make us capable of disentangling illusion and reality and seeing human life unveiled. The active discernment involved is the clarity of the Great Within, the mind of our fundamental humanity (see the introduction).

The Relationship between Stability and Discernment

Many metaphors illustrate that the two aspects of consciousness belong with each other. Discernment or discriminating awareness—sometimes called the ability to see our true face—is developed only on the basis of mental stability or calm, a calm that results from letting go of our fixation on our turbulent stream of thoughts. This calm makes the mind (consciousness) function like a mirror or clear, still water or the motionless flame of a candle. Calm is not the aim, as some people think, but the means; it leads to insight, which is the true goal. In the stories of the Christian desert fathers, we find the story of two monks who visited another monk and asked him about his progress. His answer illustrated the importance of rest for developing insight:

> He was silent for a little and poured water in a cup. And he said: "Look at the water." And it was cloudy. And after a little he said again: "Now look, see how clear the water has become." And when they leant over the water, they saw their faces as in a glass [mirror]. And then he said to them: "So it is with man who lives among men. He does not see his own sins because of the turmoil. But when he is at rest, especially in the desert, then he sees his sins.[10]

The same idea, but formulated somewhat more optimistically, is expressed as follows in Buddhism: "When the mind settles naturally in quiescent absorption, free from dullness and sensual incitement, it vividly perceives its very essence."[11] We see here the interesting paradox that the more restful the mind is, the more mobility and room for mobility discernment has.

"Rest" in the contemplative meaning is certainly not the drowsy, uninterested calm of which we usually think when we hear the word. In the contemplative sense, calm is a form of mental stabilitas, a form of internal stability. This is a steadfastness that does not allow itself to be carried along or away by our turbulent stream of thoughts and, because of that, makes the stream visible or conscious. For this reason, calm is also the basis of insight. The less our awareness is pulled along by our thought-stream, the more we can see this stream in an unbiased way. While the more open our awareness is, the more energetic and lively our discernment, and our insight begins to manifest itself. Mental calm, of which the contemplative traditions speak, appears to allow for a great deal of energy. When the energy of wakefulness begins to function, the calm appears to be a dynamic one, which in a single movement furnishes a view of both the totality and the details of each moment of experience. This wakefulness incinerates every perceptual distortion and self-deception that belongs to our typical egocentric, fixated consciousness. We will discuss later how these two aspects of calm and discernment are cultivated by the mental disciplines of contemplation.

The Contemplative Psychology of Thought

Let us now further explore the concept of thought as it is used in contemplative psychology since it is employed differently than in conventional psychology. We will discuss three points here: first, the broad meaning of the term *thought*; second, the difference between the object of thought and its content; and third, the form and content of thought.

The Broad Meaning of Thought

First of all, in many contemplative traditions, the meaning of the term *thought* is closely associated with the term *stream of thoughts*. The former is often used as a general term for all mental movement, or everything that occurs within the mind. This broad definition means that the term *thinking* is almost synonymous with "mental activity." Its use is similar to the way we use the term in everyday life. If we say, "I am thinking about it the whole time," no one is surprised to hear that our stream of thoughts includes images, desires, and even strong emotions. In academic psychology, *thought* is not defined this broadly. Rather, it is defined as a cognitive activity that does not include emotion and will or feelings and desires.

The Content and Object of Thought

The second important point involves the ambiguity of the term *thought* in our everyday language. If, for example, we ask John, "What are you thinking about?" and he answers, "My work situation," we can interpret this answer in two ways. First, we can interpret it in the sense that John is referring to a situation outside himself and outside his thoughts about it, a situation that we, as his colleagues, understand. It is independent of John's thinking about it. It is that about which John is thinking. This situation is the *object* of his thought.

This interpretation of the term considers or assumes thoughts as separate from the object of thought. The object of John's thoughts, his work situation, is separate from his thoughts about it. Whether John thinks about it or not, the work situation itself does not cease to exist. Even when we think about our actual situation at this moment, we may recognize that our thinking is something separate and does not influence the situation. We often believe that we influence our actual situation only when we begin to act. However, our thinking is also part of our actual situation. By thinking about it, our situation has already been changed. We discussed this point previously in terms of the stage metaphor.

There is still another way to understand John's answer. If John says he is thinking about his work situation, we can say that he is telling us about the *content* of his thinking. He is stating which formation of thought is occurring in his head at that moment. His thought has a certain form: images of his desk, conversations with colleagues, and so on. The content of this thought does not lie outside John or his thought but within it. In short, we have two interpretations: One that refers to the object of a thought and one that refers to the content. The object lies outside the thought and the content lies within it.

The object and the content of thinking are therefore two different things. There is often, though not always, a relationship between the object and content. The image in John's thought of his desk and his colleagues can, for example, be a more or less faithful mental likeness of his desk and colleagues. We then say that the content of the thought is a mental representation of the object of the thought. Stated conversely, the object is represented in thinking by the content.

Of course, not all contents are mental representations. We might think of a situation that does not exist: "I am thinking of a sunny island where I am lying in the shadow of palm trees while eternity unfolds before me." If that were John's answer to our question, we would view it simply as an answer about the content of his thoughts and not the object. We would not proceed on the basis that this thought was a mental representation of a certain object.

Therefore, the contents of thought do not need to have any connection to an object in experience. Also, the variety of their forms is not determined or limited by actual objects. That is determined by the wealth of our imagination, by our mental creativity, and by the material available in the form of memories in our stream of thoughts. This creativity can also be destructive and make us believe in ghosts or devils, and it is the basis of the development of ego. We saw in our previous discussion of this topic that we can form contents of thoughts and incorrectly claim that they have an object: our ego and egocentric world of thought. We begin to feel anxiety and fear with respect to imaginary dangers. We then engage in tilting at the windmills of our egocentric experience of reality.

The Contents of Thought Are the Forms of Thought

A third characteristic of the term *thinking* in the contemplative sense is that it refers to a dynamic or fleeting phenomenon. The contents of thoughts are not mental entities, meaning they are not some kind of enduring mental things appearing in a moment of consciousness. So, what are they, and how do they come into being? They are momentary formations in our stream of thoughts. In that stream, which cannot be observed by our eyes or ears, all kinds of mental formations almost constantly occur in flexible and continually changing forms. The *contents* of thought are the *forms* of thought.

In Buddhist psychology, these contents are often compared to cloud formations: Clouds come and go, take shape and dissolve again into the sky. Their forms are continually changing yet follow certain patterns. Our mental clouds have their own dynamic. They can arise and evaporate slowly or appear and disappear from one moment to the next, as when our mood suddenly changes or something occurs to us. This dynamic shows us the nature of our stream of thoughts. Another metaphor is that thoughts are a kind of "mental clay," a soft, pliable mental substance. In the mind they are continually reshaped—now a horse, then a man, then an ashtray, and finally a pancake or a rolling pin. These metaphors emphasize that the contents of thoughts do not exist as things but as forms of thoughts or thought formations. This concludes our discussion of the term *thought* in contemplative psychology for now.

Connections between Thinking, Experiencing, and Consciousness

On the basis of what we have learned about thoughts, their content (form), and their object, we can identify two important differences between thinking and experiencing. The first difference is simply that experiences have content but no object, while thoughts can have both content and an object. If we experience pain or see a cyclist, then the pain or the cyclist is what we experience—meaning it is the content of our experience. That is why we can say that we think about something but not that we experience about something. Experience does not have an object in the way that a thought does.

Thus, when we think about an experience, the experience is the object of our thinking. And *what* we think about the experience is the content of our thinking. Conversely, we can experience a thought, as when the thought is the content of our experience. To give a concrete example, if we see a blackbird, the bird becomes the content of that experiential moment. If we then think, "Ah, a blackbird," this is a thought about the experience. The experience is then the object of the thought, whereas the mental form "Ah, a blackbird" is the content of the thought. Another example is if we recall a precious memory at a certain moment, the memory is the content of that mental experience. We may begin to reflect on that memory and the content of our thinking could be something like, "That was a very special moment in my life." Here, the experienced memory is the object of the thought.

Because the content and object of thinking are two different things, the one can represent the other; that is, the content of a thought can be a mental representation of the object. However, in the case of experience, it is different. We do not have two separate things (content and object) where one can be a representation of the other. This means that experiences do not represent things. What we experience is not a representation of something else, as the content of thoughts can be. What we experience simply presents itself. It is not a representation but a *presentation*. If we experience something—either mentally or through our senses—the experience simply is; not only is it a presentation but it is also *present*. So, experiencing only happens in the here and now. It does not represent something else but is directly present to us at this moment. From a first-person perspective, the content of experience is the only thing we go through. Thoughts can be representations, but experiences—including the experience of a certain thought—cannot.

An example may help to clarify matters further, as we are dealing with an important yet somewhat difficult distinction. Let us return to seeing the blackbird in the tree. The tree and the blackbird form the content of our experience. If we turn around so we no longer see the tree, we can still think of the blackbird—that is, form the mental representation. At that moment, the blackbird and the tree are the content of our thought. The object of the thought—the blackbird and the tree—are now absent from our experience. We can claim that our representation is of the object—the blackbird—if it has not flown away, startled by so much philosophizing.

A second difference, connected with the first, between thinking and experiencing is that the term *experience*, as used in the first-person perspective of contemplative psychology, is related to what is present in the here and now. *Experiencing is always here and now.* This is a somewhat more limited meaning than the one we find in ordinary usage. There we do speak about "having experience with something," meaning that we have become acquainted with something in the past. The meaning of this term then approaches that of *memory*. In contemplative psychology, however, experience has to do with what we undergo now. For example, what I experience now is that I am writing. What you, the reader, experience now is that you are reading—this very sentence, in fact. But you are now already experiencing a different sentence. It is quite nice to communicate with you for a moment between the lines. But let us proceed with the argument.

We cannot experience what is past nor what is to come. Experience is, by definition, experience of what is now present. In other words, we cannot experience the past or the future. Experience has no temporal dimension, no extension in time. It is different in that respect from thinking. Even though a

thought always occurs only here and now, its content does
have a temporal dimension. The content of a thought can, at
any rate, be a memory or an expectation—a mental representation of something that has been or is still to come. But,
again, the experience of the memory or expectation occurs
only here and now. It would be a mistake to believe that the
experience of a memory is the experience of the past or that
the experience of an expectation is an experience of the future.
It is true that in everyday usage we play fast and loose with this
distinction. But if we think about it, we will understand that
we cannot experience the past or the future. The past no longer exists, and the future does not exist yet. What does exist
at the moment they appear are memories and expectations
as the contents of thought, which we can experience either
consciously or unconsciously. In our discussion of the mental disciplines of the contemplative life, we will see that their
focus on experience and experiential knowledge (perceptual
knowledge) corresponds closely with their focus on experience
and life here and now.

The "I" as Ding an Sich

Let us take up a related question that often arises in this context. Does experience not imply *someone who experiences*,
and does thinking not imply a *thinker*? In everyday language,
we are inclined to smuggle in a subject, to think that there
must be someone who is aware, thinks, or experiences. And
if by "someone" we mean a (human) being, we must admit
that this is so.

However, most of the time, "someone" means something
else, namely our "I" that is separate or at least different from
what we think or experience. This is our common, dualistic way of conceptualizing reality. In the context of contemplative psychology, however, the ego or "I" is the content of
a thought and not the thinker, because the assumption that

there *is* a thinker is nothing more than a thought. We identify this thinker by means of the thought, "'I' think about something." However, if we consciously experience this thought, then we see that its existence shows nothing more than the thought itself. We can confirm neither the existence nor the nonexistence of an entity called "I"—or of any entity that we can call the thinker or the one who experiences. In short, if we presuppose the existence of an "I," then the presupposition is still nothing more than a thought. In itself, a thought has no demonstrative power. We can think what we want.

We already saw in chapter 3 that from the perspective of contemplative psychology, the "I" is not assumed to be something that precedes our experience of reality. We do not presuppose the "I" is an invisible entity behind the experience nor that it has or possesses an experience or thought; we see it as a thought that may or may not turn up in our field of experience.

The idea that something exists or must be presupposed behind the experience is an old philosophical theme. Some philosophers have questioned not only the existence of the "I" but, more generally, whether there is something outside the realm of experience—whether our experience could, like our thoughts, have an object after all, even if it is an object that we cannot experience. Assuming such an object, Immanuel Kant christened it the *Ding an sich.*

Contemplative psychology says that we can at most imagine—that is, conceive of—the existence of such an object. But as we have already seen that, from this point of view, such an object exists only as a thought that we may or may not— depending on our philosophical views—want to carry along in our stream of thoughts. We have never seen and will never experience the Ding an sich itself—whether we believe in its existence or not, and whether we identify it as a subject, an ego, or an object. For if we could experience this subject, it would no longer be the one who is experiencing but that which is experienced.

Thought and Consciousness

Finally, let us look briefly at the influence that thought and consciousness can have on each other. A feature of our stream of thoughts is that its flow seems uninterrupted. This impression arises because of its speed. As soon we wake up in the morning, it seems to set its course and carries us along. On the basis of this running mental commentary, there are a great many aspects in our stream of experience of which we are not aware. The metaphor of the film—now a metaphor for our stream of thoughts—is also helpful here. Films, which consist of separate images, suggest through their speed an uninterrupted movement, a continuous cinematic reality, that weakens the intensity of our being aware of the theater and the chair on which we are sitting. Watching the film, our discriminating awareness decreases, and we become dependent on the limited space the movie allows us. In the same way, a narrowing of our awareness leads to our viewing our stream of thoughts as real. It is, at any rate, the only reality we have at that moment, the only one of which we are aware. (See the earlier quotation from Proust in chapter 3.)

We may already suspect that the spiritual disciplines of mindfulness undo this narrowing of our awareness and the fixation on our stream of thoughts by first decreasing the speed of our thinking; thus, the emphasis on first calming the mind. The disciplines of insight subsequently cultivate our ability to recognize the nature of the mind and our experience of reality. Stated another way, these disciplines make us aware of the way in which we interpret or conceptualize our experience. They are not directed at replacing one interpretation with another, a bad one with a better one. The contemplative traditions recognize that we engage in an almost continual interpretation of our experiences. However, their disciplines are directed at cultivating a discriminating awareness that allows us to see the effect of our interpretations on our experience of reality from moment to moment. For this reason, it is said that discriminating awareness leads to wisdom. What kind of wisdom is this? One that causes us to recognize the confusing and painful illusion of our egocentric experience of reality and liberates us from it. In the Christian tradition, it is called *diakrisis*; the Mahayana Buddhist tradition calls it *prajna* (literally, "higher knowing"). Prajna cuts through our being caught in *samsara*, our egocentric experience of reality, and makes samsara visible to us. It shows us the true nature of our egocentric experience: a self-created illusion. When we recognize that it is an illusion, it loses its hold on us. Then the world of phenomena, including all our illusions that have been recognized as such, appear to us in a different way—as nirvana. The egocentric experience of reality, with its accompanying emotionality, is extinguished and robbed of its power. The self-deception is broken. That is the kind of wisdom, or state of being wise (free of confusion and ignorance), that the contemplative traditions seek to cultivate. Then our humaneness comes to full bloom and can manifest itself in the world for the well-being of all living beings and society.

The development of wisdom by means of discriminating awareness is described differently in the various contemplative traditions. However, they all emphasize that the cultivation of awareness is a way to wisdom, insight, or contemplative knowledge. We will discuss the nature of this contemplative knowledge next. In part 2 of this book, we will see that all this is needed for a good understanding of the mental disciplines we find in the contemplative traditions.

Knowledge and Insight in Contemplative Psychology

Concepts such as knowledge and insight, ignorance and confusion, have their own meanings in contemplative psychology. These meanings clarify once again an aspect of what is meant by the human mind in first-person psychology. As already suggested, an important aim of the practice of the mental disciplines relates to the cultivation of insight into the nature of the human mind and experience itself. It is also said that this insight transforms the mind and experience. What kind of insight and knowledge do we refer to here?

This is a question about the *epistemology* of the contemplative traditions. The old Greek word for knowledge is *epistèmè*, and epistemology refers to the theory of knowledge. This theory explains what knowledge is and when something can be called "knowledge." I have previously outlined this aspect in detail,[12] so here we will summarize the key points of that information.

The reciprocal relationship between thinking and experience that we have established—that is, we can think about our experience and experience our thoughts—suggests two ways in which we can acquire knowledge. If we think clearly about our experience, this undoubtedly leads to a form of knowledge. We are wiser because of it. The kind of knowledge we acquire is *conceptual knowledge*, for we think in ideas, or concepts—the latter term being the one used in cognitive psychology. As we have seen, concepts are elements in our stream of thoughts.

However, this is not the only way to gain knowledge or insight. We can also try to experience clearly what goes on in our minds (stream of thoughts) by using our discriminating awareness, or mental discernment. This also yields a kind of insight or knowledge, but this knowledge is not conceptual. We could call it *perceptual knowledge*: it comes into being not through thinking but by improving our ability to look with our inner eye, our awareness. This gives us a form of knowledge or insight that is nonconceptual, meaning not based on concepts. It relies on clear vision and recognition rather than ideas. The Buddhist tradition says that it is a form of knowing, similar to a person who is mute knowing what sweetness tastes like but being unable to speak about it. In the same vein, the knowledge an enlightened person has of enlightenment is perceptual and inexpressible.

Modern psychology considers only conceptual knowledge to be scientific; however, both conceptual and perceptual knowledge were recognized in early Western psychology and considered to be valid. William James called them "knowledge-about" and "knowledge of acquaintance," respectively. He wrote, "I am acquainted with many people and things, which I know very little about, except their presence in the places where I have met them. . . . I cannot *describe* them. . . . At most, I can say to my friends, go to certain places and act in certain ways, and these objects will probably come."[13] In this sense, we can describe in only a limited way those with whom we are well acquainted. We may know the faces of hundreds of people but cannot give hundreds of different descriptions of faces. Our vocabulary and conceptual framework simply fall short. If we are asked, "What does the person look like?" we do not proceed much beyond something like "brown eyes, quite tall, curly gray hair." We can perhaps say something in addition about the nose or the way the person walks, but after that we have nothing left to say. Nevertheless, we would immediately recognize that person among a thousand. It is a different kind of knowing than conceptual knowing.

Bertrand Russell would later refer to James's knowledge-about as "knowledge by description." Since this form of knowledge is conceptual, it is closely tied to the possibilities offered by language for describing something.

In almost all contemplative traditions, we find this distinction between the two forms of knowledge. In the Christian tradition, one often finds a distinction between knowledge of the head (or understanding) and knowledge of the heart. The knowledge of the heart is understood as a form of perceptual knowledge; it is acquaintance with. Knowledge of the head is a form of conceptual knowledge; it is knowledge-about.

The Function of Knowledge in the Contemplative Traditions

If there are two kinds of knowledge, we can also expect two methods for acquiring knowledge. Let us first investigate what the function of conceptual and perceptual knowledge is within the contemplative traditions. Why are these traditions interested in knowledge? The scientific traditions (including scientific psychology) look for knowledge with the aim of manipulating the world of phenomena to our benefit. But what purpose does the acquisition of knowledge within the contemplative traditions serve?

The aim of the contemplative traditions (including their psychology) is not to acquire a great deal of knowledge about the world in order to rule over it but to change human beings. In what respect, however, are human beings to be changed? As we have seen, the traditions first focus on the opposite of knowledge: they are concerned with removing blindness, ignorance, darkness, and confusion. To that end, both perceptual and conceptual knowledge are ultimately only useful instruments in this process. The contemplative approach is not directed at gathering a great deal of information, for that can be as confusing as it is helpful. The ultimate aim is the elimination of the confusion and ignorance that comes with our solipsistic and egocentric experience of reality. The human being who has accomplished this is a wise person, a person who "knows life" in the contemplative sense.

Confusion and Ignorance

With what kind of blindness or confusion are the contemplative traditions concerned? What is the nature of our ignorance and confusion? How can we characterize this in the terms of contemplative psychology?

First of all, we can be confused because we use the concepts we possess in an illogical way. We make mistakes in our reasoning and thus arrive at wrong conclusions. This is a form of conceptual confusion with which we are all too familiar. We can also be confused, not because we draw the wrong conclusions, but because we lack the concepts or information required for having insight into something. For example, we may simply lack the conceptual framework for understanding how a DVD player works or how the human mind works. We simply do not know. I have called this *conceptual ignorance.*

Traditionally, science has had a keen eye for both conceptual confusion and ignorance. That is the reason for its interest in logic—the theory that teaches us how to reason properly—and for the gathering of reliable information by means of empirical research.

In addition, there are other forms of confusion and ignorance that lie not on the conceptual level but on the perceptual level—the level of how we perceive something. We have touched on them briefly. There are situations in which something escapes us; we do not pay attention. Someone leaves the room, and we do not notice. That is a moment of ignorance in our perception. We call it *perceptual ignorance.*

Yet another, very important phenomenon appears on the level of perception about which we have already spoken extensively—that we mistake our thoughts about a situation for the situation itself. We confuse the map with the landscape, or the content of our thought for the object of our thought. We mistake the mental representation for what it represents. We call this *perceptual confusion.*

Within the contemplative traditions, we find many examples that characterize perceptual confusion. The most well known in the Hindu and Buddhist traditions is perhaps that of the snake and the rope. In a dimly lit room in India, we step on something thin and round. We immediately think, "I have stepped on a snake," and recoil, shrieking. We *experience* a snake. Yet when we turn on the light, we see that it is only a rope on the floor, and our experience changes at once. When we stepped on it, we actually had the experience of stepping on a snake. Our experience of reality was thus confused. We have returned to the fundamental theme of contemplative psychology: the way in which we experience the world depends on how we dress it up mentally with our thoughts, concepts, memories, and expectations.

The metaphor of the map that is not the landscape has another point to teach us. Suppose you are sitting in a car next to the driver. The driver asks you where you are. You unfold the map and point to a red stripe: "Here, somewhere between Atlanta and New York." You could also have pointed outside and said, "Here. Just look out the window." That is a different type of answer, perhaps somewhat less informative, but certainly not incorrect. There is a world of difference between these two answers, and in some cases, one answer is more adequate than the other. Let us now apply this logic to answering the question "Who am I?" Would we be better off consulting our self-concept, the map we have developed about ourselves, than "looking out the window," that is, looking directly at ourselves and our minds? Looking out the window is a metaphor for the practice of the disciplines of insight (see chapter 8).

The problem highlighted by the contemplative traditions is that we are not aware of either when or where we use an internal map. We can no longer distinguish clearly whether we look at the map or out the window. The discernment of which we spoke earlier is often inactive, let alone developed. We live in our dressed-up experience without being able to recognize its magnitude or extent. The situation with the snake and the rope seems clear enough, but in everyday life, the magnitude of the problem is often much more obscure. Our enemies and friends, for example—do they exist outside us or only in our minds?

The fact that Jane is a friend to one person and an enemy to another should make us think. Where is the enemy—within or outside us? From the contemplative perspective, the answer is that both the friend and the enemy are within us; they are both the product and the object of our passion and aggression. The enemy seems to be outside only because we project the idea that Jane is an enemy onto Jane. We dress her up as the enemy and thus become aggressive because we see her.

Han Fortmann wrote an excellent work concerning the role projection plays in the religious context. He remarked, "If I experience myself as the persecuted, I must interpret the image of the other, who is so multifaceted in many respects, in such a way that he is my persecutor."[14] This does not mean that if someone follows us with a knife and eventually threatens us physically, we do not have to take action. More important, if we should at that moment become lost in the thought, "Here is an enemy," we might well be a fraction of a second too late in grabbing the knife and defending ourselves effectively. Such a thought can tear a hole in our attentiveness and readiness to fight. The basic discipline behind the Japanese martial arts is not to lose ourselves in such thoughts in dangerous situations. The consummate master in these arts "is not encumbered in any way, be it physical, emotional, or intellectual."[15] He sees the knife attack and reacts to it; he is not preoccupied with thoughts of enemies.

In a classical metaphor, the nature of our perceptual confusion is compared with the mixing of oil and water. Stated in more modern terms, our dressed-up experience is a sort of skin lotion. This lotion consists of two clear liquids: oil, representing our mental stream of experience, and water, representing our sensory stream of experience. If we mix them together, we get a somewhat more solid substance, one that is no longer clear but murky. It can consist of small droplets, all of which are clear, but because the liquids are mixed together, we can no longer distinguish which is oil and which is water, or which is our mental stream and which is our sensory stream. It is because we cannot make this distinction that we find ourselves in a self-created world, within which a number of illusory people and events, including ego, appear. Our experience is thereby dressed up by concepts and contains our self-concept, our concept of the world, our concept of God, and all the other concepts we have developed. As long as our discernment, or discriminating awareness, is not active, we cannot distinguish our self-concept from our true nature, our concept of God from God, or our concept of the world from reality. We then live in darkness. This is a central theme in almost all contemplative traditions.

Conceptual Knowledge and the Disciplines of Consciousness

We also find that the contemplative traditions emphasize that our knowledge about ourselves, reality, and God can stand in the way of our acquaintance with ourselves, reality, and God. Stated in terms of contemplative psychology, our conceptual knowledge can block our perceptual knowledge. If we think we know who we are, what is real and what not, who or what God is, why should we attempt to take a closer look? Why should we still want to cultivate our discernment? Especially in our culture, in which conceptual knowledge is considered to be almost the only valid knowledge, this danger of intellectual complacency is prevalent. We have come to accept that our ideas and presumptions are enough, that we no longer need to look closely at something, for we already know what we are supposed to see. When this idea dominates, then the intellectual understanding of the contemplative life can easily become confused with the experience of contemplative life. Again, this is a form of perceptual confusion. It actually withers the contemplative life. Instead of a willingness to tame the mind and develop wisdom, an intellectual arrogance arises—the arrogance that we know the contemplative path without ever having trodden it. We do indeed know it intellectually, but not with the heart. Nothing has happened to us yet. We might dabble in spiritual concepts, reflect on them, and believe that this occupation is the whole of the contemplative path. We may even derive a feeling of superiority from it. We then look down on those who actually practice a contemplative discipline or those without much knowledge who use a primitive prayer, like one popular in the Eastern Christian Orthodox Church: "O God, be merciful to me, a sinner" (Luke 18:13).

This is not to say that the contemplative traditions do not consider conceptual knowledge to be worthwhile. It does say that contemplative traditions hold conceptual knowledge to be a means rather than the end. It can point us in the direction of perceptual knowledge. If we understand conceptual knowledge as a pointer, it can help us on the contemplative path. It can be a clue. As it is said in the Hindu and Buddhist traditions, conceptual knowledge can be like a finger that points us to the moon. If a father wants to teach his toddler the word *moon*, he may say, "Moon" while pointing to it. If the child gazes with fascination at the pointing finger, then the pointing does not fulfill its function. The child may even believe that a finger pointing upward is called "moon." She thinks she knows what the moon is, even though she does not see the moon.

However, if we look at the pointing of the finger as a metaphor for conceptual knowledge, it can help to bring the head and heart, the intellect and intuition, together. This is why the mental disciplines in the contemplative traditions include disciplines of both the head and the heart. We will look more closely at these disciplines in the second part of this book.

PART TWO

Spiritual Practice
and Development

5

On the Way

In the first part of this volume, we explored the view and central concepts of contemplative psychology and how that psychology is different from our conventional understanding and academic psychology. Let us quickly summarize the main themes again. In the first chapter, we became acquainted with the first-person perspective of this psychology and briefly outlined in which the contemplative traditions work. In the second chapter, we discussed the metaphor of the Way and its sphere of influence: our experience of reality, including our self-experience. In the third chapter, we looked more closely at the concept of ego. We sharpened our psychological view of the origin of our dualistic, egocentric experience of reality and of the nature of a nondualistic experience that is free from ego. We also saw that such a transformation is not simply a fantasy or an unreachable goal but a real possibility anchored in being human. Finally, in the fourth chapter, we looked at a number of psychological core concepts used by all contemplative traditions yet referred to by various names, including mind, thought, consciousness, and forms of knowledge. We saw how our experience of reality, with all its emotional coloring, is formed by the interplay of experience, thought, and consciousness. We also saw that contemplative knowledge is directed at the elimination of confusion and ignorance. Thus, part 1 laid a foundation for a psychological understanding of what will be discussed in this second part: entering and proceeding on the Way.

In this part, we will focus on questions of a more practical nature. Across time and culture, people have engaged in practices such as prayer, offerings, ritual, meditation, and contemplation; studied obscure, inaccessible texts; practiced complicated liturgies; and chosen to live according to strict and supposedly edifying rules for behavior in almost all areas of life. How and why have such structures and practice forms evolved? What kind of concept of humanity do they support or rely on? Most important, how and why have people allowed themselves to be led or guided by others in all these things? If we think about it, this may seem strange from the perspective of ego and its belief in self-agency. Furthermore, doesn't life seem difficult enough without saddling ourselves with more peculiar and demanding practices? However, from the perspective of the contemplative way of life, all of these practices serve the flourishing within and are necessary both for that flourishing and as a source of ongoing inspiration to stay on the Path.

Since we have outlined a psychological framework in part 1, we have laid the ground to discuss the notion of "progress" along the Way. That is, the idea of contemplative disciplines, development, and guidance together suggest a progression the practitioner undergoes along the Path.

First Steps toward Transformation

Let us start at the beginning: Why is it that people, sometimes consciously and willingly, sometimes unconsciously and even unwillingly, set off along a spiritual path? In the contemplative traditions, this question is often answered in terms of conversion. That may be an old-fashioned word, but it is one with an important meaning that is not always easy to comprehend. We will examine it again here, not so much from the usual theological point of view, but from that of a contemplative psychological approach. Many readers may be more familiar with the term *conversion* as associated with the Christian monastic life, where it is traditionally referred to by the Latin word *conversio*, which connotes conversion to a religious tradition. However, from the perspective of contemplative psychology, the meaning of the term can be understood more broadly to refer to an internal and existential process that includes turning around a way of life that until this moment was assumed to be natural, as well as an accompanying and fundamental revision of one's own experience of reality.

From this perspective, we can discuss the idea of gradual conversion—what may be described as a not-so-spectacular transformation that entails a process of *metanoia*, "a change in attitude." For it is in the gradual transformation or conversion—such as those chronicled in the hagiographies of the Christian saints Anthony, Pachomius, and Benedict; of the Saiva saints of Hinduism; of the Immortals or the saints of Taoism; and of the Buddhist saints mentioned in the Theragatha and Therigatha—that the dynamic of contemplative psychology is clearly visible.

Although the idea of sudden transformation is also mentioned in many traditions and can be a powerful experience, we should not limit our view of spirituality to this idea. Nor are the experiences of a sudden conversion antithetical to a gradual conversion; we can have sudden moments of conversion along the Way that inspire us to maintain our practice. For our purposes here, it is the idea of progress along the Path and gradual transformation that are of interest, since they reveal the psychological nature of the contemplative life.

Open-Mindedness

Let us consider what seems to be the precursor and portal to gradual conversion. In our lives, moments of openness are always occurring, moments that clearly have their own character. Such moments can occur when we are waiting for the bus or when we are engaged in our spiritual practices. They seem to simply occur and cannot be forced; we cannot hold on to them, nor can we evoke or manipulate them. In a sense, these moments are not *ours*; they occur outside of the fortress of ego, which may in fact be threatened or confused by their presence. At the same time, they are very common moments that may contrast so strongly with ordinary experience that we do not know quite what to do with them. We experience clear moments of seeing things, but they are often too clear; there is a sense of peacefulness, but it is often too peaceful. There may be experiences of reconciliation and union, but the reconciliation or union is so complete that we cannot retreat from it, nor can we find ourselves again so easily. These are the moments when we are open-minded and not preoccupied with strengthening the fortifications of our "ego-city," moments that from ego's perspective are aimless and groundless, perhaps even frightening, but from their own perspective are peaceful, clear, warm, and joyful. That is what is both so unbearable and at times so frightening about them from ego's point of view. It is also possible, as we discussed in chapter 2, that these experiences may rarely be recognized; they are so fleeting that we miss them.

All contemplative traditions have their own names for these moments. In the Christian tradition, they are called "moments of grace." Hinduism and Buddhism use the term *adhisthana*, usually translated as "blessing." It is a movement of mind that disrupts ego—that which we think we are and to which we are attached. How can we understand these moments? Are they so unique? A very ordinary and therefore striking example that helps us figure out what happens in these moments is when we have to sneeze. Let us look at the movement of our mind at such a moment: First, we are occupied with something and then feel the prickling of a sneeze coming on. We try to concentrate on what we are doing for as long as possible but are then finally forced to succumb, to surrender to the sneeze. At that moment, the entire situation with which we were occupied is lost for an instant, and there is complete openness and union with the occurrence of the sneeze. Afterward, we get a hold of ourselves (mentally) as quickly as possible and check to see that nothing serious has happened, then we try to get back to what we were doing. This is a seemingly trivial but also classic example from the Buddhist contemplative tradition.

No less of a classic example is pointing out what happens to us mentally when we burst into laughter. At the moment we laugh, the worrying, deadly serious monitoring of ourselves briefly falls away. As Chögyam Trungpa describes it, in the moment of laughing, we often see "both poles of a situation as they are from an aerial point of view. Sense of humor seems to come from all-pervading joy, joy which has room to expand into a completely open situation because it is not involved with the battle between 'this' and 'that.' . . . This open situation has no hint of limitation, of imposed solemnity."[1] Indeed, it is precisely when we are seriously and solemnly occupied with something that we can suddenly surprise ourselves and burst into laughter. It is an absolute moment that, in a sense, stands on its own. Georges Bataille, the great unorthodox French philosopher, also used laughter as an example to indicate these absolute moments of total openness. He called such a moment an "*opération souveraine.*"[2]

We may also experience such open and spontaneous moments when suddenly confronted with a great loss, when our usual concerns and preoccupations seemingly fall away. We all know the particular atmosphere following a funeral. We have buried the one who has died and subsequently gathered together. These moments often have a special atmosphere—very subdued and open. We are briefly immersed in the situation in which one of our loved ones is gone and all other concerns have fled our mind. Equally, we can appreciate that moments of intense loss, as well as moments of great happiness, are what make all previous events and concerns fade for a brief while. Such moments lift us out of our daily routine; they often have a true sense of being carefree. We might even experience a little light-headedness—for example, after a long laugh shared with friends. However, the carefreeness that accompanies such moments is not a banal defensive measure but a response to the tenderness of the moment, of life, loss, and shared humanity. We are dazed in a positive sense. Fundamentally, such moments cut through our customary experience of reality. This is why it is said that even, or especially, our own final hour can be such a moment. The practice of the contemplative disciplines is concerned with the recognition of the sovereignty of these moments in our experience.

Cracks in the Walls of the Fortress of Ego

What is striking about such moments is that it is often difficult to recognize them for what they are. It is because these moments exist outside our egocentric experience of reality, that they cannot be interpreted or grasped from our usual perspective. While because they are "outside," they are also the basis for conversion. We are transformed at such moments. Viewed from the fortress of ego, they represent or threaten a crack in its structure. They are not part of the fortification but an opening in its walls. In the words of Leonard Cohen, "There is a crack in everything. / That's where the light comes in." Our fortress is lit up briefly from the outside and from within, allowing us to see its structure clearly for a moment. It bears repeating that the metaphor of a fortress does not refer to an object but a mental activity—the continual mental preoccupation with ourselves in relationship to the other; to our place, position, and self-importance; to our ups and downs.

In fact, we can see that these moments are the light of wisdom. In these moments, this light shines and allows us to see clearly how we are continually lost in that which is temporary and a world of our own making. We might even see that securing our relationship to this world is what keeps us involved in and preoccupied with it. It is in these moments when "the light comes in" that we can see, even momentarily, the triviality of such preoccupations. We could say that this whole process of ego's game becomes relativized by this light. When the light reveals how we are attached through our ego to a belief that either glory or downfall are determined by the world as we believe it to be, then it can be experienced as both a shock and (sometimes) a liberation.

The contemplative traditions maintain that these moments of open-mindedness occur at times in all people. They are in no way reserved only for the fortunate few. One way of understanding their occurrence is that it is simply impossible for the walls of the fortress of ego to be 100 percent watertight, or more rightly, lightproof. In the end, ego is actually a flimsy construction. The theistic traditions express this by saying that God's love and light is greater than our egotism and conceit, which leads us to blindness with respect to God. The nontheistic tradition of Mahayana Buddhism states that we can never completely repress the clarity and warmth of own heart, our own Buddha-nature.

Mental Responses to Open-Mindedness

We have two choices when these moments occur: We can either turn toward them or turn away from them toward ego. To turn toward them and learn to go along with them, we have to be aware they are there and that they are positive or trustworthy. Thus, the first phase of transformation begins not with the presence of these moments themselves but with the awareness that we can trust them and open ourselves to them. However, that awareness is not obvious, since these moments can easily be misunderstood and, in a sense, abused. That is, when we do not recognize them for what they are, we tend to make them into something special. We then want to pull this special moment in our experience toward ourselves and appropriate it: "What I have experienced is something very special, possibly even a spiritual experience!" However, because the mental action of holding on is diametrically opposed to the action of letting go, which is the essence of such moments, it actually chokes the experience. Rather than the experience actually impacting us in a positive way, we try to take possession of it and secure it to our identity in some way—"I am special because I had this special experience." This is one of the possible responses from the perspective of ego.

Another response, which we touched on briefly, is that such moments are seen as distinctly threatening when they are experienced as cracks in the walls of our familiar, egocentric experience of reality. In this response, too, the openness of such moments is not recognized for what it is. When we see these moments of openness as threatening, we experience them as *horror vacui*, the "fear of emptiness." This happens not because those moments are actually empty—far from it—but because, from the perspective of ego, they offer no support whatsoever in the ways we usually secure our sense of identity. In this sense, they are "empty," and we can fall into resisting or fighting against these empty moments when we are at a loss.

A third response that conceals the true nature of these moments from us is that of indifference, an attempt to dismiss or even ban these moments from our consciousness and memory so we can get on with business as usual. Maybe we had made a resolve not to fall apart, so we attempt to get beyond such moments. It is also true that usually we are not entirely at ease when we wave them aside as having no meaning for our lives or as irrelevant disturbances of our tranquility of mind.

Of course, as we saw in the earlier examples, we often are not able or do not allow ourselves the time or opportunity to fully appreciate the nature of these moments. We simply do not recognize these moments for what they are and therefore have no chance to learn to trust them. We may be in limbo of some kind; we may sense that our usual experience of reality is up in the air or that it has been exposed. We appreciate the beauty, tenderness, and groundlessness of those open moments. At the same time, we may also experience the agony of seeing our own ego fortifications exposed so clearly. The moment itself is open, and we may be what the famous Trappist hermit André Louf called "sinners-in-the-process-of-conversion."[3]

In these early stages of transformation, when awareness and response are so crucial to what happens next, guidance plays an important role. Having a person or teachings to help us understand that this open space, which appears so groundless, is actually inhabitable can make all the difference. A good guide will reassure us that if we allow ourselves to become more familiar with this openness, then our faith and trust in its being inhabitable will become stronger. We actually begin to develop genuine trust or faith through familiarity. We will return to this in chapter 10.

When we begin to recognize that these moments are not only happening in our lives but are essential for them, an inspiration can arise within us that is no longer constrained by fear and ego's games; it is a kind of egoless motivation. However, this does not mean it is a simple matter of replacing our ego-directed motivation with an egoless one. For most of us, both of these motivations play their roles for a long time: openness and non-ego-directed motivation and moments are present with the drive for self-improvement and self-elevation, prompting us to try to draw these moments toward us, to secure them as part of us in some way. At the same time, there are cases when we struggle with or ignore them. Within the contemplative life, the ego-directed motivation is also called spiritual materialism.[4] This motivation may lead us to practice the contemplative disciplines *outwardly*, but it is based on the desire to gain or possess something that can strengthen and protect us *inwardly*—our sense of identity and ego. If our approach to practice is dominated by this motivation, we may even ultimately turn away from these moments of openness.

How do we recognize spiritual materialism in ourselves? From a contemplative psychological point of view, it is said that we can recognize ego-directed motivation in relation to spiritual experience by the fact that it makes us unstable. We are unstable in relation to our practice in terms of consistency and discipline, and we are unstable in terms of the transformative effect of moments of openness—they come and go with little lasting impact. On one hand, we may be applying a vast effort to gain what we want, while on the other, there may be no or little actual spiritual growth occurring. Further, we may fall into the extreme attitudes of *nihilism* and *fundamentalism*, possibly going back and forth between the two. The basis of both of these attitudes is ambition in the sense of ego striving toward self-confirmation. The fundamentalist attitude is one of mentally holding on to that which is seen as unchanging, eternal, and absolute. This can include certain experiences, such as openness itself, but also fixed ideas or forms that one's religious tradition provides. When we are in the grip of a fundamentalist attitude, the value of our contemplative tradition is measured by the degree to which it offers an unshakable buttress that helps us in our struggle with a reality that seems to want to take that buttress away. History as well as our current world illustrate that such fundamentalism easily leads to damaging oneself mentally and physically and to killing people for the sake of saving one's "religion."[5] This approach may also cause us to identify frantically with the tangible, external forms of the tradition, possibly with the proud feeling that we are sitting on the right side of the line or being great practitioners. We have come to believe that we can elevate ourselves by associating with and possessing something that in our eyes has been elevated to incontestable heights—our own religious tradition, or rather, our religious tradition as we believe it to be.

If our egocentric spiritual ambition or spiritual materialism cannot be satisfied, or rather, when it is inevitably not satisfied, it is easy to veer in the opposite direction toward an attitude of nihilism. We may have started out thinking we had found gold that we could store and make ourselves feel rich and important, but that turned out not to be the case. Even though many traditions tell us explicitly that these spiritual material-ist games of ego are barriers to spiritual transformation, we may find this position an affront to our sense of who we are, an insult that leads us to discard the entirety of our "spiritual experiences" and our religious tradition (and often those of others). The materialistic attitude of valuing only what we can possess is challenged when, on closer examination within the spiritual domain, we discover there is not much there that can or should be collected the way we can collect material or intellectual property and hold on to it. Spiritual experiences and attainments—of openness, peace, or bliss—are simply not of that nature. At this point, we may be in danger of fall-ing into a nihilistic attitude; if we cannot possess something in some way, then we no longer find it valuable. Then disap-pointment and contempt are conjoined. We reject and even begin to despise that which disappoints us, thus avenging our disappointment until we once again find and chase after a new spiritual object that ambition can offer to ego as a buttress. Thus, we begin to swing back and forth between fundamen-talism and nihilism, between belief and unbelief in a spiritual buttress. In fact, belief and unbelief themselves come to serve as spiritual buttresses, often paralyzing our clarity of mind and our care for others.

However, if we persist in our practice, despite our tendencies to cling to the two extremes, the moments of openness have the power to disrupt both nihilism and fundamentalism— even simultaneously—so our clarity of mind can move freely. Naturally, at times we will feel threatened by these moments of openness and then may slip back into our fundamentalist or nihilistic attitudes. That is how it goes developmentally on the Path. At those times when fundamentalism and nihilism dominate, we may not actually encounter the tenderness, warmth, and freedom that are inherent in such experientially open moments but rather see them as a counterforce that seems to turn against us and threatens to crush us. The theistic religions call this experiencing the wrath of the gods or God. In Vajrayana Buddhism, it is the protective power of reality itself, called Mahakala, that shakes us up and out of our ego-centered approach. For ego, there is only a wrathful God or a hostile reality that threatens our possessions and buttresses and therefore *us*, that perhaps or at best can be manipulated or pacified. Conversely, when these moments of openness are recognized for what they are, they reveal their serene form and work as moments of transformation. When this occurs, then the (partial) collapse or evaporation of the fortification of ego calls us to surrender, also giving us the courage to expose ourselves and stand naked in the light of these moments. Then it is possible to become aware that we have always stood naked. Even when we believed we could hide ourselves, we were always seen by our own Buddha-nature, by the gods or God.

From Openness to Positive Doubt

Let us now take a more detailed look at what moments of openness initiate within us if we no longer pursue, repel, or ignore them and how they are the first steps to transformation. These moments have two sides: what we see clearly and the fact that we see clearly. What we see clearly is our ego-centered habits. The fact that we see clearly is characteristic of these moments themselves. In religious terms, this clarity belongs to the Holy Spirit (being moments of grace), to the *Shekinah* (Hebrew for the "presence of God"), and to our Buddha-nature when it is given the chance to work within us. We are often struck by what we see at first glance, and the gladdening fact that we can see so clearly may well escape us. As beginners, we do not yet fully recognize the nature of these moments; however, we are able to recognize them sufficiently to see the failure of ego by means of the light that these moments shed on ego-centered preoccupations and games. Most transformative in this moment is that when we see that failure, doubt can arise about the possibility of cultivating insight and joy in life within the walls of our egocentric experience of reality.

Initially, this doubt often manifests itself as a distrusting, critical attitude toward ourselves. We are no longer so sure of our motivations or intentions nor that we see things as clearly as we thought we did. In fact, this is a very positive development because this distrust is born out of the awareness and inkling of an insight that the self-serving attitude that has directed our lives up to this point may, in fact, bring only suffering and confusion. This insight comes with the moment of openness. When that moment has passed, it leaves distrust and doubt behind in the mind as wholesome fruit with the potential for further ripening. Thus, this distrust and doubt are tender and raw and usually uncomfortable. This discomfort and doubt are often at their strongest before we take the first step along the contemplative path, which is why it is important (for us and for those guiding us in this phase) not to gloss over them or reason them away but to make room for and respect them. It is precisely when we have arrived at this uncomfortable point that it is tempting to rid ourselves of this spiritual distrust by escaping into the materialist attitudes of nihilism and fundamentalism. Simply by allowing room for this distrust, a renewed search for yet another buttress can be prevented. After all, distrust is a first, albeit rather one-sided, manifestation of clarity of mind.

The distrust about which we are speaking is usually all-embracing: it is not only distrust with regard to ourselves and the way in which we have attempted to build our lives around ego but also with regard to our surroundings—the demands, expectations, and promises of the world. "If you do what is expected of you, if you have a good job, if you have a nice family, if you have nice friends, then you'll have made it. Just make sure you accomplish *that*, and you'll be happy." All these requirements and promises are usually presented in such a way as to suggest that they will lead to peace in life, if not inner peace. These promises are also disrupted by moments of openness. The resulting distrust not only affects our own attitude toward life, but it is also directed at the world around us and the attitudes to life that are held and lived there. The world around us also includes religions, which is why the distrust applies to the promises of the world as well as the promises of religions. There, too, the individual will look at them critically again or for the first time.

When the failure of our egocentric experience of reality in these moments of openness has become visible and a fundamental, penetrating doubt has been raised, several questions arise: "Yes, but what now? Are there other people who have experienced this as well and survived, or am I the only one? Is it just me? Should I just find (a) different job/friends/spouse? Is it a crisis that is caused by my puberty/adolescence/midlife/old age, or is it more fundamental than that? Are there people who talk about this, and if so, where can I find them?"

These questions make us look for possible contact with people who we think are engaged in "these kinds of things." However, we must be cautious in seeking out others so that in doing so we are not seeking out a buttress or a place to belong that makes us feel safe and secure again. A spiritual community, such as a Buddhist *sangha*, is recognized as important for spiritual development, but the journey is also characterized as a basically lonely exploration of our individual experience of reality. When looking for a spiritual community, it is important to maintain a critical attitude—for example, asking pragmatic questions of the spiritual tradition and those who express or embody its point of view is healthy. As we know, so many promises made in our lives, so much has been suggested in so many different ways from our childhood until now by those in our environment, by our culture, and by religions. It is precisely because of moments of openness that we can see clearly that many, if not most, were unrealistic. Promises or ideals may sound good, but they do not have the power to transform our experience of reality. This is why we develop a critical attitude that is nourished by what we could call an urgent sense of curiosity to assess what is real and authentic in everything, including those traditions that (appear to) discuss matters of reality and authenticity. Thus, as we venture onto the spiritual path and respond to the need that has arisen to become better acquainted with and explore a religious tradition, at the same time we need to cultivate a healthy sense of distrust or inquiry with regard to the promises a religion and its followers make.

The First Steps Along the Way

When contact is first made between an authentic contemplative tradition and a searching, critical individual, one of the tradition's first and most helpful pieces of advice is to encourage the person to relax and take the time to examine and get to know himself thoroughly. We must begin with ourselves, with our experience of reality, with our thoughts and feelings as they manifest themselves from moment to moment throughout the day.

For example, we may approach a contemplative community and be invited to taste its way of life: "Come in and join us for a day in the contemplative life that we lead in the community or congregation and just be yourself. Look at yourself as you encounter yourself while following the disciplines of work, study, and contemplation." Or we may approach a spiritual teacher who advises us, "Make room in your daily schedule to explore your mind. Here is a discipline of meditation that will enable you to do this. Practice it. Take a break from all those books about psychology and spirituality and from those deep discussions on the philosophy of life. Study the movement of your own mind."

In each of these examples, there is a genuine openness to the tradition that invites us into an open inquiry about ourselves. For if we want to investigate a tradition's authenticity, we must possess discriminating awareness. Such mental sharpening starts with coming to know our own minds and experience.

Self-Knowledge as Personal Reliability

By getting to know the movement of our own minds with the help of a contemplative method, we become acquainted not only with ourselves but also with the value of the method. At the same time, we sharpen our discriminating awareness, and this ability becomes more reliable. I have used the term *personal reliability* elsewhere to express this sense of discernment.[6] Discriminating awareness relates to the ability to distinguish habits of spiritual materialism or egocentric motivation from true inspiration on which we can rely and that will nourish us on the spiritual path. As we learn to know, trust, and discern our own mind, then our sense of personal reliability develops to the extent that we are able to recognize our tendency to flee from reality and preserve ourselves in some way. We then begin to discern that this tendency makes it impossible to look at ourselves and the tradition realistically. It may even become clear that this tendency for self-preservation comes from not wanting to recognize the truth about ourselves or our spiritual tradition even if we were staring right at it.

The development of this type of self-knowledge is very important and needs to be fostered and nourished. The more we learn to trust ourselves, that is, to trust our moments of openness, the better we can see when the mind makes that quick movement in the direction of ego habits. When we can see the route the habit wants to go down, we may be able to stop the movement of the mind in that direction simply by seeing the illusory and destructive potential of it. Thus, our inner discernment develops and, with it, the reliability of our judgment. In time, we become better at catching that ego-driven movement of mind and at returning the mind to the movement of openness. What we are discussing here was expressed by John Calvin (Jean Cauvin) in his *Institutes of the Christian Religion*: "Without knowledge of self, there is no knowledge of God. . . . But as these are connected by many ties, it is not easy to determine which of the two precedes and gives birth to the other."[7]

Openness as Surrender

The development of this form of self-knowledge is not only necessary for another step but it also makes that next step possible: we are now better able to listen and actually hear what the tradition has to offer. This is also the moment when more personal contact with the tradition becomes possible; for example, by developing a relationship with a spiritual guide and assuming the role of a student or the person being guided. During this contact, the guide is—and should be—tested in various ways, sometimes openly but often more subtly. In fact, trust in the guide (and thereby in the tradition) develops along with the growth of our trust in ourselves.

This development also contains the beginnings of a process of surrender—surrender *to* openness and *of* ego. We begin to suspect that the surrender of ego entails the open, naked acknowledgment of the mind's egocentric movement at every moment that this movement occurs, again and again, time after time. The moment we feel ourselves turning in the direction of ego's way of experiencing, we jerk ourselves back. That is not always easy, since we also know that ingrained mind movements take time to overcome. Thus, moving the mind away from its habitual routes requires a certain amount of consistent and kind self-discipline. It is also possible that our guide may function to bring us back, teaching us how and when we can do this for ourselves.

Naturally, the guide can accomplish this only if we are prepared to reveal ourselves as we are, to expose ourselves completely. In an absolute or fundamental sense, this is baring ourselves to ourselves or to God, if that is our tradition. However, in a relative or practical sense, it is baring ourselves completely to a fellow human being—our guide—and surrendering our ego in concrete, actual interaction with the other, which is not easy to do. There is also a surrender to the guide, and the trust that encourages us in that surrender is in turn based on our growth in self-knowledge.

However, because of the fact that self-knowledge is the basis of surrender in the spiritual path, the kind of surrender we are talking about is very different from the form of surrender based on the idea that "the tradition or the guide will surely know what is good, which is why I surrender myself, for I am not capable of that knowledge." This kind of surrender implies a regretful abandonment of the development of our discriminating awareness. This is why it is also called blind surrender (see also chapter 10). In fact, it shifts our responsibility for ourselves onto a higher authority that is viewed as more competent or knowing than we are; it can be regarded as a form of spiritual escapism. Blind surrender may be motivated by a fear or confusion that leads us to *not* want to face who or what we are, what our existence is about, and what can give it meaning. Blind surrender may be best described as self-protective because it is ego's attempt to imitate actual surrender: "I surrender. Do what you want to me. I trust you." Ultimately, however, such a form of surrender is not strong enough or good enough for something as fundamental as the total transformation of our attitude in life, because it does not arise out of and is therefore not supported by a bond tested by experience. As we have been learning in this chapter, the development of such a bond includes, in its initial phase, doubt and sounding out and testing our connection with the tradition and our guide. Genuine trust can develop out of this bond so that later, when we take steps that go deeper into uprooting the world of ego, there is someone who can stand by us at difficult moments—someone who encourages us to enter further into the moments of openness; someone who, through her own example, demonstrates that it is possible for people to live within those moments of openness, the no-man's-land that lies outside the territory of ego.

The saints and great contemplatives of the traditions who have preceded us speak from this no-man's-land with all the means available to them and have been calling to us all the time. Consider again the metaphor of the mind swimming in the ocean of experience while holding on to one of our limbs, thinking it to be driftwood offering support. We actually look up for a moment and see somebody waving at us: our spiritual guide. We hear him calling to us, "Look at me! Look how I swim! You can too. Let go of your driftwood. It's your own leg. That's why your life is so difficult. I will help you. Face the fear of letting go. Go through it and be free!" Little by little, we hesitatingly dare to do it, perhaps just for a moment, going back and forth. Thus, our process of transformation begins.

In the following chapters, we will examine the methods and skillful means the contemplative traditions offer us to go in this direction. In the last chapter, we will once again pick up the theme of contemplative development, the beginning of which we have discussed here.

6

The Disciplines of Thought

How do the contemplative traditions handle these first steps to transformation, the beginning of the flourishing within? We can assume they have something to offer that can support this process and take it further, but what is it?

The contemplative traditions have, in fact, quite a lot to offer in terms of an enormous wealth of contemplative disciplines and methods. Human inventiveness has been richly manifested in this area; in fact, more broadly, there is hardly any aspect of life that has not been addressed by one or more disciplines in the contemplative traditions. Naturally, these traditions differ in their emphasis on certain disciplines. The emphasis is sometimes unique to the tradition itself and sometimes has to do with the culture in which the tradition has taken root.

Before we go any further, let us look at the word *discipline*. For many people, it has a strict, almost military ring to it and seems to border on the notion of forcing ourselves and putting ourselves under pressure. In contrast to this interpretation, we can say that the contemplative understanding of discipline is much more neutral; it simply means "systematic and ongoing practice." In fact, the characteristic of these disciplines is precisely that they must be carried out with a certain gentleness and flexibility rather than in a heavy-handed way. The disciplines we are referring to are the spiritual skills of a tradition related to handling the mind, speech, and actions—as we shall call them, the three domains of spiritual practice. These skills reflect the practical insight of the tradition, circumscribed by what is possible. This does not detract from the fact that we occasionally find people in contemplative traditions who practice all kinds of seemingly outlandish exercises. However, when such exercises are prompted by self-aggression or spiritual ambition, they are certainly rejected by the traditions themselves. The Buddha, who experimented for years with extreme forms of asceticism, later warned his pupils of the two extremes of self-torture and indulgence. It is for this reason that Buddhism is known as the Middle Way. An often-recurring metaphor for the correct use of the disciplines is that of a gardener's method of working: a garden flourishes through both love and knowledge. Besides fertilizer, the gardener also sometimes uses pruning shears. The metaphor here is that the gardener's love prunes the excessive growth of self-torture, while her knowledge prunes indulgence and indolence.

As already suggested, we can speak of the disciplines in terms of a classic division into three domains: mind (mental domain), word (speech domain), and deed (action domain). There are specific contemplative disciplines or practices for each of them. We will refer to them as the *mental disciplines*, the *disciplines of speech*, and the *disciplines of action*, respectively.

The mental disciplines are naturally concerned with cultivating insight into the nature of the mind. They are the most important to the cultivation of the flourishing within—at our dealings with our thoughts and emotions, and our attitudes toward life. We can therefore practice them by ourselves in situations where we are alone with our own minds.

The disciplines of speech and action are directed at the cultivation of a gentle, caring way of communicating and relating to our fellow human beings and our environment. Their function is to help us transcend the habits of self-preservation and egocentric emotionality with which we normally respond to our environment. Therefore, we practice these disciplines toward and with one another. Of course, those who live in a contemplative communal life—the Christian tradition calls them "cenobites"—place a great deal of emphasis on these disciplines since they have an interactive and a communicative emphasis. These disciplines are obviously of fundamental importance for all of us who live in the so-called world. We could also call them "social disciplines," but this does not do justice to the importance of a compassionate treatment of nature and the material world. We can therefore more rightly speak of the disciplines of speech and action together—because of their practical orientation to everyday life—using the term *practical disciplines*.

On the spiritual path, the mental and practical disciplines are not practiced in isolation from each other. This gives the traditions their power and makes them a holistic approach since they cover all aspects of our lives. We will discuss the mental disciplines in this and the following two chapters. The disciplines of speech and action, which are concerned with the cultivation of the visible fruits of this flourishing, are discussed in chapter 9.

The Mental Disciplines

The explanation of what contemplative psychology means by the word *mind* has provided us with a certain background for understanding the how and why of the mental disciplines. All great religious traditions possess a whole range of such disciplines, which are directed at becoming familiar with and cultivating the mind in one way or another. If we look at the range of mental disciplines, we characterize them into two main groups, which we will call the "disciplines of consciousness" and the "disciplines of thought." These two kinds of disciplines are the contemplative forms of the two fundamental ways of acquiring knowledge that were discussed in chapter 4. Elsewhere, I have discussed their methodological background in terms of the so-called conceptual strategies and awareness strategies.[1] Let us consider each in turn.

The disciplines of consciousness are intended to provide and enhance our perceptual knowledge (also discussed in chapter 4). They do this on one hand by cultivating our mindfulness and on the other by sharpening our discriminating awareness. From the perspective of disciplines or methods, we can thus distinguish two kinds related to perceptual knowledge: the *disciplines of mindfulness* (or stability) and the *disciplines of insight* (or discriminating awareness). We will discuss these in chapters 7 and 8, respectively.

The disciplines of thought that we will discuss in detail here work with the creation and use of *mental content*, meaning concepts, ideas, theories, representations, images, and symbols. The term *thought* here has the broad meaning used in chapter 4. Some of these disciplines are directed at enlarging our conceptual knowledge of the contemplative life, that is, our intellectual understanding of it. Others make use of the power of imagination. They offer us mental representations and images that can help to turn our experience of reality in a direction that leads to clarity of mind and greatness of heart. We can distinguish two groups within the disciplines of thought as well: the *intellectual disciplines* and the *disciplines of the imagination*.

The Two Disciplines of Thought

These two areas of the disciplines of thought are both concerned with mental content. They could, of course, be investigated from a religious or theological perspective, which would lead us to ask, where does the mental content the disciplines use fit within the whole of the tradition's religious (and theological) content? We will not take up that investigation, however interesting it may be. Rather, we will primarily explore the disciplines of thought from the angle of contemplative psychology. That means our central question is, precisely what do these disciplines do *with* and *to* the mind and to the experience of reality of those who practice them, and how do they do it? This question involves three aspects.

The systematic use of our intellect and power of imagination are, psychologically speaking, entirely different disciplines. Of the two, the intellectual disciplines are the most well known because we live in a culture that is strongly oriented toward the intellect. In everyday life, we make great use of our intellect, albeit mainly for purposes other than the furthering of our spiritual development. The disciplines of the imagination may be less familiar to us. Although we make representations of anything and everything in everyday life, our culture—with the exception of a few modern cognitive psychotherapies—hardly recognizes or values the systematic use of the power of imagination as a means of transforming our experience of reality. Let us explore both disciplines more thoroughly.

The Intellectual Disciplines

It is part of human nature to construct theories; it occurs in all cultures and at all levels of society. We construct theories about all kinds of things—about the world of phenomena and how these phenomena cohere, about ourselves and others, about the visible and the invisible. We also attempt to test these theories against experience. We adjust them as necessary on the basis of new data or results of (our own) research and attempt to avoid intellectual errors by testing the consistency of our theories, that is, by making sure they do not contain any internal contradictions. If we do this systematically, we are practicing an intellectual discipline, one that has been primarily shaped and brought into widespread use by our Western academic tradition, in the forms of both empirical science and philosophy.

Theories consist of a set of concepts that are related to one another in certain ways. They contain knowledge about a certain area of reality, which helps us to sharpen our thinking about our experience.

Since ancient times, the contemplative traditions have also considered the intellectual disciplines to be very important and used them widely. These disciplines form the core of what we have called the conceptual strategy of the acquisition of knowledge. All religious traditions have a particular conceptual framework in the form of a more or less systematic doctrine or teaching, which is based on their holy writings: the Christian catechism goes back to the Bible; the *Tafsier* is based on the Koran; the Talmud goes back to the Torah of Judaism; the Abhidharma of Buddhism is based on the sutras and the Vedanta of Hinduism is based on the Vedas. The practice of the intellectual disciplines thus entails study as well as analyzing and reflecting on theories about the contemplative life, bringing the theories to life through experience.

In most traditions, this reflection continually gives rise to new and extensive commentaries in which the central concepts of a religion can be clarified intellectually in terms that address the contemporary reader. It is here that the importance of such literature lies: this exegesis is never completed in a living religion. Christianity has its theology; Buddhism, its *shastras* ("commentaries"); Judaism, its Talmud, which includes commentaries on commentaries; and Islam, its Tafsier. Hinduism possesses a great variety of religio-philosophical commentaries as well. In some traditions, the study of commentaries has been greatly emphasized because they are more contemporary and often contain an unfolding of insights that are present but possibly still hidden in the original texts. In some Jewish Orthodox circles, the Talmud is studied almost exclusively. Many Buddhists primarily study the shastras.

The value of continued intellectual study is well known to be emphasized in the Jewish tradition, but all traditions recognize its importance. The Buddhist traditions speak in this context of the necessity of practicing the disciplines of study (*sruta*, "hearing") as well as reflection (*chinta*) and meditation (*bhavana*), alongside the other contemplative disciplines. *Svadhyaya*—the study of the sacred books—is one of the five essential disciplines for Hindus.

That which is reflected on differs from tradition to tradition but not so much that there are no common themes. The traditions cannot, in any case, escape the existential themes of human existence: the finiteness of that existence; human responsibility and failing; the experience of good, happiness, peace, well-being, and meaning; the receipt of insight; and evil and suffering. All traditions have a conceptual framework for clarifying our thinking about these themes.

Thus, the practice of the intellectual disciplines includes intellectual training. If the training is successful, it clarifies both the conceptual framework and its application to actual concrete existence; it has a transformative effect on how we are in the world. It can inform us about how things are and consequently remove conceptual ignorance, and it also disciplines our thinking process and thus removes conceptual confusion (see chapter 4). The intellectual disciplines enable us to see the how and why of traveling the contemplative path; they can both instruct and motivate us.

The strength of these disciplines is that they are very communicable, for they work with language. If we work with concepts, we also work with language. Various ways of using language are applied, including descriptive, prescriptive, and evocative (performative) linguistic uses.[2] By appropriating the religious concepts through the discipline of study, the content of our stream of thoughts (mind) changes in a way that has the potential to help us be in a somewhat better position to clarify and intellectually investigate our own world of experience. That is the intention of using conceptual means of discipline.

The Disciplines of the Imagination

The other kind of discipline of thought also employs mental content but does not work with our intellectual and analytical abilities. Rather, it works with our power of imagination. This discipline does not involve concepts but mental representations or images: the discipline of the imagination.

The contemplative traditions use an enormous variety of mental images and representations—too many to mention them all here. The following is an arbitrary selection: images and representations of God; the image of one's own mentor, a guru or person who is an example to us; stories from the tradition and biographies of the prophets, Jesus, Buddha, Mohammed, Arjuna; images associated with various kinds of prayers such as prayers of aspiration, intercessory prayers, short prayers, prayers of thanksgiving, images in the form of sacred formulas, meaningful mantras, prayers of one word, and vows people repeat to themselves; religious representations and visualizations; koans on which people brood mentally; and reminders of mortality (*memento mori*).

Other images or representations may not have a formal place within a religious tradition but have spiritual value for us personally. These too serve to inspire us and lift us up: a precious memory or hopeful expectation, an image from a poem by Gerard Manley Hopkins or a piano concerto by Amadeus Mozart that we suddenly remember, a liberating thought that opens up new perspectives and that we keep with us. All these mental images have a place in the practice of the disciplines of the imagination.

To clarify the character of these disciplines, let us look at a few examples. In Christianity, for instance, we know the discipline of entering into the suffering of Jesus Christ by pausing at the fourteen Stations of the Cross and reflecting on the Lord's suffering. Another, more general, example from this tradition is the *lectio divina* ("spiritual or monastic reading"). The practice of this discipline is not concerned with acquiring information or gaining conceptual knowledge about a text. Rather, the emphasis is on becoming acquainted with, gaining perceptual knowledge of, or developing familiarity with the text. This way of reading (lectio) is very much like how we listen to unfamiliar music—by staying with it and listening to it again and again. Eventually, it begins to touch us and subtly transform us. It is in these ways that the experiential value of the text can reveal itself to us and, as a consequence, transform us. Of course, the lectio divina does not exclude acquiring information since that will be naturally present, but it gives primacy to the experiential effect of the text on its readers. It is by means of the word that we can come to a genuine internal intimacy with the meaning. This can be a "true encounter" when the experiential value of the text can reveal itself to us (and us to it); then transformation is possible.

Consider an example from Mahayana Buddhism, where we find the discipline of *tonglen* ("giving and taking") in which one imagines breathing in all the negativity of the world and breathing out all that is positive within oneself to the world.[3] This practice has potentially transformative effects on the practitioner, such as increasing tolerance for difficult situations and increasing compassion for the suffering of others. Vajrayana Buddhism is well known for the use of the disciplines of the imagination; for example, visualizing an anthropomorphic representation of enlightenment—the *yidam* ("deity"). Visualization and identifying (or imagining) oneself as the deity is how one binds the mind (*yid* means "mind" and *dam* means "bond") to the qualities of enlightenment and thus awaken those qualities within oneself. In Hinduism as well, we find mental exercises through which one identifies with a mental image—for example, the image of an *ishtadevata* ("divinity"). In all Buddhist schools, we encounter a mental discipline that consciously invokes images of people we know and don't know, so we can cultivate four specific mental attitudes toward all people. These attitudes are called *apramana* ("immeasurable" or "limitless") because they go beyond the limitations of ego and its ego-centered emotions. In that sense, we could also characterize this discipline as the cultivation of four egoless emotions or attitudes: *maitri* ("friendliness"), *karuna* ("compassion"), *mudita* ("joy at another's prosperity"), and *upeksha* ("impartiality"). We cultivate these four attitudes in relation to imagined recipients, imagining and rejoicing in their transformation, which results from our immeasurable friendliness, compassion, joy, and equanimity. Patanjali, the well-known Hindu master, also recommends this kind of exercise.

In the Buddhist and Hindu traditions, the disciplines of the imagination are often called "meditation with form." Here the term *form* refers to the mental content with which it works. In the Christian tradition, the spiritual disciplines that work with images are listed under *cataphatic spirituality*, which also work with the content of consciousness. This includes images, symbols, representations, and concepts, since as Willigis Jäger, the famous Christian mystic and Zen master said, "Human beings need images and concepts in order to come to God."[4]

The Purpose and Practice of the Disciplines of the Imagination

The disciplines of the imagination are directed at replacing the images and representations that prevent our fundamental humanity from manifesting itself with images that cause our humaneness to awaken and become visible. They thus act to transform—even if only briefly—our experience of reality. The efficacy of the method of using images rests on the fact that our usual experience of reality is also permeated by images. Alongside intellectual reasoning with all its concepts, images are always surfacing in our stream of thoughts in the form of memories, images of the future, metaphors, symbols, and so on. Together, the stream of conceptual thoughts and the stream of images color our experience of reality. The images that we have either consciously or unconsciously appropriated in the course of our lives—like our self-image, our image of human beings, and our image of the world—have become part of our stream of mental events. They can serve to either advance or prevent the development of our fundamental humanity. Thus, we can see why the contemplative traditions have also developed the disciplines of the imagination. These disciplines amount simply to the replacement of unwholesome images by mental representations that have a beneficial experiential value. Our experience of reality can be influenced in this way.

In general terms, the traditions offer us representations or images that, as far as their experiential value is concerned, are at odds with our usual egocentric experience of reality. When a dissonance or gap develops between our usual self-preoccupied tendencies and the open flourishing brought forth by the imaginative disciplines, then gradually ego begins to lose its grip. When this occurs, more room for openness actually becomes available in our mind stream. We could in fact characterize the disciplines of the imagination as a kind of surgery on our way of thinking: a mental transplant in which one set of images is removed and another more beneficial set of images is implanted. However, this is not an overnight process; initially our egocentric responses to these new images may be to experience them as less real or less true than the familiar images we are used to. Therefore, we may dismiss them or not trust their efficacy as a contemplative discipline. We might call such responses "symptoms of rejection," which are also recognized as a possibility by the contemplative traditions. In an attempt to overcome these kinds of responses, the beginning practitioner is introduced to images in such a way that the likelihood of believing in them is stronger; they seem truer or realer. However, this truth requires a radical shift in attitude—and here we can see how the conceptual and imaginative disciplines work together—toward the conviction that in some way the images are mental representations of our humaneness. This requires a twofold awakening of the open psychological space to which these images can appeal, since they will not appeal to ego and its self-important reality. They compete in a certain sense with our belief in the egocentric images of our own making and our experience of reality. If the "truth" of the former wins over the "truth" of our egocentric representations, then our way of thinking is transformed.

Even though these mental images are nothing more than self-created appearances in our stream of thoughts, they none-theless have experiential power since they open our eyes to the qualities of our own fundamental humanity, which lies *beyond* these images because it is not dependent on them. It is rather the reverse: all the images with which the disciplines of the imagination work sprout from and derive their effective-ness from our fundamental humanity. They are its expression, just as our profane, egocentric representations originate in the self-contained space of ego.

In every period, culture, and religion, we can see how this fundamental humanity looks for ways to make itself known and manifests in images. The disciplines of the imagination are a deliberate means for doing this in the most effective way: they are directed at the transformation of our egocentric images of ourselves, humanity, and the world—the sacred, so to speak—by substituting more contemplative images for them.

More specifically, over and against an ego-centered self-image that enslaves us into seeing ourselves—our needs and desires—as the center of the world, the theistic traditions, in contrast, provide us with images of ourselves as *subjects* of this humaneness, decentralizing the primacy of the individual self. For example, in the theistic traditions, this can be seen in such images as being the bride of Christ or the servant or even slave of God and God's will. In nontheistic traditions, such as

Mahayana Buddhism, an egoless self-image evokes the feeling that this humaneness is actually the basis of one's aspiration as a spiritual practitioner, as suggested in the following prayer:

> May I be a wishing jewel, the vase of plenty,
> A word of power and the supreme healing;
> May I be the tree of miracles,
> And for every being the abundant cow.
>
> Like the earth and the pervading elements,
> Enduring as the sky itself endures,
> For boundless multitudes of living beings,
> May I be their ground and sustenance.
>
> Thus for everything that lives,
> As far as the limits of the sky,
> May I provide their livelihood and nourishment
> Until they pass beyond the bonds of suffering.[5]

In Vajrayana Buddhism, the practitioner identifies with a yidam, an anthropomorphic visual representation of the awakened state. The yidam functions as a new or alternative self-image in which all the emotional and intellectual qualities of the egoless state of mind are symbolically represented.

The disciplines of the imagination offer us an important window into a contemplative tradition's image of humanity. For example, when an image of humanity pictures the human being to be fundamentally beastly, evil, and selfish, many theistic traditions provide counter images of human beings as created in God's image. Nontheistic traditions offer an image of humanity according to which all human beings, without exception, are in essence good, caring, and clear of mind. Nontheistic traditions like the Confucianism of Mencius asserts the innate goodness of the individual, believing that it is society's influence—or its lack of a positive cultivating influence—that causes bad moral character. In general, Buddhism would not blame society but assert that any form of misanthropy arises when we have lost contact with our fundamental humaneness and begin to build our self-image and image of humanity on distrust.[6]

Furthermore, the contemplative traditions offer an image of the world in which disappointments are challenges for the development of our humanity. Such a view is at odds with many common or taken-for-granted images of the world that, for example, portray it as a place to be rejected, one that should continually satisfy our needs but fails to, or one where the hard realities of our human existence are seen as the world's errors. Such images often function to justify habitual rancor and fear of life. Elsewhere, I have discussed these two images of the world and the mental attitude to which they give rise more extensively in terms of the sacred and profane experience of reality.[7]

This mental attitude or image of the world as sacred is expressed in the theistic traditions when they claim that human beings should be grateful to God for adversity. In the nontheistic tradition of Buddhism, one finds the proverb "Be grateful to everyone."[8] These are certainly bold statements, but we should understand that here *gratitude* does not mean that we have to resign ourselves to everything that happens. Rather, it refers to a state of mind in which we are able to approach moments of adversity—as much as moments of prosperity—in a way that makes us grow in wisdom and loving-kindness. This attitude is again dependent on our mental maturity, which grows rather than withers with every successful handling of adversity. In this way, we can see that adversity places us at a spiritual crossroads: either we can take the route of mentally succumbing to despair and fear in the face of difficulty, or we can choose the route of mentally growing by working with adversity on the Path. However, it is recommended, as in all education, to begin small. If we begin by working with smaller challenges—keeping in mind that "small" is different for everyone and depends on the situation—then more intense adversity can gradually become more manageable. It is in this sense that we can be grateful for adversity, since it can be the fertilizer for the flourishing within.

Finally, when it comes to considering the disciplines of the imagination, it is worth noting that in the theistic traditions, we find images of God that go against all kinds of egocentric representations that cut God down to human measurement in some way. The following are some of those images: God as Big Brother, an almighty ally on our side when we want to have things our way; a God who protects our egocentrism and justifies it or who watches us like a kind of superego; or a God who threatens us with reward or punishment and with whom we must remain on friendly terms. Contrary to these images, the theistic spiritual traditions offer an image of God that, with respect to its experiential value, does not fit into our egocentric experience of reality but makes us feel that we are "created in the image of God," as Christian spirituality emphasizes. Whenever we transplant that kind of image of God into our stream of thoughts, it changes our experience of reality as well.

In short, the disciplines of the imagination within the contemplative traditions are directed at transforming our egocentric experience of reality by changing our world of thought and feeling. By providing nonegocentric images, they help remove the obstacles to our inner flourishing that egocentric images produce.

The actual *practice* of the disciplines of the imagination consists in continually internalizing these images, keeping them in mind until their experiential qualities unfold. This presupposes that those images and representations have meaning and experiential value for us and that we, if we have not yet done so, could learn their significance. Once the more intellectual preliminary work has been completed in terms of bringing the image to mind, the experiential value can then begin to make itself felt. Sometimes it is a process that takes place in a flash as soon as the image is obtained, but this may be rare. Most often, it is necessary to keep the image in mind over a long period of time, to "taste" its qualities again and again, before its experiential value can be felt. This is characteristic of the practice of the disciplines of the imagination.

The Disciplines of the Imagination and the Devotional Path

Our power of imagination is strong because its products are not, on the whole, simply neutral mental pictures but emotionally charged images. They have "real" or experiential effect. As we have seen, this emotional charge can bind us in two ways—to a habitual egocentric perspective or to an egoless or fundamental flourishing perspective. The efficacy of these disciplines of the imagination rests on the fact that they work with images that both conceptually and emotionally fly in the face of the imagined reality of ego. Because of their potency, it could be said that their images offer an emotional antidote. On the basis of a burgeoning desire to liberate ourselves from the habitual preoccupation with our self-centered world, we use and finally come to master all kinds of images: some directly evoke an egoless experience of reality; others express the fundamental sacredness of reality, including our fellow human beings. In theistic traditions, images evoke the love and omnipresence of God. In short, images serve to move us to both surrender and devotion—the surrender of ego and its concerns, and devotion to reality or God.

What brings the potency to images so they can bring about such a transformative experience? It is essential that we experience these images to be, at last, as powerful as the egocentric image of reality. For this to occur, we need to focus on them with all the mental—and emotional—power at our disposal, to surrender ourselves to them. For this reason, the cultivation of devotion is seen in many traditions as a path in itself. We find this emphasized strongly within the Christian traditions by, for example, the Song of Songs, the spirituality of John of the Cross and Teresa of Avila, and Christian bridal mysticism. We also find it in the Bhakti yoga of Hinduism, which is directed at the realization of the divine through devotion and love for a God who is seen as a personal lover. In Mahayana and certainly Vajrayana Buddhism, we also see this emphasis on devotion, which mobilizes human emotionality and directs it at a certain mental representation, an object or person who stands for or embodies qualities of enlightenment.

Emotions have an object. They are always directed at something, and the heart of the devotional path is that they are no longer directed at aspects of our egocentric experience of reality but at those that are manifested in an egoless or theocentric experience of reality. Discussing the path of devotion, Akhilananda formulated it as follows in his *Hindu Psychology*:

> The vast majority of the people in the world are predominantly emotional, so it is both convenient and necessary for them to use their emotions for higher spiritual development. We can hardly find a man or woman who has not strong emotional urges, and it is considered wise to express them instead of starving or discarding them. Emotions are great powers; a seeker after truth is, therefore, asked to direct them to an aspect of God which is suitable to his own temperament.
>
> That is the very reason the devotional mystics vary in their methods of approach to God. Some few may like to think of Him as their child, while more prefer to look on Him as father or mother, and again others will love God as their friend or beloved because this attitude is best suited to their

individual temperaments and this relationship is natural and spontaneous to them.[9]

The devotional path thus uses the disciplines of the imagination intensively; choosing images that provide a good antidote for those practicing these disciplines is an individual matter in which supervision by a mentor is very important. Of course, we must not forget that the images used in any tradition also guide action and speech to cultivate them in the direction of compassion. By practicing devotion and surrender not only in the mind but also in and through actions and speech, we give up more and more of our preoccupation with our egocentric tendencies. As we have been saying, our familiarization with images that arouse an egoless experience of reality enables us to leave our preoccupation with ego behind. Thus, these images fulfill their evocative function and are no longer necessary, at which time they can be left behind.

The Limitations of the Disciplines of Thought

We find acknowledgment and awareness of the limitations of the disciplines of thought in both the contemplative traditions and Western philosophy—from Plato and the skeptics like Pyrrho of Elis to the modern philosophy of Immanuel Kant and the deconstructive philosophy of Jacques Derrida. Even though people within the theistic traditions have sought logical proofs of God's existence, the outcome has been the realization that such proof in terms of language and thought is impossible. In Western philosophy, Kant was important in exposing the limitations of reason. Interestingly, he did so to open a space for religion beyond the intellectual domain of thought. Nagarjuna, the great philosopher of Mahayana Buddhism, systematically showed the limitations of every conceptual framework, including that of Buddhism.[10] We have already learned that intellectual study and learning to understand a religious conceptual framework is not the same as following a contemplative path. It is certainly part of it, but if we think that our practice need only go as far as an intellectual discipline, it is as if we see the movement of our finger on a map as the journey itself.

The limitations of the disciplines of the imagination are perhaps somewhat less well known. In Judaism and Islam, we find an emphatic reservation with regard to making images of God. This reservation is present in other traditions as well, for it is generally recognized that the disciplines of the imagination have a number of limitations. Let us consider those now.

The first limitation is that contemplative images and representations are, in the end, no more than images. We may say that the images of the contemplative traditions are better representations of ultimate reality than our ego-centered images, but even the former are not the "original"—they are and remain representations at best. Their potency, if any, lies in their experiential value; when this has been deeply felt, we have to leave behind the image itself.

A second limitation is that these disciplines make use of our mental inclination to become captivated by images and representations and to view them as real. Because these practices make use of this existing inclination, they do not liberate us from it. They make a virtue of necessity by moving this inclination in a certain direction. However, as long as the tendency is there to be captivated by our own images and representations, it makes spiritual sense to replace our egocentric images for the time being with egoless or theocentric ones and thus change our experience of reality.

It is for this reason that, in some contemplative traditions, the disciplines of the imagination are compared to the administration of an antidote that has a neutralizing effect on the poison of habitual egocentric images. However, especially at the beginning of the Path, the antidote itself is at risk of being a poison too, since beginning practitioners are not yet immune to perceptual confusion. They may still be inclined to confuse representations with that which is represented, meaning they may mistakenly believe that the image they generate in the practice (representation) is actually the thing itself. Of course, we can say that the disciplines of the imagination actually derive their efficacy from precisely that—as long as we live in reality as we *think* it to be, the disciplines of the imagination are effective. We will see in the following chapters that the disciplines of consciousness are specifically directed at liberating us from being dominated and seized by all the products of our mind, the helpful as well as the harmful. That is why we need to supplement the practice of the disciplines of the imagination with the disciplines of consciousness.

Since the disciplines of the imagination have their limitations, it is dangerous if a tradition uses *only* these disciplines. For although they lead us in a certain direction—toward our fundamental humanity—we have not as yet uncovered or recognized its true nature. Simply holding a vivid and moving representation of Christ or the Buddha is not the same as discovering the qualities of Christ or the Buddha within us. In fact, when that discovery occurs, then the images are no longer necessary. Discovery of our true nature goes beyond every representation and is the fruit of a direct vision. To illustrate, we do not need any images of our hands because we can see our hands. Discovery occurs through the disciplines of insight and will be discussed in chapter 8.

The disciplines of the imagination lie, as stated above, within cataphatic spirituality. It is worth taking some time to consider this perspective in Christianity, since many of us may have grown up with this tradition or at least been exposed to it as the dominant religious social context. For many contemporary Christians, prayer has become identified solely with the mental disciplines that work with the content of thought, not with imagination. However, historically in the Christian contemplative tradition, the disciplines of the imagination were very much in the foreground. It is central, for example, in the tradition of Ignatius of Loyola's *Spiritual Exercises*: "Christianity has become trapped at some point by thinking that prayer is verbalization and asking. That's a wrong understanding of prayer. The Greek word for prayer, *proseukomai*, means to move in a condition or state of being in which there is no thought, no imaging, no desiring."[11]

In the traditional Christian terminology of a few centuries ago, the term *meditation* was used to refer to the mental disciplines of thought, which are central to cataphatic spirituality. The term *contemplation* was originally used for the disciplines of consciousness, which are emphasized in *apophatic spirituality*, a spirituality that is beyond or separate from (*apo*) speaking (*phanai*), as we will explore in chapter 8. Because apophatic spirituality, which held contemplation to be a central discipline, has been almost forgotten, the original meaning of the term has shifted to "thinking about something." The disciplines of consciousness have also disappeared from much of Christianity. In its original meaning, however, meditation was seen as the preparatory phase for contemplation. In this, Christianity followed the same line as the Buddhist and Hindu traditions. In Vajrayana Buddhism meditation, the use of mental representations (visualizations) is a preparatory developmental phase (*utpattikrama*) for the resultant phase (*sampannakrama*) in which representations are no longer used. In this tradition, they are described as "meditation with form" and "formless meditation," respectively. The first is a discipline of the imagination; the second, a discipline of consciousness. In Hinduism as well, the mental practices by which one identifies with mental content constitute a step toward the imageless experience of the transcendent reality itself (*para vasudeva*). In this tradition, the mind is cultivated first by means of the mental disciplines that lead to a meditative state (*savitarka samadhi*) in which we gain conceptual knowledge. But the intention of such knowledge is that it points us in a direction that transcends all conceptual and articulable knowledge. It leads to a meditative state (*nirvicara samadhi*) in which a nonconceptual knowledge breaks through.

The Carmelite Tessa Bielecki, using the terms of *contemplation* and *meditation* in their original meaning, outlined this development as follows:

> In fact, as we advance and grow more intimately into union with Christ, we may not need the preliminary step of meditation at all. John of the Cross teaches us in the *Ascent of Mount Carmel* how to discern whether it really is time to stop meditating and to move into contemplation, or whether we are simply lazy and don't want to bother meditating anymore. He also describes the necessity of letting go of meditation when it is time to do so. His instruction is, "If you find the orange peeled, eat it." You don't have to peel it again. It is unfortunate that Christianity has a reputation for being word- and activity-oriented, because contemplation is actually at the center of the tradition. [12]

For the most part, we no longer use the terms *contemplation* and *meditation* as Bielecki did here. Today, for most people the meaning of meditation has shifted to what the Christian tradition used to call contemplation, which historically referred to a discipline of consciousness.

Imagination and Intellect in Psychotherapy

Finally, let us look briefly at the relationship between the disciplines of thought and a discipline that has become very important in our Western culture and time: psychotherapy.

In everyday life, we are sometimes inclined to denigrate the human power of imagination. What we imagine does not have to be taken seriously: "Oh, you're only imagining that—it's not really true." Because of this, we may also be inclined to think that working with a mental representation is a relatively innocent, if not superficial, activity. Imagination is viewed as something outside the reality of everyday life and perhaps even a form of self-hypnosis.

The contemplative traditions certainly do not share this dismissive or suspicious view of imagination. In chapter 2, we saw why this is the case: our entire experience of everyday reality is permeated and thereby shaped by our power of imagination. We live—to an extent unknown to us—in an imagined reality. Intervening in the formation of mental images with the help of the contemplative disciplines is actually a direct intervention in our experience of reality; as a result, it is not regarded as a minor affair. These disciplines do something with our minds in a systematic, conscious, and beneficial way by using imaginative processes that we already follow in a habitual, nonsystematic, and unconscious way that is often harmful to our own well-being.

It is interesting to note that the insights on which the efficacy of the disciplines of the imagination are based are not only commonly held by many contemplative traditions but are recognized within psychotherapy. The latter also acknowledges that the images people form determine their experience of reality; they can lead to psychological problems and even psychosis as well as away from them.

Let us take a brief look at psychosis so as to clarify the enormous power of the imagination. A psychotic condition, particularly one in which hallucinations are prominent, can be seen as one of extreme perceptual ignorance (see chapter 4) with respect to our surroundings; our capacity for mindfulness and awareness are no longer functioning properly. When, as a result, our surroundings no longer adequately register with us, they no longer serve as an anchor, and we give ourselves over to the dynamic of our imagination, which has free rein. As a consequence, whatever penetrates us from our surroundings is adapted to fit into our imaginary world in the same way that an external sound merges into our dreams while we sleep. At these times, the unbridled and unrecognized power of imagination leads us further to extreme forms of perceptual confusion, and our discernment is also paralyzed.

Fundamentally, whether we are speaking in terms of disturbed mental health experiences, "normal" experiences, or spiritual experiences, in all cases our experience of reality is a tapestry that has been woven by the mind. The contemplative disciplines are directed at making that tapestry transparent to the extent that the threads and the spaces between are visible. As a result, we no longer "see" the tapestry as a solid, finished product. To use this analogy, in psychosis, this tapestry may disappear completely, namely from being torn. When this happens, we can lose our familiar egocentric experience of reality, and our power of imagination may, if it can no longer find any point of orientation, attempt to mend the tear in any way it can. For example, it may produce delusions and hallucinations that serve to create a hold or an anchor in some way. We are then psychotic. Since in the initial phase of psychosis we may experience a sense of being liberated from our conventional, egocentric, everyday reality, we may well experience it as a liberation from ego. On this basis, "the seduction of madness," as Edward Podvoll entitled his book, can occur.[13] It is often the case, as Podvoll suggested, that spiritual and religious themes and imagery often come to the fore in psychotic episodes.

If we look at the way in which psychotherapy deals with psychological problems and mental disorders, we can see that the approach is based partly on the same principles as those of the mental disciplines of the contemplative traditions. The power of the imagination, for example, is deliberately used to a great extent in the first phase of the treatment of phobias in *behavioral therapy,* where the client is instructed to form an image that has a calming effect. When that image has been established, the client is asked to gradually bring to mind an image of the situation that tends to trigger the phobia. If the client becomes too frightened, he is instructed to let go of the frightening representation and return to the calming image. The frightening representation is subsequently invoked again (and again, over time) until the experiential value of the calming representation more or less remains intact during the representation previously experienced as frightening. After this has been established, the client can then begin to work with exercises in practical situations.

Modern *cognitive psychotherapy* makes much use of what we have called the intellectual disciplines. The therapy here consists of acquiring other, healthier ways of thinking and interpretations by showing the inconsistency of the problematic ones. Cognitive and behavioral psychotherapies are thus the therapeutic counterparts of the contemplative disciplines of thought. In chapter 8, we will also look at psychoanalysis and related forms of psychotherapy and see how they work with methods that are based partly on the same premises as those of the disciplines of consciousness.

In spite of this similarity in underlying premises, however, there is a great difference between psychotherapy and contemplative traditions, and we must not lose sight of this. The difference lies in both their purpose and methods, which are in some sense almost the reverse of each other. Within the psychotherapeutic tradition, insight and loving-kindness are the means for solving problems, whereas in the contemplative traditions, problems are the means for cultivating insight and loving-kindness. Here is a well-known anecdote that illustrates this reversed approach. When Buddhism was spreading to Tibet, many Indian gurus were invited to teach the dharma. Not much was known about the Tibetans. One guru who had received an invitation heard that they were extraordinarily kind, helpful, and always friendly people. This presented him with a problem: How could he practice the great contemplative discipline of patience if there was no one around to irritate him and challenge his patience? He therefore decided to take an assistant, a Bengalese, with him to Tibet. This man was known to be extremely irritating because of his rudeness, obstinacy, and temper. Grateful that the man wanted to be his assistant, he went to Tibet. Of course, once they arrived, it became obvious that this measure was superfluous; the Tibetans proved to be no different from other people.

The Necessity of Guidance

Precisely because our imagination has such great power, the practice of the disciplines of the imagination is not without risk. Therefore, authentic spiritual guidance is a necessity in working with them. The guide must not only know the intended experiential value of the contemplative images that the traditions contain but also must sufficiently know the pupil in order to decide which images are suitable at a specific moment and which are not. Without guidance, there is a chance that we will wander around in spiritual fantasy worlds, where we may mistake the experience of our fantasies and imaginings for spiritual realization.

The consequence of this is manifold. It may perpetuate a certain measure of alienation from the world, and in extreme cases, religious delusions may occur; finally, our practice may become an endless moving from image to image. In this case, we try one image and then another; new religious images and spiritual maps that can enthrall the mind are always available. However, even after years of great effort, we may be forced to admit that we have not grown in clarity of mind, wisdom, and loving-kindness. We have devoted our time to the study of the map and have mistaken that for the exploration of the landscape.

Another reason we need personal guidance is that the images and representations of the tradition itself are not immune to the march of time. They can lose their experiential value and thus their transformative effectiveness. After all, contemplative traditions are practiced and passed on by people, and experiential value is not inextricably bound to the images themselves but lie within people's minds. If the people, their culture, and their mentality change, the intended experiential value of the images may no longer be evoked. It is even possible that their experiential value shifts in such a way that the images become obstacles, and their use may even be destructive.

However, this can happen not only because people change but also because the tradition itself changes. For example, if a tradition loses its view of the Way as a path of development, it may no longer be clear which image is helpful in which developmental phase. Images that are effective in different phases of development can potentially become incorrectly connected, as if they all pertain to the same phase. The images may even come into conflict with one another and choke the seed of spiritual growth. This phenomenon is universal; we can find it at times in all world religions. Of course, because the effectiveness of the images is also dependent on the local culture and mentality, a continual cultural and psychological regauging of the disciplines of the imagination in particular is unavoidable and necessary. Only then can the tradition survive. A process of regauging occurs within the concrete situation of personal guidance between teacher and student. It takes two living beings—a textbook cannot replace the teacher. When a text is nevertheless presented or understood as an alternative for the teacher, it easily becomes a conservative power or something the student can mold according to her own preconceptions. This is why personal guidance is also necessary for the transmission of a living spiritual lineage from one generation to the next.

At the same time, spiritual mentors need to be well-trained holders of their own lineage to be able to sense what kind of imagery and language is trenchant and helpful for the student right now. In this case, we could understand the concept of tradition or lineage as a living organism that should be cared for by teacher and student alike, as opposed to a lifeless object that should be preserved unscathed through time.

This is especially relevant to the use of the two disciplines of thought we explored in this chapter—the disciplines of intellect and the imagination. Both are very delicate disciplines because they work with cultural forms like images and concepts from within the spiritual tradition itself and the culture in which the spiritual tradition finds itself. This cultural dependency is somewhat less important with the other two mental disciplines that do not work with form—the disciplines of mindfulness and insight. We will explore them in the next two chapters.

7

The Disciplines of Mindfulness

It is a striking psychological fact that the disciplines of consciousness are found in almost all contemplative traditions. These disciplines are intended to cultivate two aspects of consciousness—stability and discernment—although these terms are not necessarily used uniformly across the traditions. Whether or not we consider ourselves to be religious, this fact tells us something about the human mind: People in all cultures have discovered that they can cultivate their consciousness by means of certain practices or disciplines. Even more noteworthy is that the reasons given for practicing such disciplines are also almost identical across the board. What are those reasons?

First of all, all the traditions recognize that the mind is predominantly scattered or fragmented. Continually carried along by the stream of our thoughts—thoughts about ourselves and our world—the mind has no rest and no stability. This becomes manifest in a continual mental agitation and lack of steadiness, which denies us the opportunity to pause and look at the mind's movement to realize where, who, and what we really are.

A second important reason for practicing the disciplines of consciousness is the phenomenon that we already touched on briefly in connection with the limitations of the disciplines of thought and imagination: the mind tends to lose itself in a self-created and egocentric mental world that obscures our vision and hangs in front of the world of phenomena like a veil (of projections). This world of our own making prevents us from seeing phenomena, including those that appear in our stream of thoughts, as they actually are. The result is that we become caught up in a consciousness that can no longer distinguish clearly between imagination and illusion on one hand and reality on the other. When this form of consciousness prevails, we lack the mental discernment that enables us to recognize the range and depth of this captivity. Thus, we do not know ourselves or our minds, and we live in an imaginary reality.

It is for these reasons that the disciplines of consciousness are directed first at overcoming the mind's agitation and captivity, and second, at making direct perceptual knowledge possible (see chapter 4). This double purpose allows us to divide these disciplines into two categories: the disciplines of mindfulness or attention on one hand and the disciplines of insight or discernment on the other. We will see how the disciplines of mindfulness or attention function mainly as preparatory exercises for practicing the disciplines of insight. In terms of perception, which we discussed in chapter 4, we can say that the disciplines of mindfulness are helpful in removing perceptual ignorance since they enhance and stabilize our capacity to be more attentive to our experience. Subsequently, the disciplines of mental discernment or insight help us to clarify perceptual confusion by seeing through our erroneous ways of experiencing.

That the contemplative traditions teach these disciplines is not important only for religious people. The disciplines are of general psychological importance because they supply us with the means for developing insight in the mind and causing our humaneness to flourish. They offer us a practical way of handling and rising above our habitual agitation and psychological blindness. Also, because they do not work with mental images and concepts (religious or otherwise), they are less bound to a particular culture or religion than the disciplines of thought discussed in the previous chapter. The disciplines of consciousness, which include the disciplines of both mindfulness and insight, cultivate the human mind in a very direct way, which is why they are so universal. We will explore the disciplines of mindfulness in this chapter and the disciplines of insight in the next.

The Disciplines of Mindfulness

A familiar metaphor for the mind's agitation is that of a wild horse—a horse that seems free to come and go as it pleases. However, because it is wild, it is extraordinarily skittish: It takes only the flutter of one leaf on a tree to send it rushing off. It is too high-strung, too vulnerable to distress, to give itself the time to take a good look around before impulsively react-ing. This is also the way of the mind when it is captured by the egocentric experience of reality: only one threatening thought needs to arise to make it (us) skittish and ready to bolt. We only have to think of one idea, and the mind rushes off with it. Zen Buddhism has a story of a man on a horse flying by at a wild gallop. A man on foot sees him go rushing past and calls out, "Where are you going?" The man shouts back over his shoulder, "I don't know! Ask the horse!" Carried along by our passions, hopes and fears, desires and aversions, honor and blame, profit and loss, we lack a kind of steadfastness and overview of our (mental) situation.

Another way to characterize this absentmindedness is to point to the lack of synchronization between the body and the mind: When we are lost in our thoughts, the mind can seem-ingly be in a very different place from the body. Moreover, if we then experience our world of thoughts as reality, the body and the situation in which it finds itself count for little. So, where the mind is and the actual place where we are physically are not one and the same. We could say that *apparently* we live in two realities, which is also like a form of break or rupture. It is on this basis that we likely will not be mindful and aware of our concrete situation, that various matters may escape us, and that we will possibly make a mess of things. When we live mentally in the situation that we either expect or remember—in what we tend to call the future and the past—we are not as conscious of our actual situation. Being led by the mind and living in two apparently different realities both mean we are not synchronized with the body and what is around the body. As a result, we can be described as absent, not completely there, or as many traditions put it, we are "asleep," not awake, not alert; we are absentminded.

The Practice of the Disciplines of Mindfulness

The purpose of the disciplines of mindfulness is to do something about this absentmindedness. Although these disciplines have received somewhat different forms in the various traditions because their religious foundations differ, all are concerned with cultivating mindfulness or attention. Here, mindfulness is related to a capacity of concentration to help us rise above, or provide a counterpoint to, the captivity that manifests as disunity or absentmindedness. To this end, we practice focusing our attention, alertness, concentration, or whatever we wish to call it on one point. This focal point can be a certain object or representation, but it can also be a process such as breathing or a certain action. All disciplines of training in mindfulness rest on the same basic instruction: as soon as you notice that you are caught up in thoughts, you redirect your attention back to the focal point prescribed by the discipline.

The disciplines of mindfulness offer us a technique for doing this systematically. In many traditions, the technique takes the form of sitting meditation—we sit erect in quiet surroundings on a chair or meditation cushion and focus our attention on, for example, our breathing. While sitting in this position, we notice that our attention again and again becomes caught up in the content of our stream of thoughts. When we notice this, we turn our attention again to our breathing, which in this technique is the focal point for our mindfulness. This is a simple yet effective instruction for training our attention. Initially, it takes a certain amount of effort and discipline to do this; after all, we are used to allowing ourselves to drift along with the stream of our thoughts. It is against this habit that the practice of these disciplines is directed.

We could compare this practice to continually grabbing a stick drifting along in a river and planting it in the river bottom. The stick represents our attention. Stabilizing the attention is like planting the stick in the stream of our thoughts. When we practice this discipline, the stick continually comes loose and once again drifts along for a short distance since our attention keeps getting caught up in the stream of thoughts. The discipline consists in grabbing the stick over and over and once again planting it in the river bottom to create a fixed point or a fixed point of view. This process actually comes down to letting go of being caught by our stream of thoughts time and again. We practice waking up from being submerged in our stream of thoughts and captive to our own experience of reality, which is also permeated by this stream of thoughts. Our mindfulness becomes like a rock in the surf and breakers of the mind.

How is it that we are able to bring our mindfulness back to its focal point at all? The human mind is apparently shaped in such a way that moments naturally occur when we notice that we have again been caught. These are crucial moments in the practice of the disciplines of mindfulness, for it is then that we can choose either to return to our stream of thoughts and lose ourselves in it, or to direct our mindfulness once more to the focal point. Each discipline of mindfulness makes use of this natural ability. When practicing this discipline, we choose to return to the focal point again and again. It is through the discipline of making this choice repeatedly that we cultivate mindfulness, which leads to a freedom that is the fruit of this discipline.

The Focal Point of Meditation: An Anchor for Mindfulness

As indicated above, the focal point of mindfulness during the practice of meditation can be anything, which is why the disciplines of mindfulness have taken so many different forms. The focal point of meditation need not be an object like a candle, a religious icon, or a stick of incense. It need not even be a thing; it can be a more or less continual process of movement like our breathing. Even a mental object, such as a representation or an image, can be used as an anchor for mindfulness. However, within the disciplines of mindfulness, a mental object like an image has a very different function than in the disciplines of the imagination discussed earlier. The disciplines of mindfulness do not try to evoke the experiential value of the mental object but only use the object as an anchor for mindfulness. Even if we use an action as an anchor for mindfulness, that does not make this a discipline of action (see chapter 9). Even so, it is striking that the natural movement of breathing is so popular as an anchor in many traditions where the discipline of mindfulness is practiced while sitting still. There may be a number of practical and psychological reasons for this. A practical reason is that we are always breathing, so our breath is always available as an anchor for mindfulness. Psychological reasons include the fact that breathing is a simple and monotonous process but nevertheless involves movement. It is a well-known psychological fact that it is easier to keep our attention focused on something that moves than on something that does not. Moreover, contemporary research suggests that there is a close psychological relationship between breathing and our consciousness.[1]

Most traditions also have forms of the disciplines of mindfulness in which an elementary, manual task serves as an anchor. This may be a chore that one performs within the contemplative community, such as gardening, sweeping floors, or washing up. The Buddhist tradition has a well-known story about a woman with twelve children who had to walk a couple of miles every day to get water from the nearest well. She longed to practice meditation, so one day she approached the Buddha to request that he instruct her in this. She added that she had no time to sit for a little while—let alone to do so undisturbed—each day and train her attention by observing her breathing. When the Buddha heard that she had to walk to a well every day, he told her to use that activity as an anchor. During her walk, whenever she noticed that she had become caught up in her (undoubtedly worrisome) thoughts, she was to focus her attention again on the movement of her body, the act of walking itself. According to the story, this is how she disciplined her mind and achieved the awakened state.

In these practices, whether one's mindfulness is focused on breathing or another fixed point such as an image, the repetition of a word, or a single action, all such focal points serve as a kind of anchor for mindfulness, a resting place for the mind. The presence of such an anchor is characteristic for the disciplines of mindfulness. In this context, the Buddhist traditions speak of meditation with an object (the object of meditation) on which we focus our attention during the practice of the disciplines. Thus, the object is not something about which we think but one on which we focus our mindfulness during the practice and to which we continually return.

Finally, the object of meditation need not be something small, but it must be something that is constantly present and that we can handle, psychologically speaking. In principle, it can therefore be the entire situation of this moment—the here and now itself—if we can handle it, since it is not the easiest choice for an object of meditation. It is certainly not recommended for a beginner in the disciplines of mindfulness—it is too easy to become trapped and confuse absentmindedness with alertness. A relevant, well-known story can be found in the Zen tradition. A *roshi* (Zen master) instructed his students in the disciplines of mindfulness as follows: "When you eat, eat. When you read, only read." In this way, he indicated that our attention must be directed exclusively or "one-pointedly" at what we are doing rather than wandering off on other matters. One day, one of his students came into his office and found the roshi reading a newspaper while eating a sandwich. Surprised, the student exclaimed, "But, Master, you taught us: 'When you eat, eat. When you read, only read.'" To which the roshi replied, "When I eat and read, then all I do is eat and read."

The Disciplines of Mindfulness in the Various Traditions

In the Buddhist tradition, the discipline of mindfulness is called *shamatha*, which is usually translated as "peaceful-abiding" or "stability." Shamatha is directed at disciplining mindfulness in the sense of stabilizing it. In this discipline, the attention is repeatedly directed at the movement of one's breathing, for example. In the Pali *suttas*—the words of the Buddha written down by his students—this practice is called *anapanasati* (*anapana*, or "breathing in and breathing out" and *sati*, or "attention," literally "remembering"). In this context, the term refers to remembering to keep our attention where we want it to be. Another common Buddhist term for the discipline of mindfulness is *satipatthana*. This is an interesting term, for it contains two notions: *sati* (or *smrti* in Sanskrit) again refers to attention, but the second part refers to a supporting power—*upasthana* in Sanskrit—that is a form of knowing or awareness that keeps track of where our attention is. The technical term for this supporting power in Sanskrit is *samprajanya* (Pali: *sampajanna*). The term *awareness* therefore has a specific meaning here: it refers to a particular type of awareness or vigilance, which is keeping check of whether your attention is still on the breath or not.

Taken from the Buddhist tradition, the term *mindfulness* has also become well known outside of its spiritual context; the practice of it is a way to alleviate stress and cope with illness, pain, and anxiety. Mainly through the work of Jon Kabat-Zinn, its application has spread from alleviating the pain and fear of cancer patients to psychotherapy and the treatment of life problems. In his classic *Full Catastrophe Living: Using the Wisdom of Your Body and Mind to Face Stress, Pain, and Illness*, he gave detailed instructions for the practice.[2] Adapting the Buddhist teachings on mindfulness, he developed an eight-week course called Mindfulness-Based Stress Reduction (MBSR), which put the practice in a medical/scientific context. In this more applied or general use of mindfulness, Kabat-Zinn removed the Buddhist framework and eventually downplayed the connection between mindfulness and Buddhism.

Whatever the context in which it is used, whether for stress reduction or spiritual practice, in the proper practice of mindfulness, sati (attention) is always integrated with sampajanna, or being aware of where your attention is. It is only when these two work together that the practice of mindfulness can fulfill its intended purpose. So, even though the technique is similar, its function in the mindfulness movement as introduced by Kabat-Zinn is different from the function that the disciplines of mindfulness have in the contemplative context. In the latter, its function is to lay the foundation for the disciplines of insight or discernment. As we will see in the next chapter, these disciplines in turn aim to bring about what the contemplative traditions see as the fruition of their spiritual path.

In the Hindu tradition, the discipline of mindfulness is called *dharana*. Usually translated as "one-pointedness," dharana is the sixth step on the eightfold path of the Yoga Sutras by Patan-jali. "Through *dharana*, our consciousness is kept in a state of attentiveness. To this end one's attention is fixed on an object and, as soon as other thoughts arise, is redirected toward that same object."[3]

In the Jewish tradition, the discipline of mindfulness is called *kavana*. Here, the discipline involves paying attention to what we are doing when we are doing it rather than allowing our minds to wander through all possible thought-worlds. The mystical schools of Islam also stress the discipline of mindful-ness. Although Muslims generally do not consider it to be an explicitly meditative practice, *dhikr* (literally "remembering") is a form of controlled attention on one's body and breathing that purifies the soul and often concludes the *Salat*, or daily practice. As with traditional meditation, these methods do much to alleviate one's daily anxieties. Spiritually, it reminds Muslims of their proper place before God and the world.

Within the Christian traditions, particularly within the so-called apophatic spirituality (see chapter 8), a great deal of importance is attached to the disciplines of mindfulness. In the Philokalia, *the* source book of the contemplative disciplines of the orthodox Christian traditions, one can find many passages on this: "After sunset, having asked the help of the all-merciful and all-powerful Lord Jesus Christ, sit you down on a low stool in your quiet and dimly lit cell, collect your mind from its customary circling and wandering outside, and quietly lead it into the heart by way of breathing."[4] Another practice in this text suggests using a word instead of breathing to redirect one's mindfulness: "[T]ake but one short word of a single syl-lable. This is better than two, for the shorter it is the better it accords with the work of the spirit. . . . [I]f any thought should press upon you to ask you what you are seeking, answer him with this word only and with no other words."[5] Evagrius Pon-ticus (fourth century A.D.), one of the desert fathers, stressed the value of one-pointed attention during prayer: "Pray with fire and dispel the cares and doubts that arise. They confuse you and deafen you with their noise, so that they may paralyze your efforts."[6] This example notes that a certain amount of concentration or mindfulness is needed to rise above absent-mindedness; otherwise, we will find ourselves in the situation Evagrius described: "If the evil spirits see that you are fervently doing your best to pray, they will put thoughts in your mind about so-called 'pressing matters' and somewhat later they once again arouse your memory of them. In this way they incite the mind to look for them again . . . so that it becomes expressed in it and thus cause the fruitful prayer to fail."[7] These examples from the different traditions reinforce the notion that the ordinary absentmindedness or distracted mind requires reining in or taming in order to make progress on the spiritual path.

Three Aspects of the Disciplines of Mindfulness

Many contemplative psychological aspects and effects are linked to the cultivation of mindfulness. Some of them have also been the object of investigation in academic (neuro) psychology.[8] We cannot discuss them all here, but some of these aspects are so typical of the disciplines of mindfulness that the latter often take their names from them. Thus, these disciplines are also called the practice of peace, the practice of simplicity, and the practice of purity. We will look at these aspects briefly.

The first aspect, which we have already touched on, is the quality of peace, or *stabilitas*—the ability to keep our attention on one thing, a mental steadfastness. This prevents us from being dragged along and drowned in the turbulent stream of our thoughts and experience. The disciplines of mindfulness are said to calm the agitation of the mind by continually returning to the focal point or anchor of our mindfulness. For instance, Cassian of the desert fathers said,

> Unless the mind has some fixed point to which it
> can keep coming back and to which it tries to fas-
> ten itself, it will flutter hither and thither accord-
> ing to the whim of the passing moment and follow
> whatever immediate and external impression is pre-
> sented to it.[9]

This also contributes to calming our stream of thoughts.
The Buddhist meditation master Chokyi Nyima provided a
helpful metaphor of this process:

> Water clears when undisturbed. If water in a pond is
> disturbed, it becomes murky; if left alone, it naturally
> remains clear. Likewise, when your mind remains
> focused on a single object, whatever it might be, and
> doesn't follow after gross or even subtle thought of
> the past, the present, or the future, it automatically
> relaxes and remains still, calm, and peaceful. This
> properly laid foundation is of great benefit for train-
> ing in the more advanced practices.[10]

From the point of view of contemplative psychology, it is
not surprising that we find exactly the same murky water metaphor in the Christian contemplative tradition in the Philokalia. After all, they talk about the same human mind.

The second aspect that is closely related psychologically to
the cultivation of mindfulness is the development of simplicity
(*simplicitas*). Simplicity is, again, such a typically contemplative concept that we find it in almost all traditions. It stresses
that practicing the disciplines of mindfulness can disentangle
the complicated, intricate jumble of the mind. After all, what
but simplicity could penetrate complexity?

By "complexity," we do not mean the sophistication that
arises when we think about an intellectually difficult subject.
Here we mean the endless complexity that arises from having

thoughts about emotions, emotions about thoughts, fantasies about thoughts about emotions about fantasies and so on, which then become inextricably mixed up with our sensory experience. This mental movement complicates our experience and clouds our clarity of mind. We wander around in our thoughts as in a castle in the air. We know that the castle is somehow connected with reality but do not see how or where. We have lost our way in this psychological labyrinth of our own creation, and whatever means we devise to escape it are, in actuality, only further extensions of this labyrinth. The complexity of which we are speaking is the result of the continually repeated mental movement of the dualistic split (see chapter 3).

Fundamentally, the simplicity of the disciplines of mindfulness does not nourish this complicating mental movement. Why not? It continually brings our attention, when lost in our mental labyrinth, back to that which is the focal point of our mindfulness practice. We do not add any more energy in the form of various thought contents but leave the labyrinth be for what it is. We stop where we are. And because this ego-driven labyrinth requires thought contents to sustain it, it slowly begins to fade and even decay over time, thereby losing its complexity. Thus, the mind and experience of reality begin to show a greater simplicity and clarity. From the point of view of our complicated minds, we become "poor in spirit" (Matthew 5:3). In this way, we also come to simplify our lives. As Chögyam Trungpa explained from a Buddhist view,

> Every situation in our lives becomes a simple relationship—a simple relationship with the kitchen sink, a simple relationship with your car, a simple relationship with your father, mother, children. Of course, this is not to say that a person suddenly is transformed into a saint. Familiar irritations are still there of course, but they are simple irritations, transparent irritations.[11]

This simplicity also applies to our attitude toward the technique of the disciplines of mindfulness themselves. As Trungpa went on to say,

> You do not try to separate yourself from the technique, but you try to become the technique so that there is a sense of non-duality. . . . [A]nd the proper attitude toward technique is not to regard it as magical, a miracle or profound ceremony of some kind, but to see it as a simple process, extremely simple. The simpler the technique the less danger of sidetracks because you are not feeding yourself with all sorts of fascinating, seductive hopes and fears.[12]

The third psychological aspect that is characteristic of the disciplines of mindfulness is purity. In a sense, this aspect is an extension of simplicity. The Christian tradition often uses the term *purificatio* ("cleansing" or "purification") for this. The term is related to breaking free of our egocentric emotions or passions. By cultivating mindfulness, the mind is deprived of space to form more egocentric dispositions and stir up the waves of our passions. Cleansing or purification, therefore, entails letting go of our world of thoughts and cultivating open-mindedness, or "nonfixation." Whereas being caught up in our emotions is the source of a continual restlessness that can not only destroy our stability but also obstruct a pure view on these emotions.

This notion of purity relates to the sense of not being caught up in emotions; this is a very important contemplative view. For example, in the Christian tradition, Evagrius Ponticus used the term *apatheia*, which means freedom from being caught up in emotional turbulence. The desert father Cassian used the term *puritas cordis*, "purity of heart," to characterize this aspect of mindfulness in relation to not being emotionally fixated. Here, the word *heart* indicates that mindfulness is also a matter of the heart, a purity that is free from captivity by ego-driven emotions and concerns. As long as we are tossed back and forth by our egocentric emotions, we lack a purity of heart that can in turn engender or facilitate a clear seeing or insight. As is also expressed in Christianity,

> But we would misunderstand "purity of heart" if we were to view it as sinlessness in a moral sense of the word. Rather, it is a spiritual condition that is pure in the sense of being free from preoccupation, from confusion and excitement. It is a serenity that has let go of everything in order to be free and open to God.[13]

By practicing the disciplines of mindfulness, we notice that we are constantly captivated by our stream of thoughts with all its emotional turbulence. At the very moment we notice that we are captivated again, we are awake. By refocusing our attention on the focal point of our mindfulness meditation, it is said that we can cleanse our minds, and our experience of reality becomes increasingly pure.

To sum up, the three aspects of the disciplines of mindfulness—stability (peace), simplicity, and purity (open-mindedness)—belong together and develop together. They lay the foundation for the practice of the disciplines of insight, which we will explore in more detail in chapter 8.

The Development of Mindfulness

An important and maybe puzzling question is, how does mindfulness develop concretely within the practice of this discipline? Or rather, how do we know mindfulness is developing in our practice? Its development is marked by all kinds of discoveries that we will look at here because they give a somewhat more tangible idea of the nature of this discipline.

Although the order in which they are presented is not the only one, the discoveries do tend to occur in this sequence.

When we begin practicing the disciplines of mindfulness, it soon becomes apparent that it is difficult. The instructions are easy enough: Keep our attention on the focal point of meditation. Most often the breath is chosen as the focal or anchor point. When we notice that our attention is getting lost in our thoughts, we are instructed to bring it back to the focal point. This instruction is so simple that we tend to think, "What can I learn from this?" However, the first and most valuable discovery occurs relatively quickly: our stream of thoughts is very compelling. So much so, in fact, that it is difficult to keep our attention on the focal point of meditation. Before we know it, we have already become lost in our thoughts. For many people, it is surprising and often shocking to discover how easy it is to be caught up in their thoughts; such thoughts need not even be important or emotionally charged. The most trivial thoughts distract us. We believed we were in charge of our own minds, but it becomes evident that that is not the case at all: apparently, we do not even have the choice of thinking or not thinking. By practicing the disciplines of mindfulness, we begin to see this.

A subsequent discovery about our minds—one that is closely related to the first—is that thoughts not only go through the mind involuntarily and often unasked for but also *almost continuously.* At the same time, we are scarcely able to remember what we were thinking about a few minutes ago, let alone throughout the entire day. A few things may have stuck in our minds, a fraction of all that we thought. Does that matter? When we discover that whether we have forgotten them or not, these thoughts have colored and shaped our experience of reality moment to moment, throughout the entire day, we may wonder. And we may want to know more.

Another discovery that is soon made is that the *content* of our stream of thoughts is hardly controlled by our will.

Thought after thought occurs, sometimes with a certain cohesion, but they can also be interrupted and broken off by the sudden recollection, "Oh! I still have to buy some milk. What time is it? Are the stores still open?" Sometimes we are able to pick up the thread of thought again, and at other times we have lost it completely. So, we drift along in a stream of thoughts—meaningful thoughts, inane thoughts, beautiful thoughts, ugly thoughts—all without having much control over the direction in which they go. Even when we seriously decide to think about something specific systematically, we notice that our thoughts wander regularly, and we must continually bring ourselves (that is, our attention) back to the topic of our thinking. If we manage to keep our attention focused and not get caught up in other thoughts, we experience it as a strain and may quickly become tired and give up. Even then, when we seem to be focused even for a short time, there is hardly a pause in our thoughts. They simply continue to coast along.

It is as if our thoughts have a certain absorptive power, which would explain why it takes so much energy to channel the stream of thoughts for a short time. We begin to see the enormous power of our thought-stream and just how much we (whoever that is) are subject to it. Perhaps we have always considered our individual freedom to think as we like ("freedom of thought") to be of paramount importance. Paradoxically, it could be said that our practice of the disciplines of mindfulness leads us to discover that we are not free to think what we want; our thoughts have a stronger grip on us than we do on our thoughts. Our "freedom" is apparently not *our* freedom but the freedom of *our thoughts* to involuntary imprison us and color our experience. In fact, we have such a poor grasp of the content of this stream that we do not know what we will think a few minutes from now.

A further discovery that we could stumble across is one that causes us to understand why our thoughts absorb our attention so easily: we take the contents of our thoughts very seriously. Actually, we are especially interested in our own commentary, which we give to the stream of our experience. That commentary is like a voice-over that "explains" to us what we experience. Our thinking mind behaves somewhat like a child who, while reading a comic book, reads only the written commentary or the text in the balloons. Increasingly, we become aware that taking this commentary so seriously actually causes us to live in a self-created reality, and we also realize the extent to which it does so.

As previously mentioned, when we begin to cultivate mindfulness, the mind is like a wild horse that needs to be tamed. We initially train ourselves—our attention—by means of the disciplines of mindfulness. This taming is a gradual process that cannot be completed abruptly or with impatience. A classic Buddhist metaphor expresses it as follows. When we want to tame a wild horse so that we can ride it later, we tie a rope around its neck and hold on to the other end. Then we shorten the rope a little but not entirely—the animal is much too skittish for that. When the horse has settled down again, we shorten the rope a little more until the tension becomes too much for the horse and it becomes skittish again, forcing us to slacken the rope. In this way, ever so slowly, bit by bit, with patience and perseverance, we pull the horse closer and closer until it is so close that it can smell us, which is a new phase, a new moment of tension. When it is used to our smell, we continue to shorten the rope until we can touch the horse. The distance between ourselves and the horse is thus further decreased. However, this cannot be achieved abruptly but only with great skill and a gentle method of give-and-take.

This is also the required approach to tame the agitated mind, which is thrown back and forth on the waves of mental and emotional movements. The focus or object of meditation is the point to which we direct our attention again and again, while the disciplines of mindfulness are the rope. We continually return our attention, after noticing that it has gotten lost in our stream of thoughts, to the focal point of meditation. We do so with great patience and without aggression. When the mind is wild, we do not shorten the rope too quickly or abruptly, but rather we give it space. When it calms down, we can then tighten our discipline somewhat. We thus develop our mindfulness.

By developing our ability to pay attention through the practice, we gradually become aware that we need not surrender—as we do habitually—to the content of our thought-stream. Although we must acknowledge it and not deny its existence, we need not yield to it and lose ourselves in it as if that is where we find ourselves and our salvation. Nor must we repress our stream of thoughts and fight it as though it were the source of hell and damnation. Our mindfulness is destroyed, not by our stream of thoughts but by being caught and submerged in it. The fundamental discovery available to us in this process is that there is more to life than existing in our stream of thoughts.

Over time, by practicing the disciplines of mindfulness, we also begin to discover that there are moments when we "wake up" from our thoughts and notice them; this also shows us that the stream does not go on ceaselessly. There are openings—the moments when we wake up from our thoughts are those openings. These moments actually make it possible for us to place our attention on the focal point of meditation once again. These moments always reappear spontaneously. We cannot summon or control them; at most, we can only give them space, which is what the practice of mindfulness helps us to do. It could be said that we briefly taste what it means to be mentally free, to find ourselves in a moment of wakefulness and experience a refreshing mental pause. At these moments, the body and mind are synchronized; we are present mentally where we are physically, in the here and now.

We often experience the transition from captivity to freedom as something opening up. It is as though our wakefulness or the situation in which we find ourselves suddenly unfolds. Our worries recede to the background, and we are briefly liberated from the play of hopes and fears, from our usual preoccupation with the future and the past; the way things were, the way they should have been, the way they should be now—all of this has evaporated for a moment. We discover that wakefulness is an aspect of the mind and that we can cultivate it.

It is often at this point that we can begin to value our practice of mindfulness because we have experienced in a concrete though small way that it is an effective instrument with which we can tame and free the mind. We develop an increasing appreciation for the open-mindedness, simplicity, and stability that appear at the moments when we wake from our thoughts. Thus, we gradually develop a certain feeling for the contrast between being lost in our thoughts and seeing them.

Initially, as suggested, we experience this freedom at moments of *wakeful thoughtlessness*, moments during which we have no thoughts and are aware of this. At this time, we are obviously free from being caught, as there is nothing in which to be caught. Since there is often a pleasant feeling associated with that sense of space and openness in such moments, we are easily tempted to hold on to them and see thoughts as the enemy. But this is, according to the contemplative traditions, a mistake that impedes the further development of open-mindedness.

At this stage of development, it may be possible for us to recognize the moment when a thought goes through our minds for what it is: a thought. At that moment of recognition, we are also free. In this phase, we begin to discover that open-mindedness does not depend on the absence of *thoughts*, or thoughtlessness, but on the absence of *captivity by our thoughts*. This is a key point. We gradually understand that both resisting thoughts and losing ourselves in them are equal forms of captivity. Initially, thoughts have such a strong grip on us that having one almost always goes hand in hand with captivity. At that point, thoughts are indeed obstacles to open-mindedness. However, the more we cultivate our mindfulness, the stronger the absence of captivity becomes. Finally, not only do we not lose our mindfulness when a thought occurs but that occurrence even becomes a signal that redirects us to open-mindedness and the absence of captivity. Our open-mindedness acquires increasing continuity; whether the mind moves or rests, it continues to endure, laying the foundation for further disciplines—the disciplines of insight. It is to these we now turn.

8

The Disciplines of Insight

In the previous chapters, we discussed a number of the mental disciplines, which we divided into the disciplines of thinking and the disciplines of consciousness. In chapter 6, we looked at the two disciplines of thinking: the intellectual disciplines and the disciplines of the imagination. In chapter 7, we explored the first of the two disciplines of consciousness: the disciplines of mindfulness. In this chapter, we will look more closely at the second discipline of consciousness: the disciplines of insight or discernment. Since this is the last of the mental disciplines that we will explore in this book, we will close this chapter with a section on the combined action of the four disciplines.

As stated previously, the Christian tradition originally referred to the disciplines of insight using the term *contemplation*. Together, the disciplines of insight form the core of what in this tradition is called apophatic spirituality. Here *apo* means "separate from," so we could translate *apophatic* as "separate from words or concepts." Willigis Jäger explained it this way: "Apophatic spirituality is directed at being conscious in a pure, empty way so that the divine can manifest itself. Contents are viewed as obstacles. As long as the consciousness [i.e., mind] holds on to images or concepts, it has not yet arrived at that point where the particular experience of God occurs. Images and contents cloud the divine rather than clarify it."[1]

A parallel is found in many Buddhist traditions in which the disciplines of insight are referred to as formless meditations. Here "formless" means that these disciplines or practices do not use mental forms such as concepts or images. This distinguishes the disciplines of insight from the two forms of discipline of thought as discussed earlier. The disciplines of insight are not concerned with arousing a certain experiential value by means of an image, a concept, a belief, or an idea. Rather, we can distinguish these disciplines on the basis of the practice of a direct, open look at the mind and our experience of reality. Open-mindedness, or moments of open-mindedness, create the state in which we can see the stream of our experience without distortion. From the perspective of contemplative psychology, this is what leads to insight and knowledge. Thus, we can say that this knowledge is a nonconceptual form of knowing (see chapter 4); it is perceptual knowledge or perceptual knowing.

This kind of knowing is the fruit of the disciplines of insight, which are the preeminent and special research tools of the contemplative traditions. The understanding and knowledge of the human mind and experience—in short, contemplative psychology as defined in this book—comes out of this first-person research tool in the disciplines of insight or discernment. This is their specialty. It is the kind of research that is not practiced in academic or conventional empirical psychology.

The most common Sanskrit term for the discipline of insight in the Buddhist tradition is *vipashyana* (Pali: *vipassana*), or insight meditation, which is practiced on the basis of shamatha, the discipline of mindfulness. In Hinduism, the term *dhyana* is used to refer generally to this discipline, the practice of which is supported by dharana, the discipline of mindfulness.

In the Western Christian tradition, the disciplines of insight have faded from sight in the last few centuries, becoming virtually unknown to the average churchgoer and the rest of our culture as well. This is why people often think that these disciplines are typical of Eastern traditions. They do not know that "the East" is a Western concept that does not correspond in any way to a cultural or spiritual unity. The Indian culture, for example, is much closer to our Western culture than to those of China or Japan, not only with respect to language but also with respect to its way of thinking.

Within the contemplative traditions of ancient Eastern Christianity, there was always a form of spiritual investigation that did not rely on concepts or language—the apophatic spirituality already mentioned. More recently, due to interreligious dialogue, these disciplines of insight have once again been brought to the attention of Western Christian contemplative practitioners. However, it is within the Eastern world religions where these disciplines have always played and continue to play a major role. From the developmental view, in these traditions, such practices are taken up when the intellectual disciplines and those of the imagination have reached a certain maturity. As they contain a very detailed analysis, we will rely mostly on the Buddhist traditions to develop a contemplative psychology understanding of the disciplines of insight.

The Practice of the Disciplines of Insight

How do we practice the disciplines of insight? Is there a certain contemplative technique for training our discernment, or discriminating awareness, just as we have trained our attention with the help of a focal point? The answer is typical for the disciplines of insight: the practice goes beyond the technique. Nonetheless, it is a very disciplined practice. How are we to understand this? The practice of the disciplines of insight is the disciplined practice of open-mindedness itself. Open-mindedness is a mind or consciousness that is free from being fixated on or lost in the contents of thought and therefore can see clearly.

Open-mindedness is the outcome or fruit of the disciplines of mindfulness, and as such it is the entrance or seed to the practice of these disciplines. We cultivate open-mindedness further in the disciplines of insight so that it becomes "unconditional open-mindedness," which means it is not being dependent on or conditioned by deliberately maintaining mindfulness or images. It is no longer vulnerable to being either driven off (or lost) or corralled (restricted) by any internal or external experience. It is this open-mindedness that creates the space in which our discernment can be active. And it is this discernment that leads to the insight that these disciplines seek to cultivate. Finally, it is this insight that in the form of experience gives us a concrete answer to the question of how the world of phenomena looks if it is viewed from the perspective of unconditional open-mindedness. That perspective shows us reality as it is, liberated from our ego-centered version of it.

The disciplines of discernment are grafted to and blossom on the same branch—the disciplines of mindfulness. If we want to speak of a "technique" with regard to the disciplines of insight, we could say that they use the same one as do the disciplines of mindfulness. However, the place that open-mindedness occupies has shifted: it is no longer a goal or outcome, as is the case in the practice of mindfulness, but the means for rousing the mental discernment that allows us to distinguish between illusion and reality. The disciplines of insight differ from the disciplines of mindfulness on this score.

A second difference is that cultivating open-mindedness within the disciplines of mindfulness comes down to developing a certain distance from our stream of thoughts, a certain *Abgeschiedenheit*, or "separateness," as Meister Eckhart calls it. In contrast, within the disciplines of insight, this open-mindedness is like that of a child who, with unfettered curiosity, stands as close as possible to everything to get a good look. At this stage, the more we develop our ability to pay attention to what we actually experience mentally and through our senses, the less absorbing is our stream of thoughts. In fact, we can see our thought-stream from a continually closer perspective without falling into the stream, that is, without losing open-mindedness.

A third difference is that the disciplines of mindfulness initially require a certain effort and manipulation of mindfulness, whereas the disciplines of insight are based on mental relaxation. For this to be possible, we must realize that open-mindedness is a natural aspect of the mind and that we can actually relax in it. The only reason that open-mindedness has so few opportunities to manifest itself is that we habitually and continually try to hold on to our egocentric experience of reality. This is where we mistakenly believe we can find refuge or ground for ourselves. Natural open-mindedness does not provide a buttress or a sense of something solid in the ways we are used to. As a result, our sense of ego rejects and even fears our natural open-mindedness.

However, through our earlier and steady practice of the disciplines of mindfulness, we have learned to appreciate our natural moments of open-mindedness. Now we can discover that these moments are not something we must produce through much effort; they occur when we cease to manipulate ourselves, our minds, and our experience of reality, when we relax into our practice. When this happens, our natural awareness is given the chance to clarify our experience of reality.

It is a key point that the practice of the disciplines of insight lead to direct perceptual knowledge of both ego and egolessness. How is this possible? Let us return to the metaphor of planting the stick in the stream. If we have developed the ability to plant the stick somewhat firmly in the river bottom—that is, if we have developed our disciplines of mindfulness to such a degree that it offers a certain stability—then, for the first time, we may also be able to observe the qualities of the water that flows past the stick. We notice the varying temperature and speed of the water as well as all its other empirical qualities.

At the moment that the stick works itself loose again and is swept along with the stream, we no longer observe any of this. The stick moves along as quickly as the water does. With respect to the water around it, it appears to be lying still and it seems that nothing happens. Our mindfulness and discernment have once again vanished as we have submerged once again and gotten caught up in the stream of our thoughts. The moment we awaken from our captivity, the stick stands straight up in the stream, and once again we notice, discern, its empirical qualities.

During these moments of stability (when the stick stands straight up in the water), our discernment once again begins to operate, offering us the ability to view our stream of thoughts openly and recognize it for what it is from the perspective of open-mindedness. Since we are able to retain stability as we discern, this stream is our total field of experience, and our discernment can penetrate and clarify our egocentric experience of reality as well as "hold" its egoless open-mindedness.

Open-Mindedness as Surrender

Cultivating open-mindedness, which is the basis for the development of the kind of insight with which this discipline is concerned, also means that we cannot afford to cling to the fruits of this discipline and other disciplines we practiced earlier. With regard to the disciplines of mindfulness, this means that we do not cling mentally to the calm and open-mindedness to which they lead. After all, clinging and open-mindedness are incompatible. With regard to the disciplines of the imagination, this means that we do not cling to the experiential value that is the fruit of these disciplines. This "not clinging" obtains a fortiori for the practice of the disciplines of insight itself: No matter which particular fruits of insight appear, we must foil any attempt to cling to them or become fixated on them. If we do, we will again be captivated, even in a subtle way, and our discernment cannot develop and bear its proper fruit. When this capacity for open-mindedness becomes stuck, it loses its quality of panoramic awareness; it can no longer fly freely and look around. In the Christian tradition, John of the Cross expressed it very well:

> For it comes to the same thing whether a bird be held by a slender cord or by a stout one; since, even if it be slender, the bird will be well held as though it were stout, for so long as it breaks it not and flies not away. It is true that the slender one is the easier to break; still, easy though it be, the bird will not fly away if it be not broken. And thus the soul that has attachment to anything, however much virtue it possess, will not attain to the liberty of Divine union.[2]

In practical terms, therefore, cultivating discernment means continually letting go of the fruit that it produces—including *the idea* that we should cling to the fruits of contemplative flourishing in order to preserve them. Practically, this means letting go of our fear of losing them and the hope of retaining them. However, the insight that we cannot possess these fruits at all, that we never have and never will possess them in a way that secures their permanency, frees us from this fear. This is a very subtle process, for we may already cling to the insight that breaks our discipline.

In practicing the disciplines of insight, therefore, there is no room left to count our blessings and attempt to hold on to our spiritual achievements of insight. There is no room for spiritual strategies and manipulation or to monitor ourselves in an anxious and strenuous way. There is not even any room to hold on to the framework of our own tradition. It goes beyond every hope of achieving and fear of not achieving. In this sense, the practice of this discipline is without hope and without fear: it is free of hope and fear. It goes beyond every goal that has previously been established. It is without a goal.

As mentioned before, the discipline thus consists of cultivating unconditional open-mindedness, not as a goal but as a means, so that our discernment can move freely and lead to insight. The practice of open-mindedness comes down to continually undoing the mental movement that leads to ego. This means undoing the dualistic split that we discussed in chapter 3—the constantly recurring split that causes us to see the world of phenomena in a distorted way by dividing it into *my* surroundings, *my* partner, *my* child, *my* body, *my* thoughts, *my* mind versus that which is not *mine*. By undoing this distorting mental captivity, we begin to see how both internal and external phenomena relate to each other rather than how they relate to the phantom of a constructed ego. Stated in theistic terms, we are now open to seeing the world of phenomena as God's world or creation instead of a world that is for or against "me." Stated in nontheistic terms, we begin to find that uncovering our humaneness and manifesting it in the world is more valuable and more interesting than cultivating *being* Mary or John or whoever we think we are.

Because of this, we could also characterize the disciplines of insight as cultivating mental surrender, a gradual process of mentally letting go of who we think we are and the dualistic mentality on which ego builds its world of "me" and "mine." Thus, complete surrender is the mental attitude that no longer possesses (anything); the mind has returned to its nakedness and also sees the world of phenomena in its nakedness. *Nakedness* here means without the adornment of being "this" or "that"; adornment is what we impose on natural openness or nakedness. Through this surrender, joy in life, tenderness, and insight are no longer bound to what ego hopes to gain or what it fears to lose or not attain. However, these qualities continue to flourish through unconditional open-mindedness. In the Heart Sutra, one of the most well-known texts in Mahayana Buddhism, those who have achieved this open insight or perfection of wisdom (Sanskrit: *prajnaparamita*) are called bodhisattvas:

"Because bodhisattvas have no attainment, they rely on and abide in the perfection of wisdom; because their minds are without obstruction, they have no fear."[3]

The contemplative traditions call this naked mind by many different names, although it cannot be known conceptually but only experientially. It is the Shekinah in the Jewish Hasidic tradition and the Holy Spirit in the Christian tradition. It is inspiration, enthusiasm. A famous passage in a Buddhist *terma* text includes the following description:

> With respect to its having a name, the various names that are applied to it are inconceivable (in their numbers). Some call it "the nature of the mind" or "mind itself." Some Tirthikas [non-Buddhist] call it by the name Atman or "the Self." The Sravakas call it the doctrine of Anatman or "the absence of a self." . . . Some call it the Prajnaparamita or "the perfection of wisdom." Some call it the name Tathagatagarbha or "embryo of Buddhahood." . . . Some call it by the name Alaya or "the basis of everything." And some simply call it by the name "ordinary awareness."[4]

Whatever we call this naked mind, it is both the invisible ground and the hidden fruit of the disciplines of insight.

The Double-Sided Function of the Disciplines of Insight

Formulated in the somewhat more prosaic terms of contemplative psychology, the disciplines of insight offer the opportunity to observe and study our stream of experience without fitting it into either religious or egocentric concepts and representations. This distinguishes these disciplines from our customary mode of observation because, as we discussed earlier, our experience is usually already adjusted to fit into certain concepts; it is usually given to us as conceptualized experience without our being aware of it. Usually, when we want to study something, we also assume a specific conceptual framework and formulation that determines and limits our experience. In practicing the disciplines of insight, we free ourselves from every formulation and conceptual framework, thus creating room for an unlimited view that offers a direct, nonconceptual form of knowledge and destroys our perceptual confusion (see chapter 4).

In chapter 2, we discussed our personal experience of reality and how it arises: at every moment of experience we dress up our experience or adorn it in our concepts; because we are not aware of this process, we simply experience it as reality. In chapter 3, we spoke of how the concept of ego structures our experience of reality, and in chapter 4, we saw how perceptual confusion arises when our discernment does not function and what its nature is:

> When the deluded in a mirror look
> They see a face, not a reflection.
> So the mind that has truth denied
> Relies on that which is not true.[5]

This is how Saraha, the great Buddhist tantric master, described it in a famous verse. The disciplines of insight are directed at developing that discernment, which allows us to see a face as a face and a reflection as a reflection. It allows us to see and know things as they are.

With regard to our self-created, egocentric experience of reality, we begin to recognize it for what it is: a fiction. Our discernment therefore begins to remove the blindness that causes us to experience this fiction as reality. It makes us aware not only of the fact that (and when) we dream but also of what we dream. Over time, our open-mindedness gradually acquires a greater continuity; whether our mind is moving or at rest, this open-mindedness can endure.

In practicing these disciplines, we cultivate another kind of relationship to our stream of thoughts that is different than that in the disciplines of mindfulness—a relationship in which the presence of thoughts does not necessarily mean that we are caught up in them. How does this relationship develop? In the previous chapter, we spoke briefly about two kinds of open-mindedness. The first occurs at moments of wakeful thoughtlessness, when our discernment is active and allows us to distinguish between being in thought and not being in thought. The second is one that is not lost when a thought arises. The open-mindedness at the stage of insight develops from this first wakeful thoughtlessness through continuing practice, while the second kind during this stage does not depend on the absence of thoughts. So again, we can see how the capacities we develop in the practices of mindfulness are the foundation for the disciplines of insight. In this case, the capacity to leave thoughts alone (that is, not get caught up in them) opens the possibility of clear sight with regard to our stream of thoughts because it is free from every kind of fixation on the world of (mental) phenomena, including our world of thought. Therefore, the discernment that functions in this second kind of open-mindedness enables us to study our thoughts without being caught up in them, to *see* what thoughts actually are, what they are made of, and what they do with our experience, instead of looking at their contents. Then we no longer see thoughts as a threat to our practice; on the contrary, their occurrence allows our unfettered discernment to explore our egocentric experience of reality freely. It is important to appreciate that this discipline of seeing our stream of thoughts is very different from reflecting on the thoughts that cross our minds; hopefully, this should be clear from what we have said about the disciplines of thought.

The disciplines of insight lead to our being less and less of a mystery to ourselves. That which is internal—our mental lives in the form of our stream of thoughts—becomes less of a frightening, unknown area, not because we know so much about it intellectually but because we know it so well experientially. Of course, this mental life continues to be unpredictable and uncontrollable, but this is something we become more and more familiar with and less reactive in response to. We develop a certain adeptness in dealing with the mind, just as a good tennis player is good because of her knowledge and skill in dealing with her opponent's unpredictable shots. In this way, we acquire a direct form of self-knowledge: firsthand self-knowledge. It is not in the form of a narrative or theory about ourselves that we have stored somewhere in our mental administration but a nonconceptual self-knowledge in the form of being acquainted with ourselves and with the qualities of our stream of thoughts. This is the first function of the disciplines of insight; it leads to perceptual self-knowledge, teaching us to know our ego's habits and its experience of reality and to realize its illusory nature.

These disciplines have a second function and fruition that are the flipside of the first; they also open up another perspective, one that gives us insight into reality, such as that which appears when we are free from ego and illusion. They reveal an experience of reality that transcends ego. This means that finally our discernment enables us to explore the egoless state of open-mindedness and to taste its qualities—qualities that are none other than those of our humaneness. In religious terms, they are the qualities of the awakened state, liberation, the Holy Spirit in us, our Buddha-nature, ultimate surrender, or obedience to God. The discernment that is now operative penetrates our entire experiential space; it is the intelligent clarity of the space itself that places everything—the worlds of ego and egolessness—in the light.

We gradually discover that this open space is inhabitable, real, and joyous and not a religious fabrication. At the same time, we do not need to look up to it nor wrap ourselves in mystery about it. We simply observe that it is possible to live outside the stream of our egocentric reality, that we do not have to be caught up in the stream and that we can rest in that space. This gives rise to an enormous inspiration that is based not on hope but on experience. As we have suggested, it is because of discernment at this stage that inspiration is possible. We can see from the perspective of ego that this space may appear (or be experienced as) groundless, lonely, and frightening; from its own perspective, it appears (or is experienced as) alive, clear, and warm. In fact, as our perspective widens, we can appreciate that this is the space in which our fundamental humanity is rooted groundlessly and from which it sprouts and flourishes constantly in our own lives and in those of others, in our culture and time, and in all cultures and times. It lets us see human existence with all its shortcomings and suffering and places it in a wider perspective that makes us milder, wiser, and more caring. This is why discovering this space and allowing it to expand and permeate our experience is cultivating the flourishing within.

Expressed in theistic terms, the second function of the disciplines of insight is that they lead to not conceptual but perceptual knowledge of God. These disciplines finally reveal a divine reality and induce us to turn toward it, which is why the disciplines of insight are also classified in theistic traditions as directing oneself toward God. Within the Islam Sufi tradition, these disciplines are called *muraqabah*, about which Javad Nurbakhsh said they "are reserved for God's saints, who see Him internally and externally, in solitude and in communion, and say: I see nothing if I have not first seen God."[6]

We can again illustrate this second function with the metaphor of the stick in the river. When the stick is planted in the river bottom, it projects out of the water, just like the hand that holds the stick. The stick appears to be standing in a bigger space than the space of the stream. A vast landscape is visible—at least, if we do not continue to be fascinated by all that we see in the stream. When we leave this fascination

behind us, we slowly acquire a view of the space itself. In terms
of Saraha's metaphor of the mirror, not only do we recognize
what appears in the mirror as a reflection but we also become
aware of the mirror itself. The discernment that sees ego is the
same discernment that sees egolessness. Chögyam Trungpa
described this discernment as the wisdom of the cosmic mirror, which is a metaphor for the

> unconditioned, vast open space. It is an eternal
> and completely open space, space beyond ques-
> tion. In the realm of the cosmic mirror, your mind
> extends its vision completely, beyond doubt. Before
> thoughts, before the thinking process takes place,
> there is the accommodation of the cosmic mirror,
> which has no boundary—no center and no fringe.[7]

Perhaps we do not have a conceptual framework and terminology at hand to express more precisely the kind of knowledge that is awakened by the disciplines of insight; even if
we do, words do not capture the fullness of the experience.
However, that does not detract from its value and usefulness,
the "truth" of the experience. We gave an example of this
earlier: we know hundreds of people by their faces, but our
vocabulary is not rich enough to describe the different outward appearances of all these people. Yet that does not detract
from the usefulness of our knowledge. This is also the case
with our knowledge of the world that we acquire by means of
the discernment cultivated by the disciplines of insight.

Of course, every contemplative tradition speaks of this
discriminating awareness in its own terms. From a Christian
view, discernment (*diakrisis*) leads us in the first instance to
see our pettiness and sinfulness in the light of the Holy Spirit,
and in the second instance it shows (and is) the activity of
the Holy Spirit. In Buddhist terms, the discernment (*prajna*)
that is cultivated by the disciplines of insight causes us to

recognize *samsara* (the egocentric experience of reality) as the greatest and most powerful illusion there is. At the same time, it reveals nirvana (egoless experience of reality) and the true nature of mind, our Buddha-nature. From this point of view, discernment itself is free of ego and an aspect of our Buddha-nature. The world of the phenomena that we first experienced as samsara is, because of the development of our discernment, now experienced as nirvana.

The two functions of the disciplines of insight show that nonconceptual self-knowledge (as in the nontheistic traditions) and knowledge of God (as in the theistic traditions) are closely related. This is because the discernment that is developed in these disciplines functions in two directions. The first direction is toward unmasking unreality, or ego's delusions; in this way, we generate self-knowledge. The second direction is toward revealing a reality that is untainted by ego (egoless) or created by God. We need to understand, however, that the moment when unreality is unmasked is the same moment that reality is revealed. We must not mistakenly believe that reality has somehow been lurking behind unreality; rather, seeing through the world of illusion *is* seeing reality. In short, the world of illusion—when one sees through it and knows it for what it is—is reality. That is why Buddhism often says that, in the egoless perspective, samsara is not separate from nirvana, and why the Christian traditions say that we are not far from the Kingdom of God (Mark 12:34) and even that the Kingdom of God is within us (Luke 17:21). From the perspective of ego, however, they appear to us as worlds apart.

The disciplines of insight teach us not only to recognize and acknowledge our blindness but also to open our eyes. They help us to see the nature and causes of ego and our egocentric experience of reality clearly by placing us in an egoless experience of reality. We can agree with Rabbi Baruch in saying, "What a good and clear world it is when one does not become lost in it, and what a dark world it is when one does become lost in it."[8]

The Interplay Between the Mental Disciplines

In the previous chapters, we classified the mental disciplines into a number of types based on various mental functions that have a central place in contemplative psychologies. We discussed those functions in chapter 4: thinking, imagining, consciousness, experiencing, knowing, and so on. In the daily practice of the contemplative life, however, the mental disciplines that we have described are used in various combinations and often in a certain order.

Combined Disciplines

First of all, let us examine the way in which certain mental disciplines are combined. In our discussion of the disciplines of mindfulness, we mentioned that these disciplines make use of an object of meditation or focal point that functions as an anchor for our mindfulness. Thus, the intention here is not to think about that object but simply to pay attention to it and, in that way, discipline our attention. Based on that principle, every aspect of our experiential world can be used for this purpose; we could therefore also use a mental object, such as a representation, word, or sentence that we repeat silently.

The disciplines of the imagination, as we know, also make use of representations; however, we do not use them as anchors but to evoke a specific experiential value. This naturally opens up the possibility of combining our mindfulness and the evocation of a specific experiential value in one mental discipline. Such combined disciplines also exist in many traditions. A central discipline in Islam is the practice of dhikr, which is a verbal formulation with a specific and deep meaning, such as *la ilaha illa 'llah* ("There is no [other] god than God"). Practitioners keep it in mind and repeat it silently to themselves. Some Christian traditions repeat the prayer "Lord, have mercy upon me, a sinner" continuously. Hinduism makes use of the continual repetition of the divine name Ram, and (Vajrayana) Buddhists often recite meaningful mantras such as OM MANI PADME HUM while visualizing a mental representation of compassion in the form of an anthropomorphic Avalokiteshvara sitting on a lotus in their own heart.

What we observe in the actual practice of such combined disciplines is that initially they may serve to cultivate mindfulness. When we become skilled in cultivating mental stability and peace, then the experiential value of the mental object can come into play. Then, when this experiential value unfolds, it can clarify our experience of reality (including our experience of ourselves and our true nature or God). This is a logical development, because as long as we have not disciplined our mindfulness, we are not capable of allowing it to rest on a mental content nor can its experiential value be revealed. Many theistic traditions use the term *prayer* for this combined discipline. The description of prayer by the Benedictine monk André Zegveld beautifully blends all the mental disciplines we have discussed:

> Prayer is primary: express *everything* and hold nothing back, for that is what pleases God, the creature that He has created in his image and not in the image that the individual has of himself. Prayer is expressing oneself, maybe not in so many words but *by looking honestly into one's own heart* [my italics]. This is how one travels along the way. Whoever has begun to travel can never say that he has achieved his goal or that he has definitively found his true self. One's proper name is always further along, and will be lost in the proper Name of God, which no human has ever been able to express adequately. This is why travelling along this way is a form of continual reorientation, of asceticism, and

of *poverty of mind* as well. Slowly and painfully it will become clear that we want to hold on so frantically to our values and ideals, our longing for justice, our love, our religiosity and even our faith that it keeps us removed from our own name and from that of God Himself. They tell us more about our "I" than about *ourselves*, more about the roles that we (want to) play than about God. Travelling along this way therefore also means a *purification*, a way of growing toward being a true *self*. Thus it is a way toward *undivided* attention so that we, looking beyond the coloring that is peculiar to each mirror, can see the name of God appear in the mirror of our own soul. It is a way in and at the same time a way out—an undivided attention to within and without, characterized by both *compassion* (a mindfulness of gentle mercy and compassion) and *universality* (a mindfulness that encompasses everything).[9]

The Order of Application of the Mental Disciplines

This developmental process we have described suggests that there is a certain order in the application of the four mental disciplines, an order that corresponds to the contemplative development of the practitioner. Let us look more closely at this aspect.

The intellectual disciplines are actually practiced throughout one's entire contemplative life. At the start, they have the function of purifying our motivation and sharpening our understanding of the how and why of the contemplative way. Later, they also furnish us with the framework for formulating and clearly communicating the shifts in our experience of reality. As we stated, intellectual understanding is a means and not a goal of the contemplative life. It offers an intellectual orientation and directions along the Way, but it does not provide us with the experience indicated by the Way. This also means that the intellectual disciplines must ultimately clear the field to make room for direct experiential and nonconceptual knowledge, for what we have called (in chapter 4) perceptual knowledge, and for the practice of mental disciplines that provide such knowledge.

In addition to study, which must be practiced from the start as well as pursued along the Way, the first discipline the traditions usually offer is the discipline of mindfulness. This helps us to curb our restlessness and absentmindedness. Through this arises room for the disciplines of insight. In the first place, the disciplines of insight are directed particularly at developing insight into ego, into who and what we (think we) are now, into how our mental patterns and our ways of acting and speaking create and maintain our egocentric experience of reality. This is the first function of these disciplines, the fruit of which is that we gradually see the illusory character of our distorted experience of reality.

However, seeing this is not always enough to cause us to let go of this habitual pattern. After all, even if we do see that our preoccupation with ego and our egocentric representations concern an imaginary world, we are not necessarily freed from this preoccupation. Our firm belief in the reality of our egocentric representation may be undermined to some extent, but this does not always conquer our constant tendency to become lost in this representation. We are like children who no longer believe in Santa Claus but are nonetheless spellbound if the jolly old man stands before them. We may be capable of recognizing these representations and the mental patterns connected with them, but letting go of them requires something more.

We have already discussed the fact that we can use the disciplines of mindfulness for this purpose since they are an exercise in letting go mentally: every time we notice that we are caught up in our stream of thoughts, we let go and direct our mindfulness again on the object of meditation. However, within the mental disciplines there is another, quite powerful way of letting go of our preoccupation with our egocentric experience of reality: the disciplines of the imagination. In chapter 6, we stated that the products of our imagination are not simply neutral mental pictures for us but are emotionally charged; this charge can link us to an egocentric perspective as well as to an egoless one. Because our experience of reality is no longer experienced as absolute, thanks to the use of the disciplines of insight, it becomes possible to change our experience intentionally by means of mastering images, which in their experiential value awaken an egoless or theocentric experience of reality. The fruit of this is, once again, that this experiential value places us in egoless or theocentric reality—a reality that exceeds the images that have roused it. The familiar metaphor of the ladder (of images) applies here, we leave the ladder behind when we have reached the place to which it leads.

In the following phase, the disciplines of insight are once again central. Now it does not function to make ego visible but to reveal the true nature of mind and experience: It makes the egoless or theocentric reality visible. It recognizes and acknowledges the space that surrounds ego, or the space that is visible when ego becomes transparent. This second function of the disciplines of insight is therefore concerned with pure vision without the support of any additional image or representation. In the famous text *The Mystical Theology* by Pseudo-Dionysius the Areopagite, this way of seeing is expressed as follows:

> And, Timothy, my friend, my advice to you as you look for a sight of the mysterious things, is to leave behind everything perceived and understood, everything perceptible and understandable, all that is not and all that is, and, with your understanding

laid aside, to strive upward as much as you can
toward union with him who is beyond all being and
knowledge.[10]

The form of knowledge realized by the disciplines of insight
is a direct, nonconceptual form of knowing or experiencing
that cannot be contained in the conceptual dualities of known
and knower, of experience and the one who experiences. In
the Eastern Orthodox Christian tradition, it is called *theoria*;
in Zen Buddhism, *Shikantaza*; and in Vajrayana Buddhism,
mahamudra and *mahasandi*. It is this experiential knowing
that reveals the ultimate nature of reality.

Many traditions emphasize that this form of experiential
knowing is not an actual experience but rather an egoless
way of experiencing. At this point, it is often said that no one
has ever seen God. This is because, ultimately, God is not an
object for our vision but rather like space; one can see things
in God. Along the same lines, the Buddhist tradition says that
the buddhas themselves never saw enlightenment. Enlightenment is not something that we can experience but a way of
experiencing within which reality is seen as it is.

The order that we have given here appears to occur often
in the practice of the contemplative life, but it is not absolute.
There are, for example, stories of people for whom simply
hearing a certain statement was enough for them to achieve
the state of enlightenment or fulfillment, although according to the traditions, such people are rare. They are likely
people who can stop smoking simply because they hear it is
unhealthy. In other words, for them, the practice of the intellectual discipline is enough to transform them existentially.
For some, just seeing ego, if only for a second, causes them to
drop their preoccupation right away. Therefore, they do not
need to practice the disciplines of the imagination that help
to bring us to the point of giving up our preoccupation with
ego's world. They may then practice only the disciplines of

mindfulness and insight. They are comparable to people who first need to see an x-ray of a smoker's lungs before they can quit smoking.

Moreover, the emphasis that the traditions lay on the use of the various mental disciplines differs. Zen Buddhism, for example, makes only sporadic use of the disciplines of the imagination, whereas many Christian traditions give only a marginal place to the disciplines of mindfulness and insight. Also, the relationship between the mental disciplines and those of action and speech differ from tradition to tradition, as we shall explore in chapter 9.

This concludes our discussion of the mental disciplines. The division used is based on the contemplative psychology of the mind that was outlined earlier. It is a functional division, in that it rests on the mental functions we discussed in chapters 3 and 4. Instead of this psychological division, one could also divide these disciplines according to their phenomenology rather than function. Our approach, however, is different because it gives an answer to the contemplative, psychological question of how the mental disciplines make use of our mental functions in order to foster the flourishing within.

9

The Disciplines of Action and Speech

Having looked at the disciplines or practices related to the mind, in this chapter we will explore the disciplines of action and speech to a certain extent. It is truly "to a certain extent" because there are so many types of these disciplines that, by means of a number of typical examples, the most we can do is give an impression of their nature, function, and form and how they accompany the mental disciplines we have discussed. The simple reason that there are so many is that our words and deeds are multifaceted and the situations in which we act and speak are enormously varied. Moreover, these situations differ with respect to time and culture, so the form of the disciplines is also relative to their time and culture. Nonetheless, they do share a number of general contemplative psychological features that we will examine here.

Let us begin with a description of the disciplines of action and speech in more general terms. The practice of these disciplines consists of observing guidelines directed at dealing with the world of phenomena, particularly relationships—what to do and what to leave undone; when, how, and about what to speak or to remain silent. In other words, they instruct us on how to conduct ourselves. All great spiritual traditions include these disciplines of action and speech; the guidelines on which they are based relate to almost all aspects of life.

The traditions trace the origin of these guidelines and often their justification to the sacred scriptures of the traditions and to the interpretation of these scriptures in the light of local culture. Thus, the Jewish tradition has its halacha. The verb *halach* literally means "to walk, to go." Halacha is the normative part of the Jewish tradition that has been passed on in the written and oral Torah; in the course of the centuries, it has been arranged in compendia or codices. Islam calls the entirety of its guidelines on how Moslems must conduct themselves *sharia*. The original Arabic word *sharia'a* translates literally to "the path that leads to water." Because of the cultures with which the tradition came into contact, these guidelines—rooted in the Koran and the *sunna* (which describes Mohammad's way of life)—have also been expanded over the centuries into a comprehensive aggregate of rules for life.

A similar development can be seen in Christianity. On the basis of central ideas in the Bible, such as the Ten Commandments, the double command of love, and the example of Christ himself, a system of rules for life has developed in conjunction with Christianity's culture that is concerned with social and contemplative life. Hinduism also contains a plurality of prescriptions for behavior, which together form a contemplative way of life. This way is called *karma marga*, or the Way (marga) of action (karma). This plurality is an unfolding of ten central rules for life called *yamas* (don'ts) and *niyamas* (do's); see Adele, 2009.[1] Both words have almost the same meaning: "to curb, limit, or control." In Buddhism, the rules for life are established in the *Vinaya*, which literally means "to lead away." It includes the five rules for laypeople, the *panchashila*, and the more extended rules for monks. The Vinaya is also a continuation of a number of central Buddhist ideas related to the *dashakushala*, or the "ten virtues."

In the Ten Commandments, the ten yamas and niyamas, and the ten virtues, we find repeated precepts not to kill, not to steal, not to conduct oneself in a sexually impure way, and not to lie. From the viewpoint of contemplative psychology, it is not surprising that similar rules for conduct exist; fundamentally within the contemplative traditions, the contours of a universal humanity are formulated here.

However, if we look at how the traditions have developed their guidelines further, differences emerge. These differences are related to the time and culture in which the tradition is found. Two motivations come into play here. The first is to contribute to the local culture and its social life through binding human action and speech to ethical norms. The second is to bind action and speech to what will specifically help in traveling a spiritual path. Elsewhere, I have called this *contemplative action*, which is "compassionate or merciful action that awakens and brings to expression the contemplative perspective and way of life."[2] In other words, it is a way of acting that causes our fundamental humanity to flourish in every situation.

However, it is also true that ethical action and contemplative action do not always go together. Think, for example, of a situation in which speaking the truth to a criminal, who is looking for someone we have hidden in our home, would lead to the death of this person. To tell the truth about his hiding place not only endangers his life but may also be the cause of the criminal creating harm or sin. From this view, telling the "truth" may be considered no more than giving our inhumanity free rein. Moreover, many actions that are viewed as ethically neutral could well be important for contemplative development, such as liturgical acts and religious practices that do not impact the well-being of others either positively or negatively. Such actions are subject to contemplative rather than ethical criteria. For this reason, many traditions have disciplines of action and speech based on precepts that have no ethical significance. We will see examples of this later.

The existence of these two different approaches, ethical and contemplative, also means that we can interpret and evaluate guidelines for action and speech in two different ways, namely in terms of their ethical value and contemplative value. We can, for example, trace the commandment not to steal to our idea of justice or to the insight that stealing intensifies our egocentric experience of reality and thus chokes our fundamental humanity. The importance that religious traditions ascribe to each of these motivations can vary to a great extent—both from tradition to tradition and within the traditions themselves. If we only employ an ethical interpretation, then judgment and condemnation, followed by guilt and self-reproach, could become the central themes. When this occurs, the educational power of the disciplines for our humaneness may be diminished, which results in the tradition having a primarily moral function; its role is reduced to being a guardian of "good morals." If, in contrast, we apply only a contemplative interpretation to actions and speech, this can lead to social alienation in that we no longer relate to the ethical norms of society.

However, for those who lead the contemplative life, the contemplative value of the guidelines for action and speech are key. This value is measured by the degree to which the guidelines promote the manifestation of our humaneness in word and deed. If we investigate the disciplines of action and speech from the viewpoint of contemplative psychology, we also approach them from the perspective that questions what their value is for the cultivation of the flourishing within and its fruit in action and speech.

The Relation to the Mental Disciplines

The contemplative approach to the disciplines of action and speech already shows that they are closely connected to the mental disciplines discussed previously. On one hand, the disciplines of action and speech serve as a kind of support for the mental disciplines. After all, our experience of reality does not develop in a vacuum but in relation to what is happening in our concrete life situation. With respect to our attitude, our life situation continually challenges us to go in either the direction of callousness and blindness or that of compassion and insight. The disciplines of action and speech give us instructions for meeting these challenges; they produce the seeds of the flourishing within.

On the other hand, we can see the disciplines of action and speech as the fruit of the flourishing within. We say, "You shall know the tree by its fruits." We can see the way in which we act and speak as a kind of test of the genuineness of our internal flourishing. Of course, if it does not bear any fruit in our action and speech, then something may be wrong. A "fruitless" internal flourishing is not possible; it is a reflection of a fantasy spirituality.

The disciplines of action and speech have something in common with the disciplines of the imagination in particular. For just as the images and representations have experiential value that can lift us up mentally, to follow guidelines also has an experiential value that influences the mind and can change our experience of reality. The situation we create through our actions and speech has an experiential value as well that either awakens our fundamental humanity or does not. And that, in turn, can have an effect on our practice of the various mental disciplines. Then these disciplines can influence our action and speech. The Catholic tradition, for example, describes the discipline of "dedicating a sacrifice," where we perform an action that we feel is difficult and imagine that the merit of this action will somehow benefit someone else we care about. In Mahayana Buddhism, a practice session is often closed with stating a wish that its merit may benefit all living beings. Thus, through dedicating any benefit or merit of good actions and speech, we reinforce in ourselves a caring attitude toward others. Within the theistic devotional way, many actions are also carried out as a sacrifice to God or with the intention that they please God. Because the disciplines of action and speech can be both the seed and the fruit of the mental disciplines, they are practiced in conjunction with them in almost all traditions.

The Function of the Disciplines of Action and Speech

In the introduction to this chapter, we touched on the function of the disciplines of action and speech. We will now investigate this function in more detail by trying to answer a question: Why do the contemplative traditions prescribe a certain way of action and speech?

As stated earlier, it is often thought that it is exclusively out of ethical considerations; in that case, it would concern becoming a morally good human being. However, the contemplative life does not, nor should it, emphasize the ethical intention exclusively. A practical insight lies at the bottom of this, namely that such a moral motivation—as the history of humankind shows—is far too weak to effect a real transformation of ourselves. Good intentions are only seldom strong enough—is the way to hell not paved with them? It is necessary that we feel connected to our own fundamental humanity, our Buddha-nature, Christ within us, or whatever name the tradition gives it and that we have the desire to cultivate. We spoke about this in chapter 5 in the context of transformation.

Within the contemplative life, the answer to the question of the why of these disciplines is inspired by the fundamental insight that has directed our inquiry—the restraint or dissolving of ego is the most effective way to cultivate our humaneness, loving-kindness, and insight. Therefore, it is not that ego should be restrained because, according to some theories, it is "bad" or ethically objectionable, but because ego chokes our humaneness. It stands in the way of the flourishing within.

The function of the disciplines of action and speech is to teach us to act and speak in such a way that ego is made visible and let go on one hand, and that our fundamental humanity is uncovered and supported by both action and speech on the other. Like we saw with the disciplines of insight, both are ways of characterizing the function of these disciplines—like two sides of the same coin.

Two Perspectives on the Function of the Disciplines

The double function of these disciplines—the exposure and restraint of ego and the discovery of our fundamental humanity—also means that we can experience the disciplines of action and speech in two ways: from the perspective of ego and from the perspective of our humaneness. We will explore these two perspectives more closely.

When we talk about the perspective of ego, we mean the point of view of the person on the Way at the moment that she is caught by an egocentric way of experiencing. Let us remind ourselves briefly what ego is and how it is manifested. We know that in contemplative psychology the term *ego* does not refer to a mental entity but to a mental activity that maintains a dualistic experience of reality. In that experience, the world of phenomena is the object of self-interest for ego and, thereby, the object of hope or fear. From this dualistic mentality, our ego psychology develops, in which greed, aggression, and indifference are the dominant forces and are considered to be normal for human beings. These forces are then manifested continually in our action and speech.

How we then experience the contemplative disciplines is also determined by this ordinary or dualistic psychology. For example, the support that the disciplines of action and speech may offer us in a given situation can be experienced as a restriction, a limitation, and sometimes even as a humiliation (seemingly hard and "inhuman"). We experience them in this way because they frustrate the self-exaltation or self-defensiveness of ego. For this reason, we can also characterize these disciplines, from the perspective of ego, as the practice of humility. The value of humility is emphasized by almost all the contemplative traditions. For example, in the Rule of Benedict, the whole contemplative development is sketched in twelve steps of humility. "Humbleness is the dwelling place of the ancestors" is a well-known saying from Vajrayana Buddhism. Here, the term *ancestors* refers to the previous practitioners—women included!—who had reached enlightenment.

In this way, the disciplines of action and speech not only remove the space for self-concern but also impact its propensity for both self-exaltation and self-denigration. That is, they frustrate ego's inclination for self-hatred—for example, our inclination to destroy ourselves through the demands for perfectionism. Therefore, we can characterize the disciplines not only in terms of being the practice of humility but also as the practice of self-acceptance, as the willingness to accept what we see in the clear mirror of our minds and to accept ourselves in friendship for who and what we are. However, this is not a conditional friendship that we can acquire and preserve only through not disappointing ourselves or by maintaining a positive self-assessment; those are the ways of ego. Rather, it is an unconditional one in which we accept ourselves with all our seemliness and unseemliness. This is the perspective of the disciplines of action and speech from ego's view.

From the second perspective, that of our humaneness, the actions and speech that the disciplines prescribe are seen as the way in which human beings conduct themselves in the state of fulfillment. "The state of fulfillment" here is the state of mind that is free from the egocentric experience of reality. What are the features of those moments when our experience of reality is free from ego and determined by our fundamental humanity? As we already stated in the introduction to this book, these are moments in which we are not preoccupied with ourselves. These egoless moments are characterized by joy in life, compassion, effective action, courage, and insight.

At those moments, we experience the disciplines of action and speech not as a limitation or as disciplines that guide our action and speech but as the natural expression in word and deed of our humaneness. All those actions that we usually think of as religious, ethical, or spiritual are now experienced as the expression of freedom. This freedom is the "spontaneity of egolessness," which is simply freedom from the impulsiveness of ego. We no longer view practicing the disciplines as a curtailment or renunciation but as a liberation and engagement. If others then judge us more often as morally highminded or good, this is a secondary issue. We will return to this idea in the last section of this chapter.

The Function of the Disciplines as Mirrors

As we can see, the disciplines of action and speech bring us into contact with the warmth and clarity of our fundamental humanity by instructing us to act and speak as if we were free of ego. At the same time, it is precisely through this kind of engagement of actions and speech that our egocentrism becomes visible to us. After all, the disciplines do away with any room for the manifestation of ego in our words and deeds. Because of this, ego continually comes up against the limitations that have been established, and in that way its forms of expression become visible to us. Ego is no longer simply another contemplative idea but has, through the practice of the disciplines, become an experiential fact that can be localized in situations. Thus, these disciplines function as a kind of mirror, which is their fundamental contemplative function. As a mirror, they show us the concrete contours of our ego, for whenever we have difficulty with disciplines of action and speech, it is because we are confronted at that moment by one of the hard walls of ego's fortification.

Our willingness to be humble and accept ourselves in those moments enables us to work with ego instead of denying it or struggling against it out of hurt pride or self-hatred. In practical terms, this means that both in following and in fighting against the guidelines that are contained in the disciplines of speech and action, the contours of ego become visible to us. In both situations, the disciplines work as a mirror. As long as we wish to travel along the Path, as long as our personal and deepest wish is to cultivate our fundamental humanity, we learn as much—and sometimes even more—from our transgressions as from closely (and piously) following the guidelines that are contained in the disciplines of action and speech.

The Relativity of the Disciplines

To a great extent, the function of the contemplative disciplines determines their form. While we have seen that the mental disciplines involve transforming our egocentric experience of reality, the disciplines of action and speech are directed at *promoting* actions, including verbal ones, that give rise to an egoless experiential value; thus, they serve to uncover our humaneness. In that way, they help us abandon actions that strongly impress on us our egocentric experience of reality. What we need to do and not to do is thus dependent on the form of ego we are each working with. This form is relative in two ways: in relation to the *phenomenon of ego* as a general mental and emotional phenomenon, and to the actual *form of ego* that every person gives it individually. The phenomenon of ego and its individual form determine two different categories of the contemplative disciplines of action and speech.

Let us first look at the disciplines whose form is determined by insight into the nature of the phenomenon of ego itself.

Ego, with its dualistic experience of reality, is a psychological phenomenon that appears in people in all cultures; it is not Western, Eastern, Southern, or Northern. It is a general, universal psychological phenomenon that we discussed in chapter 3. The disciplines of insight are perfectly suited to rendering the phenomenon of ego visible, regardless of the form it has at a certain moment, in a certain time or a certain culture. This is because the disciplines of insight are independent of the form of ego. They are universal, transcultural disciplines that can directly expose the illusion of ego in our experience of reality. Whether it is a primitive or refined ego, the disciplines of insight expose both in the same way. The form of these disciplines is determined by insight into the phenomenon of ego, so these disciplines could be called "absolute disciplines."

The disciplines of action and speech also work with the individual form or expression of ego, because the form of ego we each have can be so solid, so impenetrable, and so dominant that it is impossible for the disciplines of insight to see through it. It is so close and familiar, it is like it is actually "me." Therefore, we have to do something about the form itself to render ourselves more malleable to the introduction of alternative ways of being. For this to occur, we use not only the disciplines of the imagination but also the disciplines of action and speech. These disciplines are all relative in the sense that their form depends on the insight into our form of ego and how it is expressed. Each of us makes our own construction of ego by incorporating elements of the surrounding culture and elements from our individual history, and this is what the relative disciplines work with.

Universal and Specific Disciplines

Although the disciplines of action and speech are relative disciplines, they are nonetheless partially universal in character.

This is because the contemplative life springs from a soil that is transcultural, a soil of the experience of our humaneness that is given with our humaneness itself and with which we are in contact to a greater or lesser degree. Because this is the contemplative psychology view, we see, as we indicated in the introduction to this chapter, a great many similarities in the guidelines for behavior that the different contemplative traditions promulgate. The traditions could be said to encode the manifestation of our fundamental humanity in relation to universal forms of ego. They encode what people in all times and cultures continually discover anew as authentic human actions. In 1992, Queen Beatrix of the Netherlands, my own home country, beautifully expressed such actions as "respect for the views and feelings of others, patience, courtesy, understanding and responsibility for one another and compassion for the weak and underprivileged."[3]

In addition to the universal guidelines for embodying a contemplative view of our humaneness, there are also specific guidelines, and again, we can distinguish different kinds. First of all, each tradition has culturally bound guidelines. Their relationship to the culture consists, on one hand, in prescribing how to let go of the patterns in the local culture that confirm ego, and on the other, in identifying and incorporating the patterns in that culture that are helpful for bringing the contemplative way into a fully flourishing contemplative life. No culture is so poor that a contemplative tradition cannot integrate a few of its values, and no culture is so rich that the tradition must not correct one or more of its features. The culturally bound guidelines of the contemplative tradition thus determine how the practitioner must deal with the cultural guidelines for behavior that circumscribe the relative expression of the contemplative life. For instance, if the local culture encourages greed or ambition at the expense of helpfulness, the contemplative tradition will be alert to the fact that greed or ambition will be an influential aspect of the ego of those entering this tradition. It will direct its disciplines at that point. As Sakyong Mipham argued, if a culture or the national ego is based on distrust toward and lack of confidence in the basic goodness of human nature, the belief in the possibility of cultivating our humaneness, both personal and social, is undermined. In that case, our spiritual disciplines will need to address that attitude in word and deed.[4]

Second, there are relative disciplines that are based on specific spiritual guidelines. These disciplines work with ego on levels that are not rooted in the local culture but in the contemplative tradition itself. Here we can think of guidelines, for example, in liturgy and the form that is given to the way of life within contemplative communities. These guidelines are therefore relative to the tradition. We will give a number of examples of these in the next section.

These two forms of relative disciplines are often written down and passed on in that form. However, there is also a third category that includes relative disciplines based on individual guidelines or instructions; these are concerned with the problem of ego on the level of the individual. They are relative to each practitioner and are primarily given orally in the context of personal guidance, which we shall explore in the next chapter.

Together, all these relative guidelines determine the form of the disciplines of action and speech and thus the form of the contemplative life. The relative character of the guidelines implies that the form of the contemplative life is not, or indeed cannot be, fixed for eternity. Its form evolves with the people who practice the tradition. People are bearers of traditions, just as they are bearers of the local culture; they also have their personal histories and outlooks, their own attitudes to life. These factors partially influence the individual form and manifestation of ego. If the contemplative traditions are functioning well, they have insight into this, and their disciplines are tailored to work with it.

The Form of the Disciplines of Action and Speech

What exactly do we mean by the "form of ego"? It comprises egocentric patterns that a person has appropriated on the mental level and on the level of speech and action. The form is different for everyone and for every culture, and it primarily determines the form of the disciplines of action and speech. We will now look at the form of these disciplines in more detail using two old sources: the Rule of Benedict and the Vinaya of Buddhism, which are directed primarily to the monastic life. Of course, both Christian and Buddhist disciplines of action and speech cover a much broader area than just monastic life, but we will discuss the guidelines for monks and nuns because the psychological function of the guidelines as a mirror can be seen there most clearly.

Examples from the Rule of Benedict and the Vinaya

In the Christian tradition, the contemplative disciplines have been formulated to an important extent in Benedict's Rule, which originated in the sixth century A.D. and is the basis for the monastic contemplative life in Catholicism. The Buddhist tradition has the Vinaya, a collection of guidelines and rules that began to take shape during the life of the Buddha and were written down after his death. Although the Christian and Buddhist traditions are very different theologically, they nonetheless include similar spiritual guidelines and precepts—both universal and particular—on how to behave and speak. In fact, this similarity is the most significant in terms of clarifying the perspective of contemplative psychology. Let us look first at the Christian tradition.

In chapter four of the Rule, which carries the suggestive title "The Tools of Good Works: What Are They?" Benedict lays down the Christian version of the universal disciplines, which include but are not limited to the Ten Commandments since they include precepts for monastic commitment.[5] The discipline of action includes directives such as do not kill, do not commit adultery, do not steal, and do not do to another what you do not wish done to yourself; discipline the body, give new heart to the poor, clothe a naked person, visit a sick person, be a support in time of trouble; do not repay wrong with wrong, but suffer patiently wrongs done to you; suffer persecution for the sake of justice.

For the practice of the discipline of speech, the Rule gives a number of general precepts: do not bear false witness; comfort someone who is saddened; do not bring anger to a head; utter the truth from heart and mouth; do not criticize; do not be a detractor; guard your mouth from evil; and do not crave controversy.

These precepts have a universal character, so we find many of them in the Buddhist tradition as well. In the Buddhist sutta *The Discourse on the (Unwholesome) Causes of Karma*, they are stated in terms of refraining from the ten unwholesome deeds. The first three are directed at action: refrain from taking life, refrain from taking what has not been given, and refrain from sexual misconduct. The next four concern speech: refrain from speaking untruth, refrain from slander, refrain from sharp words, and refrain from drivel. However, the last three focus on our mental attitude but tend to appear in our actions and speech: refrain from greed, refrain from malice, and refrain from wrong ideas. These encompass the three basic emotions of ego we discussed in chapter 3; they also reflect a divergence from the Christian tradition in terms of explicitly linking mental attitudes and emotions to ethical action and speech. In Buddhism, the mental attitude or motivation is seen as the primary factor in an ethical life, since the ethical impact of actions and speech is much more dependent on the relative circumstances in which they are enacted.

In addition to these universal disciplines of action and speech, the Rule and the Vinaya contain a great number of specific disciplines that shape life in the contemplative community itself, precepts that specifically apply as Benedict described it in the "workshop," meaning monastery enclosure, "where we labor diligently at all these things."[6] There are rules governing action with respect to such practical matters as how monks should sleep: "They shall sleep singly in single beds. . . . If possible, let all sleep in one place . . ."[7] The Rule specifies whether the monks should possess any property: "Let no one presume to give or receive anything without a directive from the abbot, nor to have anything of his own, absolutely nothing, not a book, neither writing-tablets nor stylus, but nothing at all, for in fact they are not to have their bodies or desires in their own will."[8] Benedict also laid out rules concerning daily manual labor, clothing and shoes, and prayer. He also wrote instructions concerning the place and function of the abbot and the prior, and the monks' relationship to the abbot: they are to love their abbot with an upright and humble affection. In everything they are to be obedient to the abbot's orders, even if he himself acts otherwise (far be it from him to do so), keeping in mind this command from the Lord: "Do what they say but do not do what they do" (Matthew 23:3).

We find the same themes in the Buddhist Vinaya in the sections for novices (*sramaneras*) and monks (*bhikshus*). The Vinaya was originally designed for wandering mendicants but was later expanded to include rules of conduct for monks and nuns who lived in monasteries. To beg for food and teach the dharma (the doctrine) in return was an important discipline that shaped the monastic life. Therefore, the Vinaya specifies from whom and when monks or nuns might beg for food. They are not allowed, for example, to beg from one another. It spells out what they may possess: three habits at most for men and five for women; a begging bowl for food; a razor (to shave the head and eyebrows); a needle; a belt (for the habit); a water sieve (to strain the vermin from the water so they would not be killed when they drank); and a sleeping mat. There are also rules about where they may sleep: always in a different place, not with someone of the opposite sex, and so on. And, of course, the Vinaya contains rules that shape the discipline of speech, such as instructions on how, when, and to whom the dharma is to be taught; when and how to speak with one another and benefactors; and so forth.

For life in the monastic community, Benedict formulated specific rules that also shape the disciplines of speech, such as do not love much talking; listen with pleasure to the holy readings, which is for the good of our sanctification; shun pride; make peace with an opponent before sunset; do not associate with guests or speak to them at all when not given the task to do so. He naturally devoted one chapter to the discipline of silence.

The Contemplative Psychological Significance

In our age, we often view the way of life sketched in the Rule and the Vinaya with a certain skepticism, if we do not reject it outright. Nevertheless, we should examine our skepticism, particularly from a contemplative psychology perspective. We need to consider how such rules and a way of life can emerge from and nourish our fundamental humanity. For what is the core of the Rule and the Vinaya? What is their psychological significance? It is when we look at what these texts have in common that it becomes clear; both sketch a way of life that leaves no room for ego to hide or establish itself. What these texts demand is the surrender of a form of privacy in which ego can have full rein over our actions and speech. This requires the surrender of our inclination to make and keep ourselves happy above everyone else and to keep the world (and especially our fellow human beings) at a safe distance. We need to pause and consider this statement more deeply, because in many ways, the inclination toward ego has become exalted as a virtue nowadays; the individual pursuit of happiness has become "the way" of contemporary life. When we appreciate this, we may find that our skepticism toward the principles of action and speech is partly rooted in this contemporary context.

The Buddhist tradition calls the person who has literally but figuratively abandoned hearth and home an *anagarika*, "one who is homeless"; this is someone who has abandoned the struggle for privacy. This person practices being unconditionally and continually open to any situation in which he finds himself, without withdrawing physically or mentally from what the situation brings. For this person, her own well-being and the well-being of the situation have become less separate from each other. We might even say they have been united, thereby denying any room for the dualistic experience of reality of "me here" and "that there," which is the ground for ego's habit of self-preservation. At this point, caring for ourselves becomes nothing more than caring for the entire situation. It is in this way that withdrawing from the world of ego is the core of the contemplative life. In the Christian tradition, this withdrawal is called *anachorese*, which is why the first monks were called *anachoretes*. However, we do not need to withdraw to a monastery or the forest to lead a contemplative life (although we certainly may).

Monastic life, as Benedict sketched it, is permeated by the surrender of privacy. We see this theme in almost all contemplative communities. Outsiders often suspect that such communities are a refuge for ego, a hiding place from the desolate outside world, but the reality of life in a contemplative community is very different. There is extremely little room for ego in this way of life. That is why it is a fertile practice ground.

Of course, one could (and should) ask whether the disciplines of action and speech as described in the Rule and the Vinaya still fulfill their purpose today. Do they still bring about the surrender of privacy, the letting go and restraint of egocentric behavior? Do they still have the contemplative psychological function for which they were intended? To investigate this, let us look at a number of disciplines of action and speech that are also practiced in our time: staying in one place, obedience, silence, generosity, and speaking the truth.

Stabilitas Loci and Stabilitas in Congregatione

The first discipline we will explore relates to action. Many contemplative traditions contain the rule of not abandoning the monastic community or the place of retreat for shorter or longer periods (sometimes for life). If one follows this rule, it is almost always preceded by voluntarily taking a vow to keep to it. In the Christian tradition, it is known as the vow of *stabilitas loci* (remaining in one place). This place can, for example, be where one goes into solitary retreat. The practitioner then vows not to leave this place before he has completed a specific spiritual practice or attained a certain realization. This approach can be found in the Hindu tradition: the yogi draws a certain line around her place of retreat and vows not to step outside it until she has completed a certain practice (*sadhana*), until she has reached enlightenment, or until death has reached her. A well-known example of this in the Buddhist tradition is obviously that of the Buddha himself, who finally sat down under the bodhi tree and vowed not to leave that spot until he had reached enlightenment. If the place is a contemplative community (*congregatio*), the term *stabilitas in congregatione* is also used.[9] One then vows to remain in the monastery.

Why do people do this? What is the function of such a discipline? The vow to stay in one place can be understood as the physical counterpart of the mental stability described in chapter 6. The contemplative psychological function of this physical stabilitas and of the adherent vow is that we let go of the idea that we have an alternative, we give up the possibility of withdrawing. As we know, one of the characteristic aspects of ego is that it always wants to have alternatives available: ego reflects a mentality that always wants to keep an exit open and therefore can never come to complete surrender and acceptance. Through the vow of stabilitas loci, we confront and surrender an important part of that mentality. We say, "This is my place, my situation, and that is what I want to work with, however it develops, for better or for worse." In a monastic community, we have not chosen our fellow monastics, and they offer us all aspects of human company—the nice and the irritating—and the willingness to work with that is expressed in such a vow. Something similar applies to the situation of individual retreat where we are alone with the movement of our minds and our mental discipline. The mind offers us all kinds of unpredictable aspects that we also did not and cannot choose: moments of restlessness, desire, joy and sorrow, confusion and clarity; moments that sometimes seem to incite us to abandon the retreat. Our vow then entails that we are prepared to work with such moments on the spot. When we enact the vow at these moments, it appears that our situation and minds are much easier to handle than we thought, precisely because we have made the vow not to evade them. This is interesting because the limitation that this discipline imposes on ego proves to have another element: a flourishing of self-confidence and strength of mind that enables us to be in the situation we are without any reservations. The experience of those who practice this discipline teaches us that it can bear these fruits. What may seem claustrophobic or restrictive actually turns into vast and hospitable space.

Obedience

How do matters stand with the discipline of obedience, which is so characteristic of monastic life? Obedience can function as a mirror that makes the willfulness of ego visible. Within a monastic community, or when we take a vow as laypeople, we have to practice a certain mental flexibility. The flexibility of going along with the demands of our situation and learning to recognize our egocentric impulses and let them go. In its complete form, this flexibility is an unconditional obedience to the precepts or vows we have taken. This does not mean we have to put up with everything and continually do what others tell us, but that we develop the ability to be obedient in all circumstances to that which can make our entire situation flourish instead of to that which will feed our ego or meet its presumed needs. That is the key point of the discipline of obedience.

Of course, unconditional obedience seems to be asking a great deal, but we must see this discipline as a way through the problem of obedience that ego raises. What happens if we are skillfully deprived of the room to follow our egocentric impulses? From the perspective of contemplative psychology, our joy in life regains its original suppleness and spontaneity when it is liberated from the captivity of our compulsiveness and impulsiveness. The apparently harsh discipline of obedience then proves to have a much different side, a side that has nothing to do with the subjection of the will of one person to another, even though it might look that way on the outside. On the contrary, obedience subjects ego to egolessness. This means the creation of freedom, even though from ego's perspective this is not readily apparent and may initially feel like imprisonment.

In the theistic traditions, the discipline of obedience is often formulated in terms of obedience to God. We see this, for example, in Islam and Christianity. Obedience to the tradition's rules leads to the discovery of a deeper, underlying internal obedience: obedience to the voice of God within us. In the Buddhist tradition, we discover an internal obedience to our Buddha-nature. In contemplative psychological terms, we can describe this as being obedient to our humaneness. The instructions for action and speech are a means for rediscovering our true humaneness and making it the basis for our behavior.

We can thus distinguish between two forms of obedience: an external form that is anchored in following rules formulated in language and concepts, and an internal form that is not fixed in concepts but is anchored in our humaneness and its expression in word and deed.

Silence

It is also characteristic of the monastic disciplines of speech that the curbing of ego and the unlocking of egolessness are simultaneous. We can see this, for example, in the well-known discipline of silence. This discipline is widespread in the contemplative traditions and functions to restrict the possibility of and need for manipulating our situation by means of language for the sake of establishing a particular image or impression of ourselves in others. The function of this discipline as a mirror is to make our need for this language visible. The interesting part of the practice of this discipline is that through silence our relationship both to our fellow practitioners and to ourselves begins to part ways from the fixed ideas and stories that we have been accustomed to draping over ourselves and our past. We are forced to stay a certain distance from those familiar and habitual stories we have in our dealings with our fellow human beings. Silence actually forces us to rid ourselves of them, and when room for a nonverbal form of communication arises, we become acquainted with ourselves and others in a very immediate, perceptual way simply by experiencing one another. In the words of the Dutch poet Judith Herzberg: "We know each other for we have been silent together."

When we first begin with the discipline of silence, we often feel somewhat shut in and unsure. We cannot ask those who are practicing with us, "Who are you? Where do you come from? What did you do before you came here?" Neither can we introduce ourselves to others in any way. We cannot pass on our inner agenda in which we have written down who or what we are. Therefore, we have no status in this situation, insofar as we derive it from our previous history. There is no longer any room for this. We can only see the others and pick up on the "sphere" that hangs about them. It is a conceptually naked situation, which at first is often experienced as oppressive. However, as we begin to rest more and more in the discipline of silence, it proves to have its own space. It turns out to be pleasant, and it can be a relief that we no longer have to constantly sell our ourselves and our self-image. This can make our life situation spacious, clean, and pure. The discipline of silence thus proves to be very effective in making us conscious of the contours of our ego as they are manifested in communication with others. It then appears that we may no longer have to hold on to our ego, or self-image, in such a forced way, nor do we need to display it. Because we have been able to see ourselves clearly, we discover that such an image is no longer necessary.

Generosity

Many disciplines are practiced in both the monastic community and ordinary life. In both cases, however, their function is the same. An example of this in the area of action is the discipline of generosity. This discipline forces us to abandon the pursuit of self-interest. Its importance is also strongly emphasized by all contemplative traditions. In the practice of generosity, we go against our own inclination to hold on to what we think is necessary for ourselves in terms of time and possessions.

We are not talking about giving a bunch of flowers on special occasions, but about giving something that has real consequences for our own way of life: giving in a measure large enough to challenge us to let go unambiguously of our sense of self-preservation. That sense, which belongs to our dualistic experience of reality, is a source of fear, and when we go through this fear in the act of giving, we notice that there is life outside the fear. We experience this as a liberation and at the same time as the discovery of a fundamental, unconditional wealth: the whole world is given to us as wealth. This does not mean we have to give everything away. From the point of view of contemplative psychology, generosity is not a moral duty but a practical matter; we can use the discipline of generosity to become acquainted with and to let go of our egocentric mentality, which is manifested in a convulsive guarding of our own interests. The intention of this discipline is to help us to (re)discover the fundamental wealth of the world and develop an appreciation for it. Generosity is the ultimate wealth.

Speaking the Truth

Another example of a contemplative discipline of speech that is not specifically bound to a monastic context and is still found in almost all traditions is the discipline of speaking the truth. This discipline removes the space where ego can protect or exalt itself through smaller and bigger lies or half-truths of whatever kind. A little bragging, advertising ourselves, belittling others, concealing our shortcomings, awkwardness, or mistakes—this discipline deprives us of the room to do that. Therefore, it also functions as a mirror for the manifestation of ego in speech. Again, however difficult the practice of this discipline might be, it leads to a form of peace and self-acceptance, to the understanding that we may be as we are with all our shortcomings and mistakes. We do not have to conceal them but can use them; we can let loose the disciplines that are necessary for rising above them and thus advance along the Way. This is crucial, for as long as we hide our shortcomings out of shame or pride, we cut ourselves off from the Way, and our guide cannot help us. Again, from the point of view of contemplative psychology, speaking the truth is not looked on as a moral obligation; rather, it is a means for making progress on the Path. It is fine not to speak the truth if that prevents suffering for others or saves a human life.

These examples of the disciplines of action and speech show how closely they are associated with the practical issues of living. Each discipline has its own target area within which our egocentric mentality can dominate our ways of acting and speaking. It makes this self-serving mentality visible and helps us to let go of it. Each of these disciplines work as a mirror, whereas the use of the mirror is itself the wisdom and manifestation of our fundamental humanity.

The Application of the Disciplines of Action and Speech

How are the disciplines of action and speech applied and when? Can or must all disciplines that the tradition contains be applied at the same time? Or does the practitioner take them up gradually?

The contemplative traditions do not give only one answer to these questions. On one hand, the answer depends on the power of our motivation for wanting to liberate ourselves from our egocentric experience of reality and to cultivate our fundamental humanity. On the other, it depends on our level of insight into the form of our ego and the function of the contemplative disciplines. Finally, the power with which we cling to ego also plays a role. If we have little insight and little motivation, we cannot bring ourselves to take up a contemplative discipline consistently or with much effectiveness. If we have little insight but a great deal of motivation, we are capable of making progress on the Way. Conversely, if we have a lot of insight, we can also progress along the Way with a small amount of motivation. If we have both, we can progress more quickly. To a certain extent, insight can compensate for motivation and vice versa.

This can be explained with an example we have already used. Some people are capable of giving up a bad habit, such as smoking, as soon as they hear it is harmful to themselves and those around them. With others, insight does not dawn on them by hearing but by feeling. Only when they begin to experience the consequences personally does insight dawn and they become motivated to give up the bad habit. They are then ready to impose a discipline on themselves that gradually frees them from this habit. Many of those who live the contemplative life have approached the matter in this way.

It is also possible that our life situation works for us: in that case, our daily circumstances do not allow us any choice but to let go of our egocentric experience of reality either entirely or partially. For the possibility of letting go to occur, we need to experience that holding on to ego is too painful or obviously foolish. Often our life situation forces us into a contemplative discipline without our being conscious of it.

What all of this amounts to is that the measure in which one should take up the contemplative disciplines is different for everybody, and the choice for a specific form of the contemplative life—the monastic or so-called lay life—is also different for everyone. A nice illustration of this is a classification found in Tibetan Buddhism. Here, three kinds of practitioners are distinguished: those with the highest capacity, those with medium capacity, and those with the lowest capacity. A famous text from the sixteenth century, written by the Mahamudra master Karma Chagmey, characterizes the three as follows:

> The person of the highest capacity does not need to
>   renounce worldly actions,
> But can practice while mixing mundane actions with
>   the practice.

This partaking of sense pleasures as the Path, without
   abandoning them,
Is the example of King Indrabodhi.
The person of medium capacity abandons most
   worldly actions.
He practices while keeping the behavior of a monk.
Trying to acquire food, drink, and clothing
Is the life-style of most learned and accomplished
   masters of India and Tibet.
The person of lowest capacity cannot fulfill his aims
   while keeping two frames of mind.
He is unable to engage in both Dharmic and mundane
   pursuits,
And practices having to cast away concerns for the
   food and clothing of this life.
This is the life-style of such masters as Milarepa and
   Gotsangpa.[10]

It is interesting that Milarepa, the poet-yogi who lived as
a hermit and did nothing but contemplative practices, without worrying about food or clothes, is celebrated as one of
the greatest saints. At the same time, people like Milarepa,
who spent all their lives and energy in liberating themselves
from the illusion of ego, are called practitioners of the lowest
capacity. Why? Because Milarepa's ego fixations were strong
and unyielding, yet he was greatly motivated to free himself
from them. He devoted his whole life to this, and it is in that
that his greatness lies.

King Indrabodhi did not have such a difficult and deep-
seated ego. The following saying applies to him: "Small
potatoes boil quickly." Under the guidance of his guru, he
continued to live in his palace and take care of his subjects.
Milarepa's guru, Marpa, was not a monk but a gentleman
farmer, a good businessman, and learned in the dharma and

many languages. He had a wife and children. He loved to drink beer and was hot-tempered. Like King Indrabodhi, he was of the highest capacity because he was capable of using his worldly life situation to cultivate total open-mindedness and unconditional compassion.

Between the contemplative life of the hermit Milarepa and the contemplative life in the world lies the contemplative life of the person of medium capacity. To make progress on the Way, such people need to simplify their lives down to the basic necessities; to this end, they withdraw from worldly life and often live (part of) their lives as monks or nuns.

Which contemplative way of life is suitable for us, which contemplative disciplines could be beneficial for us, and when, are practical questions rather than ideological ones. Our self-insight and—if that is missing—our mentor's insight into us, our motivation, and the circumstances of our lives are the determining factors. We will return to this in the last chapter.

The Practice of the Disciplines of Action and Speech

Let us see, finally, if there are certain stages of development to be detected in the way practitioners discipline their actions and speech. Many traditions offer their disciplines of action and speech in a certain succession that seems to be guided by insight into the development process undergone by the practitioner. As we have seen, the emphasis in many traditions lies primarily on disciplines that curb the manifestation of ego in word and deed. The freedom of acting out of ego is shackled. Just as the disciplines of mindfulness are primarily concerned with taming the mind, here the concern is primarily to tame egocentric behavior. It is because of this that instructions for the disciplining of action and speech chiefly have initially the character of prohibition—they advise against certain behavior—do not do this and do not do that.

Again, it is tempting to give an ethical interpretation of these prohibitions—for they are often ethical—but from the viewpoint of contemplative psychology, the issue is not to be a good person. Rather, it is to make our egocentric blindness and emotionality visible by having them run up against the limitations imposed by the disciplines. The function of these disciplines as a mirror is and remains central here. At the same time, we are deprived of the possibility of engraving our egocentric patterns of behavior even deeper. We plane ego down, knowingly if not willingly. That leads to what Meister Eckhart called *Gelassenheit*, a "detachment" that contains an element of freedom—we do not, like the idiots we have been, need to follow the impulsiveness of ego any longer.

By curbing ego in this way, a certain room for further disciplines that are directed at the cultivation of egoless action and speech comes into being. Our humaneness flourishes to the degree that our preoccupation with ego lessens. We begin to experience our humaneness more consciously and become inspired to cultivate it by bringing into play disciplines that take our experience of our fundamental humanity as their starting point. The disciplines of action and speech therefore begin to have more of the character of positive recommendations. They positively advise certain actions. The discipline of generosity that we discussed earlier is an example of this. That discipline entails the positive action of giving, which goes a step further than just refraining from being stingy. More generally, we can appreciate how these disciplines contain instructions about how we can cause our environment to flourish.

Of course, the one phase does not follow the other in strict succession. It is more a question of shifting emphasis: the disciplines are directed first at acquiring insight into and refraining from egocentric behavior. After that, we add the disciplines that are directed at conducting ourselves in the world on the basis of this tamer state of affairs: we gain

practice in the doing of "good works." For without first taming our egocentricity to some extent, our ability to do good in
the world is limited. We continually run up against the borders of our ego, while not yet having developed the flexibility
to open these borders or at least to thrust them back. When
still at this stage, observing or not observing the commands
easily becomes a source of self-exaltation or self-reproach, of
honor and blame—in short, of internal, if not external, strife.
"Do well without expecting thanks" is still a utopia for us.
We then distance ourselves even further from the cultivation
of our humaneness and the chance is great that we are not
inspired but exhausted by our service to others; we may end
up with "compassion burnout." We are vulnerable to losing
the courage and faith that the cultivation of our humaneness is
even possible. However, whenever we mature in both phases,
then the prohibitions and recommendations lose their limiting
character. The practitioner, as Benedict said,

> will begin to keep everything which hitherto he
> used to observe not without fear, no longer now by
> fear of hell but by the love of Christ, and the good
> habit itself, and the delight of virtues.[11]

Finally, in this change of attitude lies still another, third
stage of development. The more we become established in the
practice of the disciplines of action and speech, the more they
awaken the openness of the spirit from which the prohibitions
and commands originally came. We discover that we can live
in that state of mind and begin to trust it. The possibility of
acting and speaking on that basis begins to open directly for
us. This stage changes the character of our practice of the
disciplines in an essential way. The focus of the practice now
shifts from an external discipline of following the prohibitions
and recommendations to the internal discipline of remaining
in this open state of mind *while* acting and speaking. The

discipline takes the form of making this egoless state of mind a starting point for all our actions.

At the beginning of this third phase, it is as if we are once again babies, as if we need to learn anew how to walk and speak. Here, "as if" is not putting it too mildly. We must indeed learn to act and speak again—to act and speak out of the open state of mind, to learn to act and speak not out of ego but directly from of our fundamental humanity. At first, we have little experience in this; we have to practice, and it is at this that the disciplines of action and speech are directed in the third phase. This may even seem to be a precarious affair. For letting go mentally of the security offered by the prohibitions and commands, and resting instead in the state of intelligent gentleness and care for others and being guided by this, gives us little certainty. We are now on our own, and the only thing we have is our fundamental humanity.

Because we have barely learned to trust our humaneness, and because this final phase of the disciplines of action and speech is about acting out of this humaneness, the third phase is often initially joined with an immense feeling of uncertainty and risk-taking. For our connection with our own fundamental humanity is, as we have (re)discovered it in ourselves, like a young plant. Nevertheless, this young plant grows only when we give it room and expose it to our concrete life situation, with no guarantee that it will survive. Of course, it is not that the behavior that has been modeled by the prohibitions and commands, by dos and don'ts, has now disappeared. Rather, we are no longer guided by them; our behavior is now prompted by our fundamental humanity and not by the ethics of duty. All our action becomes contemplative action.[12]

All the contemplative traditions agree that this is the most advanced, difficult, and risky form of the disciplines of action and speech. It is risky because the disciplines are no longer limited or contained by the safety ropes of the guidelines. It is also extremely difficult not only because the practice now becomes continuous, twenty-four hours a day, but because in this phase, we must sustain the practice of not withdrawing into ourselves under any circumstances. This means being continually available to our environment—to our fellow human beings, to the situation that presents itself—and doing so without hesitation is what causes the situation to flourish. This is the discipline of action and speech that lies beyond (or should we say, below?) guidelines and was stated by Augustine as *Ama et fac quod vis*, meaning "Love and do as you wish."

Mahayana Buddhism speaks here of the practice of unconditional compassion. This is no small task. We cannot bring this about because we have decided to do so on the basis of all kinds of moral considerations. We can only do it because we have learned that this practice causes the natural, nondualistic state of our fundamental humanity, which we have discovered by means of earlier disciplines, to flourish even more. In this state of openness, we and our environment are no longer two different things that have to manage to coexist; our separateness has melted into one whole.

In Vajrayana Buddhism, the practitioner who has completed this deepest discipline of action and speech is called a *siddha*. A siddha speaks and acts out of "crazy wisdom," that is, out of a wisdom that is united with a completely uncompromising and unconditional compassion with respect to ego. This wisdom is free from every hesitation to subdue what must be subdued, to destroy what must be destroyed, and to care for what needs care, as it is traditionally stated. From the perspective of ego, the manifestation of this way of acting and speaking is completely unpredictable and incomprehensible—crazy or wild, not tamed by ego's perspective. It works outside the logic of ego. The most well-known siddha in this tradition is Padmasambhava, who, as the embodiment of crazy wisdom, is called Dorje Trolö. He is most often depicted as riding on a pregnant tigress, who represents this uncompromising compassion:

The symbolism of the tiger is also interesting. It is connected with the idea of flame, with fire and smoke. And a pregnant tigress is supposed to be the most vicious of all tigers. She is hungry, slightly crazy, completely illogical. You cannot read her psychology and work with reasonably. She is quite likely to eat you up at any time. That is the nature of Dorje Trolö's transport, his vehicle. The crazy-wisdom guru rides on dangerous energy, impregnated with all kinds of possibilities. This tiger could be said to represent skillful means, crazy skillful means. And Dorje Trolö, who is crazy wisdom, rides on it. They make an excellent couple.[13]

What this ultimate form of practice adds to the previous ones is our potential to grow beyond the idea that spiritual success is guaranteed if we only follow the guidelines closely and piously. This is, as Taoism most emphatically stresses, not the Way. Because all actions can, in principle, be contemplative actions, the opposite is also true: actions that are prescribed in the disciplines can also become unskillful actions. There is no guarantee that the rule-based practice of the disciplines of action and speech will have the intended effect. The decisive factor is not that we perform these actions but that we perform them with insight into their contemplative function and with the right motivation, the motivation to let go of ego and manifest our humaneness. That is why Meister Eckhart said,

We ought not to think of building holiness upon action; we ought to build upon a way of being, for it is not what we do that makes us holy, but we ought to make holy what we do. However holy the works may be, they do not, as works, make us at all holy; but, as we are holy and have being, to that extent we make all our works holy, be it eating, sleeping, keeping vigil or whatever it may be. It does not matter what men may do whose being is mean; nothing will come of it. Take good heed: We ought to do everything we can to be good.[14]

10

Development and Guidance

In chapter 5, we explored the psychological nature of transformation and the moments of open-mindedness that not only help us break through our usual egocentric experience of reality but also make it visible. In the intervening chapters, we have discussed the disciplines that are designed to cultivate those moments.

We have seen that there are many kinds of contemplative disciplines; the question now arises as to when and to what degree they can be applied so as to bring results, bearing in mind that this is a different matter for each individual. These are practical questions that require us to immerse ourselves in the theme of contemplative development and guidance. Every tradition gives its own name to those who offer personal guidance. The Christian tradition has its *abbas* (pastors) and *magisters* (elders). The Jewish tradition has its rabbis and its *maggidim*; Islam has its *oelama* (scholars). Hinduism has its gurus. Theravada Buddhism has its *staviras* (elders) and Mahayana Buddhism its *kalyanamitra* (spiritual friend). Vajrayana Buddhism uses the term *guru* as well. Throughout this chapter, we will use the universal term *mentor*, which harks back to the Latin word *mens*, meaning "mind." A mentor is thus someone who minds our business, someone who is concerned with our mental growth.

Although each tradition has mentors, the position they hold does vary from tradition to tradition because of the role ascribed to the mentor. In some theistic traditions, God is regarded as the original—if not the only—mentor. In contrast, a nontheistic tradition would naturally regard the human mentor as the one who can render the contemplative way concretely accessible. Practical concerns also determine the position of the mentor—for example, are there (still) good mentors available? What view does the local culture have of what it is to be a mentor?

The bond that ideally exists between mentor and practitioner is also viewed in different ways. Many traditions strongly emphasize the value of a *personal* bond. We see this, for example, in the Jewish (Hasidic) tradition, as well as in Hinduism and Buddhism. Of course, it is not necessary to be constantly by the mentor's side; the quality (for example, of openness) of the contact is more decisive than its duration. On the basis of this personal bond, the mentor is someone who knows us (and our ego) well and can therefore instruct us personally. Although instructions are often given verbally, they are also relayed through the mentor's exemplification of a way of being in that personal contact. The latter is often more important than formal instruction. For example, in the Jewish tradition, Rabbi Loeb made the following statement about his *maggid* (master): "I did not search out the maggid to get instructions from him, but to see how he tied and untied the shoelaces of his felt shoes."[1] In monastic Christianity and Sufism from the Islam tradition, the mentor occupies a very personal place. There are also schools within these traditions in which the mentor has a somewhat more distant position and where the emphasis is not so much on individual guidance as on general instruction in the doctrine. Christianity has its theologians; Islam has its mullahs; Hinduism and Buddhism have their pandits.

Whatever the case, some form of spiritual guidance along the Way can always be found in the contemplative traditions. The goal of guidance across contemplative traditions is also the same: the task of the mentor is to aid the practitioner in avoiding obstacles along the Path wherever possible. That is, each tradition has an expressed understanding that where there is growth, there can also be stagnation or lopsided growth; where there is growth, there is also the chance that development will be hindered. There are many aspects related to the obstacles to contemplative growth, and most spiritual traditions have access to an extensive contemplative psychological knowledge about the kinds of obstacles that can arise, as well as how the disciplines can help overcome them. Whereas some of this knowledge is committed to writing, for the most part, it is passed on orally in the contact between mentor and practitioner.

In the Buddhist traditions, we find an extensive discussion about the teacher or mentor, including how to assess the qualities of a teacher and his role on the spiritual path. As a nontheistic tradition, we also find a more explicit articulation of how the nature of that relationship is founded in our basic humaneness. It is both the basis and purpose of the relationship to nurture the flourishing of basic humaneness in the practitioner. Therefore, we will rely on Buddhism here to explore the role of the student-mentor relationship in relation to contemplative psychology; as a result, the themes explored will be relevant to varying degrees to the student-mentor relationship in other contemplative traditions. We will direct our exploration to two general themes: the nature and development of the relationship of trust between mentor and student, and the way in which the mentor can help the student in dealing with obstacles along the Way.

The Relationship of Trust between the Mentor and the Student

The mentor's most important task is to provide instructions to the student that are tailored to her needs and in a way that she will be able to understand and implement. This raises questions about both the practitioner and the mentor. Is the practitioner prepared to follow instructions? Under all circumstances? Is the mentor trustworthy and reliable? Usually we accept personal instructions only from those we trust; trust is not something that can be decided on a good day (or perhaps even a bad one)—it is something that must be nurtured over time. Let us look at three quotations from Chokyi Nyima, a contemporary Buddhist teacher, that concern the conditions necessary for the development of the relationship between mentor and practitioner. He addresses a number of universal themes.

Three Quotes

The first quote emphasizes the importance of mutual examination for the growth of a true bond of trust:

> Traditionally, it is said that the student should examine the teacher, and the teacher should examine the student. If a disciple fails to examine his [sic] teacher well and follows a wrong teacher, it will kill the life-force for liberation. Like blindly jumping off a precipice while holding someone else's hand, it is detrimental. If the teacher fails to examine the student well, and if the student is someone who will turn against him later on, this is the same as eating poison. Therefore, before entering a close relationship, it is extremely important that the teacher and the student both examine each other carefully.
>
> After finding that they can trust each other, the student should be very constant, and practice the teachings that he has been given with trust and confidence.[2]

The second quote concerns the possibility of judging the teacher's outward behavior and frame of mind:

Of these, the frame of mind is the important aspect, though it is invisible. Although we can see how people behave, we cannot judge from this alone. Some Chinese ministers for example are experts in behaving nicely even in the face of the enemy. They will shake hands, joke, laugh and so forth, but we never know exactly what they keep inside their minds. On the other hand, some practitioners or masters reach a certain level of realization and their outward behavior begins to change and sometimes becomes a little strange. Their actions don't really fit a normal human being's way of behaving. Sometimes it doesn't even fit a Dharmic [spiritual] way of behaving. This may cause someone to wonder, "What is going on?" This sometimes slips out of one's mouth.

That's how it is. It is best to think, "Whatever he does is excellent, whatever he does is perfect," and to mingle one's mind with his. This attitude is very important, but difficult for a beginner. If one sees one's teacher doing something completely strange, then it is better to think, "This is beyond me, I don't understand," and not try to judge or evaluate his actions, but to leave the thought aside. One should not consider or judge him as one might an ordinary human being.[3]

The third quote concerns the development of the student's relationship with the teacher:

A traditional teaching says that the master should first be a real person, a human being. Next, your teacher can be a book. Finally the master should be one's own mind. In order to have a book as a master, you must first have received personal instructions on how to practice according to the text from a truly

qualified living master. Having heard these instructions, since staying continually near to a great teacher
may not always be possible, you should take the oral
instructions to heart and practice in solitude, using
the text as a guideline. As you gradually become more
experienced, you can follow along with the text trying to correct your own mistakes. Finally, the master
will be your own mind, the naked awareness itself.[4]

Unconditional Trust

No one will disagree with the content of the first quote in
terms of the need for the mentor and the student to get to
know each other; this is relatively straightforward. Simply,
the emphasis here is that trust can only come about by getting
to know each other well. This situation is comparable, say, to
that of an experienced mountain climber who begins a climb
with a trainee. The two are connected by a rope, and a necessary first condition for them to climb successfully together
is that they know and trust each other's ability enough to
begin. When this condition is satisfied, the risk of the climb
is decreased, and the trainee is in a position to learn from the
experienced climber.

In the second quote, however, much more sensitive themes
are brought to the fore. First of all, it states that such getting
to know each other is not a simple matter—especially for the
student. In this case, the student needs to have developed a
certain degree of discernment in order to be able to recognize
whether or not his ego is the primary adviser in this inquiry
as to whether to trust a particular mentor. If so, there might
arise all kinds of negative or critical appraisals of the mentor
that serve to keep the student at a distance from the mentor. However, this quote introduces yet another aspect that
makes such an inquiry even more risky and uncertain: the
external behavior of the mentor is not the most important

criterion. The student's examination should focus more on the teacher's mental attitude of the teacher than on his external behavior. This quote touches on a central point of the contemplative life with respect to the position of the teacher. In Christianity, for example, the question is, can we still trust Jesus if he violates the Sabbath by plucking grain (Luke 6:1–5) or by healing someone (Luke 6:6–11 and 13:10–17), to say nothing of his starting a fight in the synagogue (John 2:13–25)? Should everything the mentor does be "good" by definition? And by whose definition? How do we engender unconditional trust when some of the mentor's actions seem to defy even social conventions? Can we continue to judge the mentor according to our usual standards? Or should we look at him against some idealized "spiritual" conventions we project onto mentors?

Of course, we may often think that it is only in our day and age that we have become painfully aware of the risks involved in trusting a spiritual mentor. However, this theme is present in all great contemplative traditions and in all eras. The Jews were very much aware of this in Jesus's time. There is a passage in the Buddhist songbook of the Karma Kagyu lineage in which the Indian guru Naropa speaks of this with his student Marpa before the latter returns to Tibet for good to resume his own work as a mentor:

> In the view of some impure ordinary men, you will appear to gratify yourself in this life with sense pleasures. Your desires will seem unchanging, like carrying a rock, so solid and so great. On the other hand, since you yourself have seen *dharmata* [things as they are], *samsara* [the egocentric experience of reality] will be self-liberated, like a snake uncoiling. All the future students of the lineage will be like the children of lions and garudas and each generation will be better than the last.[5]

Naropa thus has great trust in his student, in spite of the expected reactions of the ordinary person. However, to enter a student-mentor relationship, we are confronted with a genuine dilemma. On one hand, we cannot necessarily judge the mentor by conventional standards only, and on the other hand, blind trust should not be a realistic basis for one's relationship with a mentor either.

The Fear of Trusting the Mentor

Can we gain a better view of this dilemma from the perspective of contemplative psychology? Our dilemma arises because behavior can be interpreted in two ways: socially and contemplatively. In the social interpretation of human relationships and behavior, for example, self-interest and power play important roles. In fact, our interpretation of actions is often based on the use of behavioral criteria to determine if there is evidence of abuse of power and unbridled self-interest that negatively impacts one party or unfairly rewards another. From the social interpretation, self-interest and power should ideally be divided fairly among people. If we were to judge the mentor-student relationship solely from this view, self-interest and power would be interpreted as skewed toward the mentor. In fact, if we are accustomed to viewing human actions constantly and exclusively from this social perspective, then the notion of unconditional trust is unimaginable to us. How can (and even why should) one person submit unconditionally to the power of another? If we see the specter of a dictator or a cult leader in this kind of relationship, then our fear and hesitation regarding unconditional trust seems justified. However, there is also the danger that we absolutize this fear, so that it acquires the character of being unconditional: we believe that this fear and distrust is justified always and everywhere. If this occurs, we then live under the dictatorship of our distrust.

To help us navigate this situation from a contemplative perspective, let us consider the example of the practice of the discipline of silence. This is not a social measure motivated in terms of silencing people or stripping them of their right to speak up. Rather, the discipline of silence requires a contemplative interpretation in relation to its function and practice. In the same way, we could say that the relationship between practitioner and mentor is not just social either; rather, it is also contemplative. When we interpret this relationship as only social, we are in danger of missing its contemplative function. We may no longer be open to seeing the mentor's action for what it is: contemplative action. This does not mean we should ignore the social or ethical aspects of such relationships; however, remaining open to the contemplative function of the student-mentor relationship means that sometimes the behavior of the mentor can be difficult for us to understand. This can result in the dilemma being real to us at those times when we are forced to choose what we find more important in terms of interpretation. Do we follow our own moral and political ideas, or our thinking in terms of interest, power, or good manners? Or are we able to maintain an open relationship to the mentor, one that is not limited by our own familiar ideas?

From the contemplative psychology perspective, although care or compassion will (and should) manifest in the form of resistance to the abuse of power and unbridled self-interest, these qualities themselves are not bound to ideologies or political principles but spring from a soil that is separate from them; they precede ideology because they originate from the experience of our fundamental humanity. If we understand this, then it is not our ideas but the experience of our fundamental humanity that forms the basis of our relationship with the mentor. It is the foundation on which a genuine mentor stands and also the perspective from which she should guide us. This fundamental humanity is the source of any true human relationship, the principle on which all guidance is based and to which all guidance is directed—in this case, directed to enhance its flourishing within the student.

This turns the question around: Do we dare to trust and submit ourselves to humaneness? When we ask ourselves this question, we may find that the issue of trust often lies even deeper than we thought. This question may cause us to become aware that trust itself is a major problem for us. That is, when we lose contact with our own humaneness, we become estranged from trusting ourselves from this fundamental perspective. When this happens, we may struggle to trust the perspective of fundamental humanity as the foundation for the student-mentor relationship. If this is the case, we need to be aware of it. Our political and moral interpretations could simply be attempts to gloss over this problem, leading us to use political notions such as self-determination and independence—which are valuable in their own right—to avoid the contemplative meaning of trust in the mentor's action. When this occurs, we may experience the contemplative function as too threatening; our egocentric mentality, which strives for safety and security, may not want to enter a relationship with a mentor at all, and certainly not a competent one.

Blind Trust

Of course, the reverse can also happen—namely, that we gladly surrender to the mentor in order to rid ourselves of the responsibility for our own lives. Obviously, this attitude is not based on open-mindedness but on fear of life. Maybe we think that transferring the responsibility for our lives to our mentor is a convenient, if not clever, maneuver that enables us to sail through our existence. We could fool ourselves into believing that this is actually what the mentor asks of us. Did he not ask for unconditional trust? We may even be somewhat proud that we are able to offer such trust so easily and willingly.

This strategy, which is often paired with a form of hero worship that we will talk more about in the last section, seems unconditional, but it is actually blind. It is dependent on a certain presupposition: "The mentor knows what is good for me; he is infallible. I must try to follow his commands." Everything that we undergo in our dealings with the mentor is no longer approached openly but on the basis of this presupposition. Whatever the mentor does or says is always met by a positive judgment. Nothing is too great to stand in the way of such a judgment, for much depends on it: our chosen dependence, our buttress, our certainty. This approach, called *transference* in psychotherapy, is a strategic maneuver for the ego. In order to avoid the uncertainty of open contact with the mentor, we choose *in advance* to view this relationship as akin to a master-slave relationship and conform to it as such. The mentor has not asked for this, but we have. Such an approach is blind because it encloses us in our own interpretations and hinders our growth, which conversely requires openness and genuine trust. Moreover, if mentors are not strong, they may even fall prey to the power of the blind trust students offer them. They fall prey to what is called *countertransference*, meaning they may enjoy being trusted so "unconditionally" instead of cutting through it. They might congratulate themselves with having such wonderful students. However, nothing truly happens.

The Awakening of Unconditional Trust

One of the contemplative functions of a true or genuine mentor is to make us aware of political maneuvers that are based on either blind fear of trusting or on blind trust. For that purpose, the mentor plays an important role in creating the kind of psychological space where we are not caught up by our positive or negative judgments about her. This includes creating a bigger container in which relationships can be viewed beyond the terms of interest and power. In fact, it is in this open space that our discernment or discriminating awareness can begin to grow and function. When discernment functions freely and clearly, it can lead to unconditional trust in the contemplative sense. It is this trust, which is no longer based on opinions or judgments, that Nyima's second quote addresses. How does the mentor create this kind of psychological space? By means of contemplative actions, not only in the form of giving personal instruction but also by creating situations in which we observe that our strategic interpretations have no sense or meaning. This is how the mentor shows loving care toward us.

In contrast, a nonauthentic teacher takes advantage of our preconceived ideas and is careful to avoid shocking us. For example, such a mentor may always be friendly, caring, and predictable. In the Christian tradition, we could say that he does not use a whip in the synagogue like Jesus did. From the Buddhist tradition, he does not behave in a radical way against the pandits (the Buddhist philosophers) as did Padmasambhava, the great Indian yogi, who converted Tibet to Buddhism. Nonauthentic teachers may present themselves as a visible support and anchor, as a fixed point of certainty. However, in reality, these presentations are merely ideal allies for ego. Such a teacher is engaged in manipulation more than in contemplative actions. Instead of uncovering our humaneness and awakening it, she meets ego and nourishes it by means of social ideologies of power and interest.

In short, if the mentor is authentic, she leaves no room for blind trust, since blind trust is not part of the contemplative way. However, even if the mentor is *not* authentic, there should be no room for blind trust. Blind trust is even more dangerous in the latter situation because the "mentor" will not do anything to counteract it. In both cases, the student has to face this issue. Blind trust is spiritually and often even socially destructive, yet this does indicate a specific direction. In the first quote, this direction is expressed as the need to examine the teacher. In the second, which actually refers to a later phase of the student-mentor relationship, it is worded as the need to remain open to the mentor's actions. This means that, after we have completed our examination and our trust is beginning to increase, we do not apply our preconceived ideas to the mentor's behavior but apply her behavior to our ideas.

When we do so, we may open ourselves to experiencing the contemplative value of the mentor's actions more clearly. As a result, the relationship becomes an authentic means to challenge our ego and cultivate open-mindedness. When this occurs, the possibility begins to emerge that we are ultimately on the path to awakening the internal mentor within ourselves. That is, we can wake ourselves up. The internal mentor is not driven by the mentality that has never learned to trust and says, "I trust no one other than myself." It is not the mentality of ego that plays it safe in that way. Rather, the internal mentor arises from an egoless mentality that has gone beyond striving for safety. This mentality has learned to trust the world of phenomena through contact with an authentic mentor and, on this basis, has discovered and learned to trust itself. It is then possible, as the third quote states, that "finally the master will be your own mind, the naked awareness itself." The aim realized at this point is to be in touch with and have the means within ourselves to cultivate the flourishing of our basic humaneness. As we know, this is what contemplative psychology is about.

Development and the Guidance that Accompanies It

What role does the mentor's contemplative action play in the practitioner's development once a realistic basis of trust has developed between them? Naturally, this differs from individual to individual, but nonetheless we can roughly estimate the psychological time line. This time line influences the way in which the mentor aids the student in overcoming the

obstacles along the Way and in developing a certain steadfastness or stability within their practice. Let us explore this
development further.

We have already characterized progress along the Way—
the continual change in our experience of reality—as a process of transformation. Obviously, this does not occur in a
day. Although there can sometimes be moments of a more
spectacular nature, the process of transformation usually
takes place almost unnoticed; it is only when we look back
that we realize we have freed ourselves from a certain illusion or heartless attitude. Overall, the process of transformation has its high and low points, its periods of progress
and stagnation.

In a fundamental sense, guidance is both an expression of
true care for the student and of the mentor's insight into the
psychology of the student. Guides can give this kind of insight
only if they are experienced in viewing their own egocentric
experience of reality from the perspective of the open space
of their fundamental humanity. Their own awareness of their
egocentricity—in thoughts, words, and deeds—then becomes
an instrument, a valuable source of knowledge. For example,
in Christian terms, the guidance of this process aims at creating room for the activity of the Holy Spirit, so the student's
egocentric experience of reality can be made transparent and
the Holy Spirit can begin to work from the practitioner's heart
and in his life.

With respect to the practitioner, there must be a point of
application for guidance to begin. Using the metaphor from
chapter 5, where we spoke of ego's fortification and the space
around it, there must be some cracks in the fortification, and
the practitioner must be prepared to allow the mentor to see
what becomes visible. However, before the student dares to
do so, many things must have happened beforehand, and that
is what we will look at first.

The Double-Sidedness of Moments of Transformation

In chapter 5, we discussed the first steps of the beginnings of transformation. Let us recapitulate a few points from that chapter. We discussed the fact that moments of transformation are double-sided. We can experience and describe that double-sidedness in many ways; such moments appear as moments of freedom that make us aware that we are being held captive mentally and emotionally. We begin to experience the fortification of ego as claustrophobic because we are now sometimes aware of experiences of openness. Or we notice the staleness and despair within us because we have experiences of the freshness of life, a moment of joy, even if only briefly. It is at those moments when we feel warmth and compassion that we see how self-concerned we usually are. We begin to notice our continual and deep fear of life precisely because we experience moments of courage. And when we recognize and value moments of clarity, it is because at such moments we are aware of the fact that we are or go through life blind.

This double-sidedness is characteristic of moments of transformation, which is how they differ from our usual experiential moments. Usually, we feel free or caring one moment and caught or indifferent the next. Our experiences usually cause us to go first one way and then the other. However, these moments of transformation we have described suggest that experientially both sides are present *at the same time.* Because of this, we have nowhere to go—at least, not the usual places. Expressed in Christian terms, we become sinners-in-the-process-of-conversion, a term that also expresses double-sidedness. At this point, the psychology of ego begins to crumble and the so-called world around "me" begins to lose its self-evident quality. We begin to sense that there is another attitude to take in life.

The Development of External Stability

In chapter 5, we also discussed the fact that the result of such moments of transformation is often initially accompanied by a sense of great doubt; a doubt in the sense of a critical attitude that arises from the shocking awareness that we have been fooling ourselves, that we have lived in a way that nourishes a lack of truthfulness, and this is actually the cause of dissatisfaction in our lives. Simultaneously, the desire not to become even more lost in this lack arises, which is important to propelling us to take up the spiritual path. Developing a critical and curious attitude toward ourselves and our habitual way of seeing the world is primarily a good and positive development.

In addition to this positive questioning, moments of transformation also awaken an increasing restlessness because something deep-rooted has been shaken. We not only begin to see our ego-mind but are increasingly shocked by it. We become more impressed or taken by what is now more clearly in front of our eyes instead of actually appreciating that a transformation that makes this seeing possible has begun. At this stage, people often say they are getting worse; for example, in mindfulness meditation, they claim their minds are getting busier rather than appreciating that they are seeing their minds more clearly. It could be said that we grab the stick by only one end: the inadequacy of our egocentric way of life. We see self-interest, blindness, confusion, and self-deception in ourselves and around us, and the suffering that arises as a result. When we focus only on this end of the stick, then we can be dominated by a critical attitude on the intellectual level and a restlessness on the emotional level; at this point, we have no sense of where to rest in the midst of this seeing—that is, the other end of the stick.

When someone in this phase knocks on the door of a contemplative tradition, the mentor who knows the process of transformation will first say, "Stop. Take a break rather than pushing yourself and being so critical of yourself." This advice is like stopping and getting out of the car in which we have been speeding through the countryside. Once outside the car, we see the sunlight and the blue sky and feel the wind brushing past our cheeks and rustling in the high, scented grass. Perhaps we see a wide, slow river and hear the sound of birds in the distance. In this moment, the hectic and constricting pressure of our life project briefly falls away; we feel a moment of calm and have time to look around us. This is what the mentor may offer us in this phase. For some people, staying in a contemplative community or monastery, with its fixed schedule and simple external order of the day, may be a way of getting out of the car, a way of entering into simply *being*. Others may need to make room in their daily schedule for practicing a discipline of mindfulness, a time for doing nothing but resting wakefully in simply being. In both cases, we create room for catching our breath spiritually by putting ourselves in a situation of *external stability*. We stop and let the mind rest in the body, the senses, and the physical environment; simply remaining where we are, with ourselves, instead of with our smartphone or whatever alternative reality we imagine we live in.

It is important during this phase of the Way that we be guided in terms of what obstacles we may encounter and how to work with them, as the preceding example illustrates. If there is no guidance and encouragement at this point, the beginning practitioner can become discouraged and fall into negativity or even depression, which may lead him to abandon the Path. In particular, it is in this first phase that we often experience daily life in its totality as an obstacle because we are unable to distance ourselves from it. We are in some way obsessed by it—caught up in the habitual sense of the "importance" that our egocentric mentality projects onto our life situations. This is how we live our lives normally; no wonder it is so difficult to interrupt or change our attitude to make time and space for spiritual practice when our lives seem to demand our full attention! For this reason, it is often beneficial to withdraw physically from our daily situation in life, abandon the pursuit of all those matters from which we hope to attain satisfaction, and gain a solid grip on life.

When we temporarily banish what we see as external obstacles, we create some respite and the necessary distance to see our habitual way of being more clearly. Of course, there is a caution here also—this way of dealing with obstacles has its limitations, especially if used as an escape, but it is nevertheless helpful. After all, as we learned in the disciplines of mindfulness, we first need to calm down and slow down, and we need to create the right external conditions to support this happening. Guidance in this initial phase that takes into account the importance of creating both regular and extended periods of withdrawal from the demands of our lives is crucial. Creating conditions of external stability and experiencing the positive effects it has are important elements in this initial stage of entering the Way.

The Development of Internal Stability

When this external stability has more or less acquired regular form in our lives by way, for instance, of a daily spiritual practice, room for further development arises. This next phase of development is instigated by the discovery that the restlessness and anxiety that seem to underlie our day-to-day experience do not arise from our external circumstances but are created and maintained through our own minds. The extent and intensity of our inner restlessness and fear actually become more visible than ever against the background of periods of external stability that contemplative practice brings to our lives.

This discovery can sometimes be shocking, albeit in a different way than we have already discussed. At this point, we may not be so shocked by the discovery that we live in illusions, but more by the extent to which this world of feared and threatening situations is mostly of our own making. Having arrived at this point, we need a mentor more than ever, in a very personal way, to navigate this stage. The mentor no longer functions as someone who simply invites us to stop and helps us create an externally stable situation in our daily lives. We now need someone to whom we can and dare to reveal ourselves. We need someone who knows the contemplative process of transformation firsthand—someone we can trust. This trust will grow when we experience the mentor as someone who knows what we are talking about when we discuss our inner restlessness, our fear of life, and especially our fear of ourselves and the mind, now that it has proven to be the creator of our egocentric experience of reality with all its negative emotions and pain. We now need a spiritual friend, and that is what the mentor becomes.

Mentors primarily provide and demonstrate an appreciation for the practitioner who dares to reveal herself; they know this is not easy. In fact, at this phase a mentor will point out that the discovery of inner restlessness is in itself valuable and necessary and that it can be trusted. Further, he may reassure us that this inner restlessness is manageable; we need not walk, or indeed run, away. We need not be scared of ourselves, of our pettiness. No matter how high the seas rise, they are of our own making, arising from our own energy, and that is why we are strong enough to deal with them. We are as strong as those seas. Our practice of the mental disciplines is directed here at this juncture because the important lesson at this stage is to trust that we *can* work with whatever we experience as internal obstacles. The more we discover this in our practice of the disciplines, the more internal stability takes root within us.

However, we also need to be guided to understand that this internal stability is not the absence of restlessness but a mental steadfastness that can accommodate the turbulent movements of the mind. If we think back for a moment to the metaphor of the stream in which we planted a stick (chapter 7), internal stability is not the stability of quiet waters or the absence of water but the ability to keep the stick upright and thereby feel the restlessness of the water. It is independent of the water. If we experience our stream of thoughts from the perspective of this internal stability, then this whole picture turns around: the greater our restlessness, the greater our internal stability. It is as though the turbulence of our stream of thoughts only plants the stick of our internal stability more firmly in the bottom of the stream. The stick takes on qualities of solidity and steadfastness that are more like a rock. Our internal stability is now nourished by mental turbulence. It is like a mental reversal that makes us see and work through the turbulent movements of our blinding self-centeredness. Therefore, what was initially such a shock to us now becomes a cause for further insight and inspiration. As a result, we begin to feel increasing joy in our honesty with ourselves and the clarity with which we see our confusion.

At first, we were shocked when we began to see in a concrete way that we (the mind) are the creators of our egocentric experience of reality. This may have been accompanied by self-reproach, shame, and guilt. We may have been disappointed with ourselves; we (ego) thought more highly of ourselves. We were so preoccupied with ourselves, so impressed by our egocentricity and the world it created, that it escaped us that there was another side to it. There is more good news in that seeing ego in action tells us that we as human beings have the capacity to recognize our blindness and callousness, even though they are often enormous, because clarity and compassion are part of being human as well. As my mentor, Chögyam Trungpa, often put it, "The bad news is the good news." With this discovery, we arrive at the other side of the double-sidedness of our moments of transformation. Continuing with the metaphor of the stick, we begin to grab hold of the other end, the transformation end. Shame and regret about our egocentric attitude become positive regret—a felix culpa, as the Christian mystics call it—that helps free us from forms of self-reproach and self-hate.

Thus, the development of internal stability is not something cold and distant from ourselves or our lives. On the contrary, it leads to a more intimate attitude toward life. This is due to four essential characteristics of internal stability. The first characteristic of this stability is honesty with regard to our world of thoughts and our innermost feelings—an honesty that brings us ever closer to ourselves and brings often less visible emotions such as compassion and care to the fore. The second characteristic is that it contains self-acceptance; we gradually become friends with ourselves as we are, with all our pettiness and magnanimity. We no longer need be ashamed of ourselves or behave differently so that others will not suspect us of being "bad" or inferior in some way. Like a caring parent and not without humor, we see the futility of promoting our ego and our endless service to ego's version of self-respect. A changed attitude of self-acceptance actually creates room for conceding or exposing our blinding self-interest. With this, the third characteristic develops: discernment. As we mentioned previously, the Christian tradition calls this diakrisis, and it enables us to see what comes from our ego-mind and what comes from the Holy Spirit. The Buddhist tradition calls it prajna, and it enables us to discern between what is based on ego and what uncovers our Buddha-nature. Or in terms of contemplative psychology, it is the insight that enables us to distinguish between ego and our fundamental humanity.

At this stage, diakrisis or prajna gives us a sense of direction for the first time. We are no longer groping about in complete darkness concerning what we should do but can begin to see how and where we must go to cause our fundamental humanity to flourish. This introduces the manifestation of the fourth characteristic of internal stability in our attitude in life: a sense of trust in the Way and in its concrete viability. The Christian tradition uses the old Greek word *pistis* for this, a good translation of which is "faith." The Buddhist term *shraddha* is also usually translated as "faith," meaning "a conviction in the qualities of meditative stabilization and its fruits."[6] Faith at this point serves as the basis for generating an aspiration for wholesome qualities that have not as yet been produced.

Together, these four characteristics of internal stability make our egocentric mind manageable, and thus our attitude toward our surroundings is reinforced and extended. We gradually discover not only that the obstacles to experiencing and manifesting our fundamental humanity do not lie in our surroundings as we previously believed but that they arise primarily on the basis of our egocentric projections. Furthermore, we now see that the egocentric emotions that have accompanied this projection are themselves the obstacles to our own well-being, as well as to the spiritual path. When our practice of the disciplines of insight begins to bear fruit in this way, we find we do not necessarily need to avoid or seek out certain situations as much as we did while developing external stability. We find that our internal stability supports and nourishes our ability to work with our egocentric emotions and representations *directly*, to see through them and free ourselves from them on the spot. We find we can tackle our jealousy directly rather than the object of our jealousy. Instead of trying to conquer or eliminate our enemies, we find it much more important to conquer our own aggression on the spot. Instead of avoiding things that might arouse our greed, our discipline consists of recognizing our greed and letting go of it in order to step back into the open space of egolessness. Our everyday situation—which used to be an external obstacle—now becomes fertile soil for our practice.

When we thought the world existed outside of "me," our surroundings may have filled us with some deep underlying fear of losing or being out of control. Now we see that this egocentric world exists only within our minds, as it also exists in the minds of others. It is only present as personal experience. If we want to free ourselves from that egocentric world, then avoiding or seeking certain external circumstances is no longer the most important thing. Freeing our being from egocentric attitudes that lead to this egocentric world and dominate our mind, speech, and actions to the detriment of ourselves and others has now become the key point of our practice.

Of course, certain situations will still trigger egocentric emotions, but now we can use them to overcome those emotions at the moment they arise instead of avoiding situations that trigger them. That such a thing is possible is a wonderful discovery, because it means that uncovering our fundamental humanity in this phase is no longer a utopia but a concrete mental skill through which we systematically begin to leave our egocentric emotions and ideas behind. It is because of this that the world of the phenomena no longer appears to us simply as the object of our emotions. It does not appear exclusively as that in which our ego is involved but reveals itself more and more as it is—in its original nakedness. We begin to have an inkling of what the contemplative traditions mean when they speak of the fundamental sacredness of the world.

The Changed Attitude toward the Mentor

When our internal stability begins to develop to this extent, then our relationship with our mentor changes as well. It causes our trust in the mentor to acquire a different quality, moving from the kind of trust that we have in a good friend to devotion and admiration.

Admiration is an ambivalent thing. In the mentality of ego, it easily takes the form of hero worship, and hero worship is easily followed by jealousy and, sooner or later, revilement of the hero. Ego's version of admiration therefore is not characterized by stability. In addition, it does not inspire us to see ourselves as we are but prompts us to show ourselves to the best advantage possible—or even as helpless as possible—to the one we admire. In that case, we often try to get as close as possible to the object of our admiration so what we admire—certain qualities or status—may rub off on us, and we may be admired to some extent by others. To that end, depending on what seems the best strategy, we put our best or worst foot forward. What actually happens is that we try to charm the mentor without giving up the fortification of ego. We try to manipulate the mentor: "I admire you very much and value your guidance. In gratitude, I offer you a hospitable welcome in my fortress. Please, come live with me." Or we say, "I trust you so much that you may approach my fortification. To make it easier for you, I have set a bench in the open space close to it." If the mentor should fall for such a proposal, the situation would no longer be fruitful because the possibility of guidance would be thwarted. Guidance would then occur under the student's conditions; however, as we have seen, a genuine mentor does not fall for this. These forms of manipulation are known to genuine mentors, and often rather than responding to them, they work around them. Interestingly, authentic mentors do not take a fixed position with regard to our ego and remain unmoved by its displays and demands. Their attention is toward that leg that we are clasping.

With this in mind, admiration in the contemplative sense evokes something else—trust, surrender, and in particular, a readiness to reveal ourselves as we are. We no longer put our best or worst foot forward, but our admiration manifests itself increasingly as naturalness; as simplicity in conversation; as complete, unarmed nakedness in being who we are. Only then is true contact with the mentor and his world possible. In true contact, we also see the extent of the insight and care the mentor employs in working with the manifestations of our ego. The way his actions exemplify this is now clearer to us. We gradually see the degree to which the mentor embodies fundamental humanity in word and deed. Then we begin to realize that our admiration for our mentor is based on some kind of resonance. Our admiration resonates with our own true humaneness.

The Development of Stability Within

When our internal stability develops, we gradually develop skill in working with our ego and internal obstacles along the contemplative way. We become familiar with the ins and outs of the mind and adept in the disciplines that we practice. However, there is a potential obstacle at this stage that all this, too, can become routine. When our practice becomes routine, then the feeling that we are making progress slowly disappears, and our spiritual ambition and trust in the Way is no longer nourished. If this occurs, a new kind of disbelief or uncertainty arises: Will we ever reach our goal? Whatever goal we may have set, and even if we have embraced the idea that there is no goal, the question of whether there is a Way at all now returns.

Many contemplative traditions say that when this occurs, we enter a phase or possibly only a moment (or moments) of despair. All forms of the tradition—its approach and insights, its disciplines that we have appropriated—have become as familiar to us as the back of our hand. And somehow, everything seems predictable or cozy like an old hat. Perhaps we cling to the forms of the tradition and feel that it is we who are old hat. It is as if there is no longer any sense of moving forward in our contemplative development. If this occurs, then it is easy for an attitude of nihilism to arise: we come to disregard and think nothing of the disciplines or of the contemplative life. Of course, it may be the other way around. We may find something in the contemplative life but think nothing of ourselves. We are first testy and then desperate, first aggressive and then depressed. We experience the Way, our contemplative life, as a dead end. Externally we may still hold on to its forms, even if it is only out of habit or for something to do, but deep in our hearts, we have lost faith in the whole affair, ourselves included. It may still look good and convincing on the outside, and we still work internally with our obstacles as we should, but we no longer believe in it.

We can express it better, perhaps, in the following way: Our disbelief is not a disbelief in *something* but disbelief *in itself*—disbelief without an object. It is disbelief as a state of being, a state of despair that exists on its own, for there is no longer something to which we can turn (and we now know this). It seems that we can no longer choose to follow a contemplative path to do something about our disbelief because we are already doing that. Nor is quitting an alternative, because we feel that is exactly what we have already secretly done. Caught between a rock and a hard place, there is nothing toward which we can direct our disbelief, no object for it, and no possibility for shrugging the whole thing off. It is as if everything to which we had so fully applied ourselves has fled, as if the Way has expanded itself into an endlessly wide landscape. We cannot say that we have arrived at the end of the Way, because we have not seen an end anywhere. Nor has the Way ended, but its contours and direction have disappeared from sight. There is no longer a Way to see, because we have somehow become the Way. We do not know what to do when we discover that there is no (longer a) Way. At this stage, it is possible that we have stepped through the Gateless Gate; we have resolved all the koans of the Mumonkan.

In connection with this, the Greek Orthodox Christian tradition speaks of *akèdia* ("despair")—despair with no way out, because there is nothing about which to be despairing. It is despair in the sense of an unfathomable mental low. In this tradition, akèdia is viewed as a great sin, because this total despair is the warding off from complete openness, not recognizing it as such. To arrive at that recognition, we have to discover that this mental low, this insecurity, only appears because we still see the egoless experience of complete openness in a subtle way from the perspective of a remnant of ego, a remnant of spiritual ambition and expectations about the Way. This understanding of the Way itself and our ambition to make progress along it are the hidden obstacles before which we now stand. The experience of despair is the result of this subtle ambition. When we let go of this ambition, it becomes possible to rest in this complete openness. In Buddhism, it is said that at this point the "bodhisattva doesn't identify himself with the path any longer because he has become the path. He is the path. He has worked on himself, trod on himself until he has become the path and the chariot as well as the occupant of the chariot, all at the same time. He is vision, energy, skillful means, generosity, knowledge, panoramic awareness."[7]

In theistic terms, we could say that this stability lies very close to the hidden intercourse with God, to the hidden activity of the Holy Spirit within us. The first two forms of stability, the external and internal ones, are relevant to our progress along the Way, to working with our egocentric side and rising above it. However, now our internal stability has deepened even more into a third and even deeper stability that we call *stability within* or *hidden stability*. This is a state of being— not as it appears in contrast to ego but as it appears to itself. Many traditions use the term *sacredness* or *holiness* for this, but from its own perspective, this state is not experienced as sacred or spiritual. What has happened is that, without our noticing, we have begun to live outside the ruins of ego and thus outside every spiritual Way, since any Way exists only as long as (and because) ego rules our way of experiencing.

When we still lived within the fortifications of ego, we saw what was outside as light because it was so dark within. Now, however, we stand in a blinding light that initially appears to be darkness because it is so blinding. This darkness for John of the Cross was the light of the Holy Spirit. In the Buddhist traditions, there is no path to see anymore because the light (Sanskrit: *prabhasvara*) of our Buddha-nature now shines unhindered.

When we learn to rest in this unconditional hidden stability, its fruits also become freely manifest in the form of
unconditional clarity of mind, unsolicited joy in life, courage
in life, and compassion because that is its nature. Just as it is
the nature of the sun to give light and warmth and thus cause
the earth to flourish; just as it is the nature of flowers to bend
toward the light, not because they have made that their goal
but because it is their nature.

Many traditions speak about this hidden stability in terms
of the internal mentor (*magister interior*), the internal guru.
When it develops and we dare to trust in it, it becomes our
guide. Prior to that, we may have wanted to trust it, but it
was still drowned out by the voice of ego. It is now that we
can understand the wordless speech of the magister interior.

At this stage, we discover that there is no fundamental difference between our mentor (magister exterior) and the internal mentor, except the fact that the first one talks and the
second one does not. This fills us with deep gratitude for the
ingenuity and goodness of our mentor and the tradition. For
they turn out to be the reflection and manifestation of our
own humaneness in a world that is hopelessly caught up in
ego's callousness and fear of life.

Ultimately, from the final perspective of the stability within,
the Way and ego are truly existing illusions. Thus, all contemplative psychology is an illusion as well. However, it is precisely because of this truth that we do and should value the
contemplative traditions, which through their psychological
insight have developed the spiritual disciplines that can set us
free from these illusions.

Conclusion

As we have seen throughout the ten chapters of this book,
the contemplative traditions of the world religions contain a
way of thinking about and exploring the human mind that is

different from what we find in Western psychology—in both its scientific and its popular forms.

Since my first book on contemplative psychology appeared in the Netherlands in 1987, quite a few new developments have taken place in the field of psychology. We have seen the appearance of positive psychology, the development of neuropsychology, and the rise of the mindfulness movement within the field of psychotherapy, just to mention a few. These developments within scientific psychology, particularly related to neuropsychology, go in the direction of a monistic view by rejecting the usefulness of the concept of mind and define human beings in terms of having a body and a brain. However, most of what has been called "folk psychology"—the psychology that ordinary people use in everyday life —is based on the assumption that human beings have both a body and a mind as distinct and nonidentical entities. This view leads to the well-known and insoluble mind-body problem: How do the two relate to or communicate with each other? Still, this dualistic view of mind or consciousness living in one's body (or brain) is commonly held to be a plausible one, although it is evident that neuropsychology on the whole rejects or bypasses this view.

The interesting thing about psychological thinking and investigations in the contemplative traditions is that their approach fundamentally avoids both this dualistic view and the monistic view of materialism. How? By deliberately limiting the object of study to first-person experience—that is, to my (or our) experience, my field of experience as it is present continuously, right now. No dualistic assumption or claim is made here nor is there any opposite claim that reduces mind to body (or brain) or even body to mind. Within this deliberately chosen limitation, the contemplative traditions make use of our human ability to clarify our experience by sharpening and using awareness (consciousness) to investigate the effects of the thinking mind on experience. They make use of the mental disciplines that we described in chapters 6, 7, and 8, which are in turn, supported by the disciplines of action and speech from chapter 9. The results of these investigations lead to the kind of psychology that were described in part 1 of this book.

As this volume testifies, the psychology of the contemplative traditions, with its methods of investigation, stands on its own. It offers a contribution to our ways of understanding human mind and experience, a contribution that has been overlooked, even ignored, for a long time.

As we saw in part 1, from the side of science, this approach has been disregarded because science has defined empirical research as third-person research only. On one hand, this serves to avoid getting lost in metaphysics and wild speculation about human experience; on the other hand, it relies on propagating the view that the mental domain is not directly observable in a reliable way. As a result, first-person empirical research, which is based on forms of introspection or contemplation, has been neither accepted nor developed in the Western empirical science of psychology.

From the side of philosophy, contemplative psychology has been overlooked because philosophy tends to look at the contemplative traditions in terms of its own dilemmas. For example, the philosophy of perception explores the realism dilemma: Does reality only exist as a mental phenomenon, shaped by our thoughts and ideas; or does reality have an absolute existence independent from our thoughts, ideas, and even consciousness? The position of the contemplative traditions is again hard to conceive in terms of this way of thinking because, as we have discussed, these traditions have what we could call the great paradox of contemplative psychology as their pragmatic basis; the world we live in is the world we think we live in, but the world we think we live in is not the world we live in. This paradoxical statement again sidesteps the need to answer the kind of dilemmas Western philosophy considers. Furthermore, because of the foundational role this paradox plays in the contemplative traditions, it means that it is incorrect to characterize the psychology of the contemplative traditions as idealism, as realist thinkers tend to do.

It is from this position of the great paradox that contemplatives all over the world, in different cultures and at different times, have explored and come to understand the nature of human experience and mind. Even though Buddhism provided me with the framework and concepts to pursue this engagement with other traditions, I hope I have shown—in the spirit of my mentor, Chögyam Trungpa—that this understanding goes beyond the cradle of the particular religion into which it has, in most cases, been born. As such, it offers a contribution to and broadening of what we nowadays call psychology. At the same time and most importantly, its disciplines of mind, speech, and action open new ways of cultivating our fundamental humanity. With this book, I hope to have given a voice to this psychology that is the fruit of the contemplative methods of exploring our own minds.

Notes

PREFACE

1. Wilhelm Wundt, *Grundriss der Psychologie* (Stuttgart, Germany: Kröner Verlag, 1896).
2. Frits Staal, *Exploring Mysticism: A Methodological Essay* (Berkeley, CA: University of California Press, 1975).
3. Han F. de Wit, "On Contemplative Psychology," in *Current Issues in the Psychology of Religion*, ed. J. A. Van Belzen and J. M. Van der Lans (Amsterdam: Rodopi, 1986), 82–89. Reprinted in Philosophy Study 7, no. 8 (August 2017): 414–419.

INTRODUCTION

1. Leo Tolstoy, *Anna Karenina* (Harmondsworth, UK: Penguin Books, 1954), 272–72.
2. Chögyam Trungpa, *Shambhala: The Sacred Path of the Warrior* (Boston, MA: Shambhala Publications, 1984), 35.
3. Michael Amaladoss. "Mission: From Vatican II into the Coming Decade," *Vidyajyoti, Journal of Theological Reflection* 54: 269–80, 1990.
4. Sakyong Mipham, *The Shambhala Principle: Discovering Humanity's Hidden Treasure* (New York: Harmony Books, 2013): chap. 4.
5. Augustine, *The Nicene and Post-Nicene Fathers: The Confessions and Letters of St. Augustine*, The Nicene and Post-Nicene Fathers: First Series, vol. 1, ed. Philip Schaff (Grand Rapids, MI: William B. Eerdmans Publishing Company, 2007), 88.

CHAPTER 1: CONTEMPLATIVE PSYCHOLOGY

1. See, for example, William James, *The Varieties of Religious Experience* (Glasgow: Collins/Fount Paperbacks, 1977); H. M. M. Fortmann, *Als ziende de onzienlijke*, book 1 (Hilversum, the Netherlands: Gooi en Sticht B.V., 1974); and Adrian van Kaam, *Formative Spirituality*, 5 vols (New York: Crossroad Publishing, 1983–1992).

2. See, for example, Vasubandhu, *L'Abhidharmakosa*, trans. Louis de La Vallée Poussin (Bruxelles: Institut Belge des Hautes Études Chinoise, 1971), 1:15.

3. Han F. de Wit, *Contemplative Psychology*, trans. Marie Louise Baird (Pittsburgh, PN: Duquesne University Press, 1991), 19f.

4. van Kaam, *Formative Spirituality*, vol 1.

5. Han de Wit, "On the Methodology of Clarifying Confusion," in *Current Issues in Theoretical Psychology*, eds. W. M. J. Baker, M. E. Hyland, H. Van Rappard, and A. W. Staats (Amsterdam: Elsevier Science Publishers B.V., 1987): 37–48.

6. Matthieu Ricard, *Altruism: The Power of Compassion to Change Yourself and the World* (New York: Little, Brown and Company, 2015).

7. Pema Chödrön, *The Wisdom of No Escape* (Boston, MA: Shambhala Publications, 1991).

8. Chögyam Trungpa, *Meditation in Action* (Boston, MA: Shambhala Publications, 1969), 19ff.

CHAPTER 2: PERCEIVING REALITY AND THE METAPHOR OF THE WAY

1. H. M. Kuitert, *I Have My Doubts: How to Become a Christian Without Being a Fundamentalist*, trans. John Bowden (London/Valley Forge, PA: SCM Press, Ltd./Trinity Press International, 1993), 216.

2. Jacques Lacan, *Ecrits: The First Complete Edition in English*, trans. Bruce Fink (New York: W.W. Norton and Company, 2006).

3. Compare Geoffrey Bennington and Jacques Derrida, *Jacques Derrida*, trans. Geoffrey Bennington (Chicago and London: The University of Chicago Press, 1993), 141–42.

4. See, for example, K. K. Inada, *Nagarjuna: A Translation of His Mulamadyamaka-karika with an Introductory Essay* (Tokyo: The Hokuseido Press, 1970).

5. Marcel Proust, *Swann's Way*, trans. C. K. Scott Moncrieff (New York: The Limited Editions Club, 1954), 19.

6. See also Tenzin Gyatso, *The Opening of the Wisdom-Eye* (Wheaton, IL: Theosophical Publishing House, 1981).

7. André Louf, *Tuning In to Grace: The Quest for God*, trans. John Vriend (Kalamazoo, MI: Cistercian Publications, 1992), 51.

8. Chögyam Trungpa, *Cutting Through Spiritual Materialism* (Boston, MA: Shambhala Publications, 1973).

CHAPTER 3: THE DEVELOPMENT OF EGO

1. Nissan Mindel, *The Philosophy of Chabad* (New York: Kehot Publication Society, 1985), 12.

2. Augustine, *The Nicene and Post-Nicene Fathers: The Confessions and Letters of St. Augustine*, The Nicene and Post-Nicene Fathers: First Series, vol. 1, ed. Philip Schaff (Grand Rapids, MI: William B. Eerdmans Publishing Company, 2007), 137–38.

3. Chögyam Trungpa, *The Myth of Freedom and the Way of Meditation* (Boston, MA: Shambhala Publications, 1976), 6.

4. Keiji Nishitani, *Religion and Nothingness* (Berkeley, CA: University of California Press, 1982), 21.

5. J. T. P. De Bruijn, "Vroomheid en mystiek," in *Islam: Norm, ideaal en werkelijkheid*, ed. J. Waardenburg (North Holland, the Netherlands: Weesp, 1987), 200.

6. Rainer Maria Rilke, *The Duino Elegies*, trans. Leslie Norris and Alan Keele (Columbia, SC: Camden House, 1993), 45.

7. See, for example, Mark Epstein, *Thoughts Without a Thinker: Psychotherapy from a Buddhist Perspective* (New York: Harper Collins Basic Books, 1995); and John Welwood, *Toward a Psychology of Awakening: Buddhism, Psychotherapy, and the Path of Personal and Spiritual Transformation* (Boston, MA: Shambhala Publications, 2000).

8. See, for example, Joseph Campbell and Bill Moyers, *The Power of Myth* (New York: Doubleday, 1988).

9. Jean-Paul Sartre, *La Transcendance de l'Ego. Esquisse d'une description phénoménologique* (Paris: J. Vrin Librairie Philosophique, 1972), 32.

10. Chögyam Trungpa, *Cutting Through Spiritual Materialism* (Boston, MA: Shambhala Publications, 1973), 123.

11. Ibid.

12. See H. M. M. Fortmann, *Als ziende de onzienlijke*, book 1 (Hilversum, the Netherlands: Gooi en Sticht B.V., 1974), 349.

13. Marcel Proust, *Swann's Way*, trans. C. K. Scott Moncrieff (New York: The Limited Editions Club, 1954), 85.

14. Beatrix, "Kersttoespraak koningin" *NRC-Handelsblad* (December 28, 1992), www.nrc.nl/nieuws/1992/12/28/kersttoespraak-koningin-7167701-a988373.

CHAPTER 4: MIND AND KNOWLEDGE IN CONTEMPLATIVE PSYCHOLOGY

1. See Martin E. P. Seligman, *Authentic Happiness* (New York: Simon and Schuster, 2002).

2. Eugen Drewermann, *Wort des Heils—Wort der Heilung* I/122-3 (Patmos, Greece: Verlag, 1992).

3. W. Y. Evans-Wentz, *The Tibetan Book of the Dead* (London: Oxford University Press, 1927).

4. John Myrdhin Reynolds, *Self-Liberation Through Seeing with Naked Awareness* (Barrytown, NY: Station Hill Press, 1989), 71ff.

5. Tenzin Gyatso, *The Opening of the Wisdom-Eye* (Wheaton, IL: Theosophical Publishing House, 1981).

6. Han F. de Wit, *Contemplative Psychology*, trans. Marie Louise Baird (Pittsburgh, PA: Duquesne University Press, 1991), 95f.

7. David Ross Komito, *Nagarjuna's "Seventy Stanzas": A Buddhist Psychology of Emptiness* (Ithaca, NY: Snow Lion, 1987).

8. Jamgön Kongtrul, *Indo-Tibetan Classical Learning and Buddhist Phenomenology*, in The Treasury of Knowledge, Book Six, Parts 1 and 2, trans. Gyurme Dorje (Ithaca, NY: Snow Lion, 2013).

9. Bhikkhu Bodhi, ed., *Comprehensive Manual of Abhidhamma: The Abhidhammattha Saṅgaha of Acariya Anuruddha* (Onalaska, WA: Pariyatti Publishing, 2012).

10. Owen Chadwick, *Western Asceticism* (Philadelphia, PA: The Westminster Press, 1958), 43.

11. Takpo Tashi Namgyal, *Mahamudra: The Quintessence of Mind and Meditation* (Boston, MA: Shambhala Publications, 1987), 35. Namgyal is quoting the third *Bhavanakrama*.

12. De Wit, *Contemplative Psychology*, chap. 3.

13. William James, *The Principles of Psychology*, vol. 1 (Cambridge, MA: Harvard University Press, 1981), 216.

14. Han M. M. Fortmann, *Als ziende de onzienlijke*, book 1. Hilversum, the Netherlands: Gooi en Sticht B.V., 1974), 351.

15. Daisetz T. Suzuki, *Zen and Japanese Culture* (Princeton, NJ: Princeton University Press, 1970), 62.

CHAPTER 5: ON THE WAY

1. Chögyam Trungpa, *Cutting Through Spiritual Materialism* (Boston, MA: Shambhala Publications, 1973), 113–14.

2. Georges Bataille, "Méthode de méditation," in *Oeuvres Complétes*, vol. 5 (Paris: Gallimard, 1981).

3. André Louf, *Tuning In to Grace: The Quest for God*, trans. John Vriend (Kalamazoo, MI: Cistercian Publications, 1992).

4. Trungpa, *Cutting Through Spiritual Materialism*.

5. See J. Harold Ellens, ed., *Destructive Power of Religion: Violence in Christianity, Judaism, and Islam*, condensed and updated (New York: ABC-CLIO, 2007); and Vladimir Tikhonov and Torkel Brekke, eds., *Buddhism and Violence: Militarism and Buddhism in Modern Asia* (London: Routledge, 2013).

6. Han F. de Wit, *Contemplative Psychology*, trans. Marie Louise Baird (Pittsburgh, PA: Duquesne University Press, 1991), 172ff.

7. John Calvin, *Institutes of the Christian Religion*, vol. 1 (1536) (Louisville, KY: Westminster John Knox Press, 2006).

CHAPTER 6: THE DISCIPLINES OF THOUGHT

1. Han F. de Wit, *Contemplative Psychology*, trans. Marie Louise Baird (Pittsburgh, PA: Duquesne University Press, 1991), 102ff.

2. For the specific role of these linguistic uses in the contemplative traditions, refer to de Wit, *Contemplative Psychology*, chap. 4.

3. See, for example, Chögyam Trungpa, *Training the Mind and Cultivating Loving-Kindness* (Boston, MA: Shambala Publications, 1993); and Pema Chödrön, *The Wisdom of No Escape* (Boston, MA: Shambhala Publications, 1991).

4. Willigis Jäger, *Contemplation: A Christian Path* (Liguori, MO: Triumph Books, 2012), 72, Kindle.

5. Shantideva, *The Way of the Bodhisattva*, trans. Padmakara Translation Group (Boston, MA: Shambhala Publications, 1997), 50–51.

6. See, for example, Sakyong Mipham, *The Shambhala Principle: Discovering Humanity's Hidden Treasure*, vol. 4 (New York: Harmony Books, 2013).

7. De Wit, *Contemplative Psychology*, 192f.

8. Jamgön Kongtrul, *The Great Path of Awakening* (Boston, MA: Shambhala Publications, 1987), 18.

9. Swami Akhilananda, *Hindu Psychology: Its Meaning for the West* (London: Routledge and Kegan Paul, 1948), 178–79.

10. See, for example, the classic *Mūlamadhyamakakārikā* as in K. K. Inada, *Nagarjuna: A Translation of His Mulamadyamaka-karika with an Introductory Essay* (Tokyo: The Hokuseido Press, 1970).

11. George Timko, "Sin: The Alienated Self," in *Speaking of Silence: Christians and Buddhists on the Contemplative Way*, ed. Susan Walker (New York: Paulist Press, 1987), 216.

12. Tessa Bielecki, "Long, Loving Look at the Real," in *Speaking of Silence: Christians and Buddhists on the Contemplative Way*, ed. Susan Walker (New York: Paulist Press, 1987), 208.

13. Edward M. Podvoll, *The Seduction of Madness* (New York: HarperCollins, 1990).

CHAPTER 7: THE DISCIPLINES OF MINDFULNESS

1. See, for example, Stanislav Grof and Christina Grof, *Holotropic Breathwork: A New Approach to Self-Exploration and Therapy* (New York: SUNY Press, 2010).

2. Jon Kabat-Zinn, *Full Catastrophe Living: Using the Wisdom of Your Body and Mind to Face Stress, Pain, and Illness*, rev. ed. (New York: Bantam Books, 2013).

3. N. Giri, "Meditation in Hinduismus," *Dialog der Religionen*, vol. 2 (1992): 63.

4. E. Kadloubovsky and G. E. H. Palmer, trans., *Writings from the Philokalia: On Prayer of the Heart* (London: Faber & Faber, 1972), 195.

5. Ira Progroff, trans., *The Cloud of Unknowing* (New York: Dell Publishing Co., 1957), 76–77.

6. Evagrius Ponticus, *The Praktikos and Chapters on Prayer*, 2nd ed., trans. John Eudes Bamberger (Collegeville, MN: Liturgical Press, 1972), 115, statement 9.

7. Ibid, 115, statement 10.

8. See Deane H. Shapiro, Jr., and Roger N. Walsh, eds., *Meditation: Classic and Contemporary Perspectives* (Piscataway, NJ: Aldine Transaction, 1984); Daniel Goleman et al., *Measuring the Immeasurable: The Scientific Case for Spirituality* (Boulder, CO: Sounds True, 2008); Andy Fraser, ed., *The Healing Power of Meditation: Leading Experts on Buddhism, Psychology, and Medicine Explore the Health Benefits of Contemplative Practice* (Boston, MA: Shambhala Publications, 2013); and Adeline van Waning, *The Less Dust, the More Trust: Participating in The Shamatha Project, Meditation and Science* (Winchester UK: Mantra Books, 2014).

9. Owen Chadwick, *Western Asceticism* (Philadelphia, PA: The Westminster Press, 1958), 198.

10. Chokyi Nyima, *The Union of Mahamudra and Dzogchen* (Hong Kong: Rang Jung Yeshe Publications, 1986), 153–54.

11. Chögyam Trungpa, *The Myth of Freedom and the Way of Meditation* (Boston, MA: Shambhala Publications, 1976), 47.

12. Ibid, 45–46.

13. Willigis Jäger, *Contemplation: A Christian Path* (Liguori, MO: Triumph Books, 2012), 84, Kindle.

CHAPTER 8: THE DISCIPLINES OF INSIGHT

1. Willigis Jäger, *Contemplation: A Christian Path* (Liguori, MO: Triumph Books, 2012), 72, Kindle.

2. John of the Cross, *Ascent of Mount Carmel*, trans. E. Allison Peers (Grand Rapids, MI: Christian Classical Ethereal Library, 2005), 95, www.ccel.org/ccel/john_cross.

3. Daniel S. Lopez, Jr., *Religions of Tibet in Practice* (Princeton, NJ: Princeton University Press, 1997), 520.

4. John Myrdhin Reynolds, *Self-Liberation Through Seeing with Naked Awareness* (Barrytown, NY: Station Hill Press, 1989), 12.

5. Herbert V. Guenther, *The Royal Song of Saraha* (Boston, MA: Shambhala Publications, 1973), 66, stanza 15.

6. Javad Nurbakhsh. *The Paradise of the Sufis* (London/New York: Nimatillahi Publications, 1989).

7. Chögyam Trungpa, *Shambhala: The Sacred Path of the Warrior* (Boston, MA: Shambhala Publications, 1984), 174.

8. Martin Buber, *Chassidische vertellingen* (Cothen, the Netherlands: Servire, 1967), 133.

9. André Zegveld, "Gebed en leven," in *Benedictijns Tijdschrift*, vol. 3 (Egmond-Binnen, the Netherlands: Adelbertabdij, 1991), 107f.

10. Pseudo-Dionysius, *The Mystical Theology*, trans. Colm Luibheid (New York: Paulist Press, 1987).

CHAPTER 9: THE DISCIPLINES OF ACTION AND SPEECH

1. Deborah Adele, *The Yamas and Niyamas: Exploring Yoga's Ethical Practice* (Duluth, MN: On-Word Bound Books LLC, 2009).

2. Han F. de Wit, *Contemplative Psychology*, trans. Marie Louise Baird (Pittsburgh, PA: Duquesne University Press, 1991), 216.

3. Beatrix, "Kersttoespraak koningin" *NRC-Handelsblad* (December 28, 1992), www.nrc.nl/nieuws/1992/12/28/kersttoespraak-koningin-7167701-a988373.

4. Sakyong Mipham, *The Shambhala Principle: Discovering Humanity's Hidden Treasure* (New York: Harmony Books, 2013), chap. 4.

5. Benedict, *The Rule of Benedict: A Guide to Christian Living*, trans. Monks of Glenstal Abbey (Dublin, Ireland: Four Courts Press, 1980), 84.

6. Benedict, *The Rule of Benedict*, 65.

7. Ibid, 154.

8. Ibid, 183.

9. Compare, for example, Benedict, *The Rule of Benedict*, 65.

10. Chokyi Nyima, *The Union of Mahamudra and Dzogchen* (Hong Kong: Rang Jung Yeshe Publications, 1986), 167–68.

11. Benedict, *The Rule of Benedict*, 98.

12. For a more extensive discussion, see De Wit, *Contemplative Psychology*, 212ff.

13. Chögyam Trungpa, *Crazy Wisdom* (Boston, MA: Shambhala Publications, 1991), 174–75.

14. Meister Eckhart, *The Essential Sermons, Commentaries, Treatises, and Defense*, trans. Edmund Colledge and Bernard McGinn (New York: Paulist Press, 1981), 250–51.

CHAPTER 10: DEVELOPMENT AND GUIDANCE

1. Martin Buber, *Chassidische vertellingen* (Cothen, the Netherlands: Servire, 1967), 142.
2. Han F. de Wit, *Contemplative Psychology*, trans. Marie Louise Baird (Pittsburgh, PA: Duquesne University Press, 1991), 127–28.
3. De Wit, *Contemplative Psychology*, 129.
4. De Wit, *Contemplative Psychology*, 189.
5. Chögyam Trungpa, *The Rain of Wisdom*, trans. Nalanda Translation Committee (Boston, MA: Shambhala Publications, 1980), 11.
6. Jeffrey Hopkins, *Meditation on Emptiness* (London: Wisdom Publications, 1983), 72.
7. Chögyam Trungpa, *The Myth of Freedom and the Way of Meditation* (Boston, MA: Shambhala Publications, 1976), 123.

Bibliography

Adele, Deborah *The Yamas and Niyamas: Exploring Yoga's Ethical Practice*. Duluth, MN: On-Word Bound Books LLC, 2009.

Akhilananda. *Hindu Psychology: Its Meaning for the West*. London: Routledge and Kegan Paul, 1948.

Amaladoss, Michael. "Mission: From Vatican II into the Coming Decade." In *Vidyajyoti, Journal of Theological Reflection* 54: 269–80, 1990.

Augustine. *The Nicene and Post-Nicene Fathers: The Confessions and Letters of St. Augustine*. Edited by Philip Schaff. Vol. 1 of The Nicene and Post-Nicene Fathers, First Series. Grand Rapids, MI: William B. Eerdmans Publishing Company, 2007.

Bataille, Georges. "Méthode de méditation." In *Oeuvres Complétes*. Vol. 5. Paris: Gallimard, 1981.

Beatrix. "Kersttoespraak koningin." *NRC-Handelsblad*. December 28, 1992. www.nrc.nl/nieuws/1992/12/28/kersttoespraak-koningin-7167701-a988373.

Benedict. *The Rule of Benedict: A Guide to Christian Living*. Translated by Monks of Glenstal Abbey. Dublin: Four Courts Press, 1980.

Bennington, Geoffrey, and Jacques Derrida. *Jacques Derrida*. Translated by Geoffrey Bennington. Chicago: The University of Chicago Press, 1993.

Bodhi, Bhikkhu, ed. *Comprehensive Manual of Abhidhamma: The Abhidhammattha Saṅgaha of Acariya Anuruddha*. Onalaska, WA: Pariyatti Publishing, 2012.

Buber, Martin. *Chassidische vertellingen*. Cothen, the Netherlands: Servire, 1967.

Calvin, John. *Institutes of the Christian Religion*, vol. 1 (1536) Louisville, KY: Westminster John Knox Press, 2006.

Campbell, Joseph, and Bill Moyers. *The Power of Myth*. New York: Doubleday, 1988.

Chadwick, Owen. *Western Asceticism*. Philadelphia, PA: The Westminster Press, 1958.

Chödrön, Pema. *The Wisdom of No Escape*. Boston, MA: Shambhala Publications, 1991.

De Bruijn, J. T. P. "Vroomheid en mystiek." In *Islam: Norm, ideaal en werkelijkheid*. Edited by J. Waardenburg. North Holland, the Netherlands: Weesp, 1987.

De Wit, Han F. *Contemplative Psychology*. Translated by Marie Louise Baird. Pittsburgh, PA: Duquesne University Press, 1991.

———. "On Contemplative Psychology." In *Current Issues in the Psychology of Religion*. J. A. Van Belzen and J. M. Van der Lans, eds. Amsterdam: Rodopi, 1986. Reprinted in *Philosophy Study* 7, no. 8 (August 2017): 414–19.

———. "On the Methodology of Clarifying Confusion." In *Current Issues in Theoretical Psychology*, edited by W. M. J. Baker, M. E. Hyland, H. Van Rappard, and A.W. Staats. Amsterdam: Elsevier Science Publishers B.V., 1987, 37–48.

———. "Psychotherapy, Buddhist Meditation and Health." *Journal of Contemplative Psychology*, Vol. VII. Boulder, CO: The Naropa Institute, 1990: 57–93.

Drewermann, Eugen. *Wort des Heils—Wort der Heilung*. Greece: Patmos Verlag, 1992.

Eckhart, Meister. *The Essential Sermons, Commentaries, Treatises, and Defense*. Translated and introduced by Edmund Colledge and Bernard McGinn. New York: Paulist Press, 1981.

Ellens, J. Harold. *Destructive Power of Religion: Violence in Christianity, Judaism and Islam*. Condensed and updated. New York: ABC-CLIO, 2007, Nook.

Epstein, Mark. *Thoughts Without a Thinker: Psychotherapy from a Buddhist Perspective*. New York: HarperCollins Basic Books, 1995.

Evagrius Ponticus. *The Praktikos and Chapters on Prayer*. 2nd ed. Translated by John Eudes Bamberger. Collegeville, MN: Liturgical Press, 1972.

Evans-Wentz, W. Y. *The Tibetan Book of the Dead*. London: Oxford University Press, 1927.

Fortmann, H. M. M. *Als ziende de onzienlijke*. Book 1. Hilversum, the Netherlands: Gooi en Sticht B.V., 1974.

Fraser, Andy, ed. *The Healing Power of Meditation: Leading Experts on Buddhism, Psychology, and Medicine Explore the Health Benefits of Contemplative Practice*. Boston, MA: Shambhala Publications, 2013.

Giri, N. "Meditation in Hinduismus." *Dialog der Religionen* 2, no.1 (1992): 32–45.

Goleman, Daniel, Bruce H. Lipton, Candace Pert, Gary Small, Lynne McTaggart, Gregg Braden, and Jeanne Achterberg. *Measuring the Immeasurable: The Scientific Case for Spirituality.* Boulder, CO: Sounds True, 2008.

Grof, Stanislav, and Christina Grof. *Holotropic Breathwork: A New Approach to Self-Exploration and Therapy.* New York: SUNY Press, 2010.

Guenther, Herbert V. *The Royal Song of Saraha.* Boston, MA: Shambhala Publications, 1973.

Gyatso, Tenzin. *The Opening of the Wisdom-Eye.* Wheaton, IL: Theosophical Publishing House, 1981.

Hanh, Thich Nhat. *The Miracle of Mindfulness.* London: Rider Books, 1991.

Hopkins, Jeffrey. *Meditation on Emptiness.* London: Wisdom Publications, 1983.

Inada, K. K. *Nagarjuna: A Translation of His Mulamadyamaka-karika with an Introductory Essay.* Tokyo: The Hokuseido Press, 1970.

Jäger, Willigis. *Contemplation: A Christian Path.* Liguori, MO: Triumph Books, 2012. Kindle.

James, William. *The Principles of Psychology.* Vol. 1 of *The Works of William James.* Cambridge, MA: Harvard University Press, 1981. First published in 1890.

———. *The Varieties of Religious Experience.* Glasgow: Collins/Fount Paperbacks, 1977. First published in 1902.

John of the Cross. *Ascent of Mount Carmel.* Translated by E. Allison Peers. Grand Rapids, MI: Christian Classical Ethereal Library, 2005. www.ccel.org/ccel/john_cross.

Jung, Carl G. *Psychology and Religion.* New Haven, CT: Yale University Press, 1938.

Kabat-Zinn, Jon. *Full Catastrophe Living: Using the Wisdom of Your Body and Mind to Face Stress, Pain, and Illness.* Rev. ed. New York: Bantam Books, 2013.

Kadloubovsky, E., and G. E. H. Palmer, trans. *Writings from the Philokalia: On Prayer of the Heart.* London: Faber & Faber, 1972.

Kaufmann, P. "Imaginaire et imagination." In *Encyclopaedia Universalis.* Vol. 8. Paris: Encyclopaedia Universalis, 1971.

Komito, David Ross. *Nagarjuna's "Seventy Stanzas": A Buddhist Psychology of Emptiness.* Ithaca, NY: Snow Lion, 1987.

Kongtrul, Jamgön. "Indo-Tibetan Classical Learning and Buddhist Phenomenology." In *The Treasury of Knowledge, Book Six, Parts 1 and 2.* Translated by Gyurme Dorje. Ithaca, NY: Snow Lion, 2013.

————. *The Great Path of Awakening*. Boston, MA: Shambhala Publications, 1987.

Kuitert, H. M. *Everything Is Politics but Politics Is Not Everything: A Theological Perspective on Faith and Politics*. Translated by John Bowden. London: SCM Press, 1986.

————. *I Have My Doubts: How to Become a Christian Without Being a Fundamentalist*. Translated by John Bowden. London/Valley Forge, PA: SCM Press, Ltd./Trinity Press International, 1993.

Lacan, Jacques. *Ecrits: The First Complete Edition in English*. Translated by Bruce Fink. New York: W. W. Norton and Company, 2006.

Lopez, Daniel S., Jr. *Religions of Tibet in Practice*. Princeton, NJ: Princeton University Press, 1997.

Louf, André. *Tuning In to Grace: The Quest for God*. Translated by John Vriend. Kalamazoo, MI: Cistercian Publications, 1992.

Mindel, Nissan. *The Philosophy of Chabad*. New York: Kehot Publication Society, 1985.

Mipham, Sakyong. *The Shambhala Principle: Discovering Humanity's Hidden Treasure*. New York: Harmony Books, 2013.

Namgyal, Takpo Tashi. *Mahamudra: The Quintessence of Mind and Meditation*. Boston, MA: Shambhala Publications, 1986.

Nishitani, K. *Religion and Nothingness*. Berkeley, CA: University of California Press, 1982.

Nurbakhsh, Javad. *The Paradise of the Sufis*. London/New York: Nimatillahi Publications, 1989.

Nyima, Chokyi. *The Union of Mahamudra and Dzogchen*. Hong Kong: Rangjung Yeshe Publications, 1986.

Ornstein, Robert E., and Claudio Naranjo. *On the Psychology of Meditation*. London: Allen and Unwin Ltd., 1972.

Podvoll, Edward M. *The Seduction of Madness*. New York: HarperCollins, 1990.

Progoff, Ira, trans. *The Cloud of Unknowing*. New York: Dell Publishing Co, 1957.

Proust, Marcel. *Swann's Way*. Translated by C. K. Scott Moncrieff. New York: The Limited Editions Club, 1954.

Pseudo-Dionysius the Areopagite. *The Mystical Theology*. Translated by Colm Luibheird. New York: Paulist Press, 1987.

Reynolds, John Myrdhin. *Self-Liberation Through Seeing with Naked Awareness*. Barrytown, NY: Station Hill Press, 1989.

Ricard, Matthieu. *Altruism: The Power of Compassion to Change Yourself and the World*. New York: Little, Brown and Company, 2015.

Rilke, Rainer Maria. *The Duino Elegies*. Translated by Leslie Norris and Alan Keele. Columbia, SC: Camden House, 1993.

Sartre, Jean-Paul. *La Transcendance de l'Ego. Esquisse d'une description phénoménologique*. Paris: J. Virn Librairie Philosophique, 1972.

Seligman, Martin E. P. *Authentic Happiness*. New York: Simon and Schuster, 2002.

Shantideva. *The Way of the Bodhisattva*. Translated by the Padmakara Translation Group. Boston, MA: Shambhala Publications, 1997.

Shapiro, Deane H., Jr., and Roger N. Walsh, eds. *Meditation: Classical and Contemporary Perspectives*. Piscataway, NJ: Aldine Transaction, 1984.

Staal, Frits. *Exploring Mysticis: A Methodological Essay*. Berkeley, CA: University of California Press, 1975.

Suzuki, Daisetz T. *Zen and Japanese Culture*. Princeton, NJ: Princeton University Press, 1970.

Tikhonov, Vladimir, and Torkel Brekke, eds. *Buddhism and Violence: Militarism and Buddhism in Modern Asia*. London: Routledge, 2013.

Tolstoy, Leo. *Anna Karenina*. Harmondsworth, UK: Penguin Books, 1954.

Trungpa, Chögyam. *Crazy Wisdom*. Boston, MA: Shambhala Publications, 1991.

———. *Cutting Through Spiritual Materialism*. Boston, MA: Shambhala Publications, 1973.

———. *Meditation in Action*. Boston, MA: Shambhala Publications, 1969.

———. *The Myth of Freedom and the Way of Meditation*. Boston, MA: Shambhala Publications, 1976.

———. *The Rain of Wisdom*. Translated by Nalanda Translation Committee. Boston, MA: Shambhala Publications, 1980.

———. *Shambhala: The Sacred Path of the Warrior*. Boston, MA: Shambhala Publications, 1984.

———. *Training the Mind and Cultivating Loving-Kindness*. Boston, MA: Shambhala Publications, 1993.

Van Kaam, Adrian. *Formative Spirituality*. 5 vols. New York: Crossroad Publishing, 1983–1992.

Van Waning, Adeline. *The Less Dust, the More Trust: Participating in The Shamatha Project, Meditation and Science*. Winchester, UK: Mantra Books, 2014.

Vasubandhu. *L'Abhidharmakosa*. Translated by Louis de La Vallée Poussin. Paris: P. Geuthner, 1924.

Walker, Susan, ed. *Speaking of Silence: Christians and Buddhists on the Contemplative Way*. New York: Paulist Press, 1987.

Welwood, John. *Toward a Psychology of Awakening: Buddhism, Psychotherapy and the Path of Personal and Spiritual Transformation.* Boston, MA: Shambhala Publications, 2000.

Wundt, Wilhelm. *Grundriss der Psychologie.* Stuttgart, Germany: Kröner Verlag, 1896.

Zegveld, André. "Gebed en leven." In *Benedictijns Tijdschrift.* Vol. 3. Egmond-Binnen, the Netherlands: Adelbertabdij, 1991.

Index